Letters
of
Transit

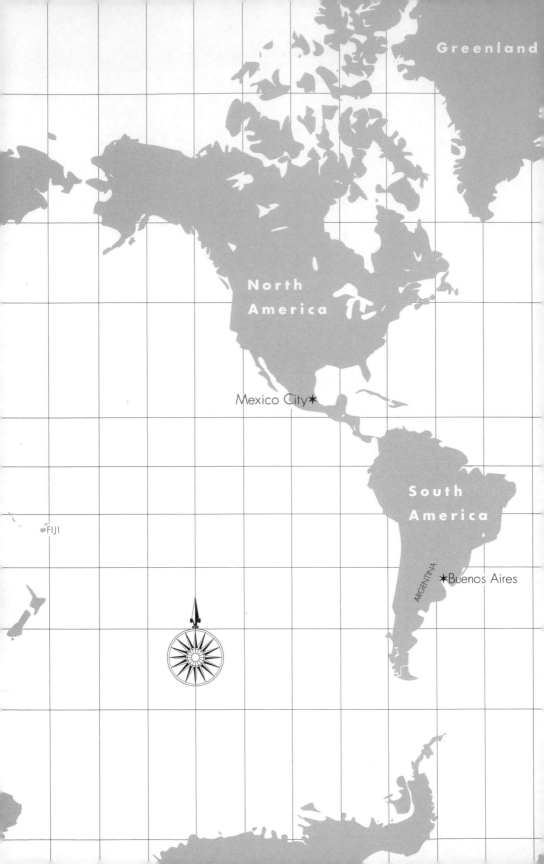

Matthew Stevenson

Letters of Transit

Essays on Travel,

History, Politics,

and Family Life Abroad

ODYSSEUS BOOKS

ISBN 0-9709133-0-3

For information, address: Odysseus Books c/o Pathway Book Service, 4 White Brook Road, Gilsum, New Hampshire 03448. Toll free: 1-800-345-6665. Fax: 1-603-357-2073. E-mail: pbs@pathwaybook.com

Please use the same contact numbers for special or direct orders, group sales, or special promotions, for example, those available to book and reading clubs.

Please visit the book's Web site: www.lettersoftransit.com

To contact the author on any matter, such as to arrange a speaking engagement, please use: matthewstevenson@freesurf.ch or lisa@booknote.com c/o Lisa Guida Tel 203-483-7035. Fax 203-488-6049

Some of these essays first appeared in Harper's, American Scholar, American Spectator, Bucknell World, and American Enterprise, in a somewhat different form.

This book was printed on acid-free paper in the United States at Thompson-Shore, Inc., located in Dexter, Michigan. It was edited by Sandra Costich. Jacket and book design by Albert M. Cetta. Artistic and map consultation: Harriett Barton. Martin Daly kindly read the galleys.

Library of Congress Cataloging-in-Publication Data

Stevenson, Matthew Mills, 1954-
Letters of transit : essays on travel, history, politics, and family life abroad / Matthew Stevenson.
p. cm.
ISBN 0-9709133-0-3
1. Stevenson, Matthew Mills, 1954—Journeys. 2. Voyages and travels.
3. Family life—Switzerland. I. Title.
G465 .S744 2001
910.4--dc21
2001003158

---

10 9 8 7 6 5 4 3 2 1

This book is

dedicated, with affection and admiration, to my parents,

Nick and Shirley Stevenson,

who take delight in travelers' tales.

Acknowledgments

As many of these essays were published in various magazines, they have had the benefit of careful editing, from editors whose element of style has enriched my own. Wladislaw Pleszczynski, the managing editor of the *American Spectator*, has edited a number of these pieces, over the past nineteen years, with the same grace, humor and insight that are his trademarks. I have the same affection for the writing and editing of my friend, Joseph Epstein, for more than two decades the editor of the *American Scholar*, who leads his readers and writers by the example of excellence. Jean Stipicevic and Sandra Costich, also at the *American Scholar*, are the finest line editors in my experience, and I am indebted to Sandra for editing this collection with her jeweler's eye for misplaced modifiers. A few of these pieces were published in *Bucknell World*, the alumni publication of Bucknell University, which has had the good fortune to have editors as professional as Marsha Scott Gori and Sally Atwood. I have transoceanic admiration for the work of Karl Zinsmeister, editor at the *American Enterprise*. Richard Kagan, as the editor of Pan Am's *Clipper* magazine in the 1980s, often made it possible for me to be the man in motion.

Although only one of these essays appeared in *Harper's*, the influence of Lewis H. Lapham, its editor, runs through most of these pages. For twenty years I have borrowed heavily from his reading lists, not to mention his own essays and the debts of friendship. Another friend, William H. Rodgers, read only a few of these pieces before the legions of time laid waste to his incisive mind. But his thoughts on writing and language preface any blank page I confront. I have always appreciated the enthusiasm that Tom Wallace—publisher, agent, friend—has brought to this project, in much the same spirit that Albert M. Cetta designed the manuscript and Harriett Barton nurtured other artistic details. From the wilds of Alaska, my sister Nanette, also a book designer, gave assistance that reached over the long horizon between our lives in Anchorage and Geneva, Switzerland. More than a few of the books mentioned in these essays came from my younger sister, Julie.

Nothing would give me greater pleasure than to list those friends, colleagues, and family members who helped to shape these essays. But the fear of omission outweighs the commission of gratitude. My hope, however, is that the themes of family and friendship run strongly enough through these essays, to make it easy for the many to whom I owe thanks to connect the dots of my appreciation.

Of course, I do want to single out Constance Scott Fogler, my wife and often fellow traveler. We met in New York in 1977, married in 1984, and moved to Switzerland in 1991. Two of the pieces in this collection replay our honeymoon to Argentina and South Africa, which, despite the jet lag, the dark politics, and the rain, remains the trip of my dreams. Since 1987, we have had four children—Helen, Laura, Henry and Charles, who with humor, fortitude, and a steady supply of souvenirs have mastered the not-so-easy details of life in a foreign land. Connie and I do have our differences: she does not share my enthusiasm for the published works of Joe Willie Namath, at least during childbirth. But mostly we enjoy the same books and friends, and—along with her cats underfoot—unraveling the thread of life's conversation.

Table of Contents

Letters
of
Transit

Scenes from a Fatherhood

(1998)

As the office-bound father of four small children, who descend in ages from eleven to two, I arrive home in the evenings during what friends call "the arsenic hour," although it has never been clear to me if the intended victims are the kids or their parents.

The telltale sign is fallout from what appears to be a four-megaton toy bomb that has hit ground zero, usually the living room. Not far from the epicenter are sofa cushions, over-turned chairs, knotted pieces of rope, dolls, a jungle of stuffed animals, and the words "Fisher-Price" laced among the debris.

Many nights, as I view this wreckage from the front door, I wonder what the Federal Aviation Administration would write in its report if it discovered the black box of our lives:

"Hi, everyone, I'm home."
[Sounds of a toddler emptying the dishwasher.]
"Daddy, how many days are there to Christmas?"
"Laura hit me."
"But it's not fairrrrrr."
[Sound of the mail being checked.]

"Either you come to dinner or I'm turning that computer off."

"I *hate* soup."

"You call *that* doing dishes?"

[Muffled sound of the bath overflowing.]

"Why aren't you in bed?"

"Daddy, telephone . . ."

The first casualty of such long afternoons is my wife. Come
dinnertime, she can have the defeated look of a woman I
remember from a cartoon in *The New Yorker*. The husband,
just home from the office, is consoling his wife near the front
door. From across the room comes the scowl of a defiant,
small child. "I have spoken to Jonah," the husband soothes
her, "and I think he's willing to work with us."

When we married, during the last days of disco, my wife
was working for a New York publisher. We had a subscription
to the Philharmonic, played softball in Central Park, and
organized late-night dinner parties while riding home on the
subway. But the last nine years have been spent in the company of a permanent two-year-old. As much as we want to eat
out or take travel-magazine vacations, we spend our free time
at the kitchen table—wondering which of us has the strength
to pick up the living room.

Although it is at odds with current sensibility, not to
mention federal statutes, in the family organization chart the
children report to their mother with, as they say in corner
offices, a strong dotted line to their father.

To her they turn for cough medicine at 2:00 A.M. or for new
shoes after school. She runs their schedules with Swiss-watch
precision, organizes pickups and drop-offs as if jockeying gypsy
cabs, and serves more crustless sandwiches than Martha
Stewart. Often she does all this in less time than it takes me,
over a business lunch, to share the pain of a client's golf story.

As someone who vanishes every morning in a suit, I see myself cut in the mold of fathers who arrive breathless for school plays, ponder report cards as if the oracle at Delphi, or somehow expect that the conversation at the evening meal will touch on the Albanian question. My idea of helping out around the house is to check for faxes or e-mail. I haul garbage, empty bottles, and cases of wine, but skirt diapers as if they were filled with plutonium. When I clean something, it is usually my bicycle.

To use the analogy of baseball, whose scores I have sometimes checked while supervising the evening bath, my role is that of middle relief—someone who takes the mound when the game is out of reach. I go a few innings on Saturdays at the car wash or the movies. I might also get the nod during family vacations. But with harp lessons or earaches on the line, my wife trots in from the bull pen.

All this is not to say that I don't relish fatherhood. I delight in reading bedtimes stories, playing Parcheesi and backyard soccer, and leading fishing expeditions as if in search of the white whale. During school holidays, I invite kids to the office. Other times I shuttle kids to school, the ice cream parlor, and the beach. My evenings are devoted to taped recordings of "The Lone Ranger." But in Orwellian terms, mine is the ministry of fun—not health, education, or welfare.

We live in a small village, west of Geneva, in a broad Rhône River valley that recalls the rolling vineyards of Burgundy, two hours to the west. Our house, although in the village, is part of a farm, so out the front door are tractors and plows, not to mention a field of sheep and nearby donkeys.

As I grew up in the New York suburbs, with cats and a dog, and those dime-store turtles that occasionally shared the evening bath, I have little say as to what wildlife passes through the front door. On the other hand, my wife was raised in Maine on a dairy farm, which allows her to feed stray cats or cast the deciding vote whenever the children present evidence to the grand jury for household pets.

When the girls made their case for a rabbit acquisition, I dropped into the conversation the fact that, across the border in France, rabbits were almost given away at the Sunday market. "Daddy, no," was the gist of the response to my cost-saving idea. Market rabbits, everyone pleaded, if spared from the stew, grow to the size of small dogs with large droopy ears. So we ended up buying two *lapins nains*, or dwarf rabbits, from a pet store chain—for roughly the cost of a small poodle in Hollywood.

Obviously our Snow Whites wanted to take their dwarfs home immediately. But the store manager explained that the baby rabbits needed a period of bonding with their biological mother. The girls negotiated visitation rights, so we spent the month before the adoption papers cleared driving carrot shavings to the mall, wondering if the adoption might later be challenged or which cage held the deadbeat dad.

We enjoyed the rabbits, who, because they loathed each other, lived in stacked cages like rent-control tenants in New York City. Sadly, after a year, one rabbit died from what we suspect was inbreeding—the unwritten story about bonding—and the other answered a call of the wild.

In their place, after closure on the VISA bill, we adopted several hamsters. When I was growing up, hamster cages looked liked the New Mexico State Prison—square metallic holding pens that had sawdust, water, and the occasional uprising. But hamster cages now look like Swedish apartment buildings.

I thought the hamsters lived lives of quiet desperation until the family left ahead of me for summer vacation and I became in loco parentis. Disoriented in a house of bedlam suddenly gone quiet, I reached out to the hamsters, who took that as a sign to nibble on my neckties. They spent their nights on the wheel, turning it fast enough to light a mid-western city. During the day they slept on bedding that I suspect my wife ordered from Lands' End.

My great fear was that they would starve to death in my care and that my fate as a father would be put to a show trial. (District Attorney: "Daddy killed Pete and Cinnamon. . . .") Consequently, every night I kept overstocking their food dishes from a box of rodent-endorsed nuts, from which, I am sure, they fished out only the cashews. In hindsight, it would have been cheaper and saved time had I taken the hamsters to a cocktail lounge.

On the weekends, when we're not reading mail-order catalogues as if they were Aladdin's lamp, we dream of the places we would have seen in Europe if, while abroad, we had not always had a toddler. We conjure oases of Greek beaches, Scottish castles, and French chateaux.

Before having children, we spent several weeks in the Middle East with luggage smaller than today's diaper bag. On another vacation, we rode our bicycles across Poland during the worst of its martial law. But now, even weekend ski trips make us feel like Hannibal crossing the Alps, not just with elephants, but also with a portable crib.

Some of the fear in traveling, beyond car rides longer than forty-five minutes, has to do with eating in restaurants. Strangers seeing the home video of our family alfresco might think they were watching a prison movie. During the long sentence between ordering Coca-Cola and a waiter pushing pizza through the bars, the prisoners have been known to overturn dishes, spill water, pound their bowls, or open negotiation on dessert as if they held hostages. Recently in Burgundy, the youngest inmate took off all his clothes under the table—not the kind of etiquette that gives the wine much of a chance to breathe.

To escape this parent trap, I decided, with the optimism of Clark Griswald, to promote the idea of camping: We would avoid costly hotels and see Europe as it should be seen, through the prism of a mosquito net.

Before our first night under the stars, however, my wife had to equip the family as if Robert Redford might want to film us in Africa. Flashlights, backpacks, sleeping bags, and a full set of pioneer dishes were delivered from L.L.Bean, which in its promotional literature announced that during a blizzard near Mount Everest forty-four Sherpas had squeezed into the tent that we were now acquiring. That it barely accommodates our four children is testimony to a Sherpa's ability to brave nature's sternest tests without pillows, extra blankets, books-on-tape, or alarm clocks that glow in the dark.

If our camping trips start with *Out of Africa*'s great expectations, by the second day they usually take turns like those in *The English Patient*. Much of our bad luck has to do with the dreary central European climate, which I associate with the cold gray mists of World War I poetry.

On one excursion to a medieval village near Lyon, the fog turned to hail, and I found myself hammering stakes into a ground covered with icy stones. As if caught in a sandstorm, my wife never stirred from the car. We broke camp when lightning mixed with the thunder.

One June in Switzerland, snow tested the tent's waterproof guarantee. This was also the trip on which the family hunter-gatherer forgot the grill and had to cook the evening meal over burning trash—one of those oil-drum fires often found at construction sites.

As Americans who live abroad, my wife and I spend a lot of time in conversation wondering who we are. The children attend the local public schools and do their lessons in French. We speak English at home and spend summers in Maine or New York, visiting our friends and families. But as my friend Peggy Brucia likes to say of transatlantic living:

"Once you have moved across the ocean, no matter which side you're on, it's the wrong one."

Sometimes I think we're living in Switzerland to give our children an American childhood. We live in a village that, were it not Swiss, could be the Great Plains in the 1950s. The surrounding farmland evokes the novels of Willa Cather. Few families among the 505 inhabitants have divorced. The children come home for lunch and, after school, ride a neighbor's ponies. We get by without television. None of the kids recognizes the name Monica Lewinsky.

Our dilemma is whether, after the sixth grade, to continue the children in the Swiss public schools or start them up the expensive slopes of private education, part of which could be in English. It goes to the deeper question of whether we are raising Swiss children with American accents or Americans on a distant frontier.

Like Switzerland itself, the local public schools are well-ordered places. Children graduate from high school speaking three languages, understanding science, and writing clearly, albeit in French. That most erudite American, Benjamin Franklin, chose Geneva as the place to educate his cherished grandson. But by age fifteen, Swiss school children can also be shuttled off to make watches or pour chocolate. Below Switzerland's international sensibility is the caste of an apprentice system very much alive.

By contrast, the international schools are English corners of a foreign field. The curriculum is that of an American high school or a British boarding school, delivered with French accents. Students graduate to American universities as if living in Rye. But children arrive and depart these schools with the ebb and flow of incoming and outbound planes. Their worlds are neither here nor there, but a cloister of resorts and townhouses within the orbits of London, New York, and Paris—customs of a country that Edith Wharton so well understood. But perhaps—and this is what we discuss over long cups of coffee—it is a world closer to our own than the good earth of Suisse Romande.

A lot of the travel that we do is to bring our children together with their grandparents or us together with our siblings. I take kids with me on business trips to New York, and my wife makes the great trek to Maine every summer. But often it means that one of us is left alone holding down not just the fort, but also some of the cowboys and Indians.

When my mother-in-law came to visit last Christmas, we decided that she might enjoy a weekend trip to Venice with my wife and our daughters, then ages eight and ten. I volunteered to stay behind with the boys, five and two, like one of those Russian cosmonauts who is occasionally forgotten by mission control.

Confident that I was ready to take charge of the boys and the house, my wife left me one of those house-instruction letters the length of a computer manual, using the jargon of her profession, such as: " . . . or, if necessary, you can give him a suppository."

As any manager would, I delegated the house cleaning to my son. He flooded the kitchen with murky water and then, stripped to the waist, swabbed the deck, as if he were an oiler on a tramp steamer.

Although my wife left enough pre-cooked meals to last even the *Apollo 13* crew to the moon, we battened on the cocktail-party circuit, it being the weekend before Christmas; we also made occasional fast-food excursions.

For Sunday dinner, the boys chose Burger King, on the solid marketing grounds that they had most of the MacDonald's toys. We carried our trays upstairs and took the last free table, near the slide, amidst what otherwise looked like a skinhead convention.

"Why does that man have a snake on his arm?" was the drift of the conversation until the boys discovered a television suspended from the ceiling. The remainder of the happy meal passed in silence, as the children, their chins aloft, soaked up French fries with the same deadpan expression with which they absorbed MTV.

On Monday morning, the travelers returned with as many stories as Marco Polo. Venice had flooded, and they had spent the weekend wading in newly acquired hip boots. Of the Doge's Palace and Venetian splendor, I heard as little as I remembered from my own trip there as a child, when my sisters and I discovered the Renaissance pleasures of go-carts set up near St. Mark's Square.

I tried to make my own account of the weekend sound like a chapter from *Little House on the Prairie*. We had brought home the Christmas tree but resisted the temptation to trim the base with a chain saw. Everyone had slept well. Milk had been served at each meal.

My cover held until the girls, in their delight to be home, sang "Old MacDonald" with the two-year-old. After they had mooed and oinked and neighed but not gotten a reply, they pressed on: "What does Old MacDonald have on his farm, Charles?" At first there was confused silence, and then came the two-year-old's answer: "Ketchup."

Most of what I know about being a father undoubtedly I learned from my own. We played catch in the yard and carried hot chocolate to cold stadiums. Camping did not interest him—World War II having sated his appetite for tents—and wood work was limited to splitting logs.

Then, as now, he worked hard and traveled often. But he left the impression that he was always around. If he went to the office on Saturdays, he often brought along one of his children. He also took us to conventions in Chicago and to Marine Corps reunions. Even if he was not in the house, he was easy to imagine.

One pleasure of my childhood was that it coincided with the twilight of American railroads. It was the era before sales became marketing, and during vacations I would often join my father while he called on the trade. My first trip, at age five, was through the coal fields of Pennsylvania. Later came the Twentieth Century Limited, the Broadway Limited, and the Silver Meteor.

During his meetings I would idle near a secretary, flipping through the waiting-room magazines or reading the sports pages. At night, we would board a Pullman that would race through the darkness toward the bright lights of Kansas City, St. Louis, or New Orleans. I would lie in my berth and watch phone poles, like the reels of an old movie, frame scenes of the American tapestry.

The trains I ride now with my children are in Switzerland, usually during that vacation black hole between Christmas and the New Year. In Europe, the tradition of thermal baths has merged with the American obsession with theme parks, and every holiday we crisscross Switzerland to take the cures.

Last year, we rode the train three hours to Zurich, changed to a local, and then boarded a postal bus that stopped in front of a gloomy concrete structure with great plastic chutes coming from the walls—Los Alamos with a water slide.

The wave pool, just beyond the entrance, looked like the River Ganges near Benares. Pilgrims with their palms aloft stood in knee-deep water as if expecting divine revelation, which appeared as breakers swelling from a wall in the deep end. The faithful would laugh, scream, and writhe in ecstasy until they got bored and drifted toward the snack bar.

For reasons known only to class-action lawyers, the children were encouraged to go down the water slides on large inner tubes, which, in the turns, started spinning like split atoms. Separated from their rings, the children would then crash head first either into logjams of inner tubes or pools of churning water, making the same shriek when they laughed or cried. I got cold after the first slide. They tired after four hours.

Late in the afternoon, we swam outdoors through the kind of trap doors that, in a James Bond film, would lead to the shark tanks. But instead we breast stroked into a chapter from *The Magic Mountain*. There were hot tubs and cold baths, and one murky iodine pool, which at the water's edge listed the ailments for which an immersion would be helpful.

We discovered a great outdoor pool, from which it was possible to watch dusk and snowflakes fall on distant mountains. We drifted in eddies of hot springs, as if the family of Emperor Franz Josef, until the attendant, who looked like Tom Selleck, turned on some air jets, and I had that great parent panic watching the children swirl away as if being taken down the Colorado River.

I worry that the children, with so much of Europe in their lives, are missing an American childhood. Only on occasion do they carve pumpkins, celebrate the Fourth of July, or join a traffic jam outside a national park.

To connect the dots of a nation that stands for more than Larry King, Paula Jones, or the evening news, I decided to take the two girls to Washington and New York. I made reservations for a White House tour, bought tickets to *Flight* at the Air and Space Museum, and laid plans for Independence Hall and the Statue of Liberty.

The hardest part of fatherhood is knowing when to push and when to ease off. At what age do they take in more than French fries? What builds better character: vacations at home with their make-believe games or the new worlds of jet-set travel? As another Stevenson often asked: Are treasure islands places that we visit or imagine?

I knew from an earlier trip with the girls to Paris that even if the splendors of the Champs-Elysées are outside the front door, children travel so they can jump up and down on hotel beds.

In Washington, we almost missed our early-morning slot at the White House after the girls discovered that the M&Ms were free at the breakfast buffet. During the tour, while a burly Secret Service agent in the Blue Room tried to explain the tranquil realism of Thomas Eakins or what was a gift to the nation from Mrs. Madison, my younger daughter, then seven, broke the hush with a loud stage whisper: "Daddy, I forgot my underwear," words no father wants to hear in the Clinton White House.

To get the girls into the Capitol Rotunda, I had first to feed the squirrels on the steps of the Supreme Court. In Philadelphia, the cost of my speech on the frailty of liberty was a ride in a horse-drawn carriage.

So that guards could inspect our handbags, we waited two hours before entering the Statue of Liberty, lest any visitor try to emulate what Samuel Adams and his Sons of Liberty did to earlier symbols of power. From the pedestal, we took in the skyline of lower Manhattan, and I tried, without much of an audience, to tell the stories of relatives who had knocked on the golden door.

As always, the gift shops of freedom proved a greater allure than the ideals. But in the museum, the French connections to liberty, among the letters that dedicated the statue, struck a chord in two girls who live every day in its language and customs.

Finally we were doing more than feeding squirrels. That gift from the Old World to the New, which spoke of earlier passages from the Swiss countryside to New York harbor, lit a torch both for this Father of Exiles and his daughters.

Globetrotting

(1989)

> *I have fallen in love with American names,*
> *The sharp names that never get fat,*
> *The snakeskin-titles of mining claims,*
> *The plumed war-bonnet of Medicine Hat,*
> *Tucson and Deadwood and Lost Mule Flat.*
>
> *Seine and Piave are silver spoons,*
> *But the spoonbowl-metal is thin and worn,*
> *There are English counties like hunting-tunes*
> *Played on the keys of a postboy's horn,*
> *But I will remember where I was born.*

Stephen Vincent Benet,
"American Names"

By happy coincidence my childhood overlapped with the fading twilight of American railroads. I spent many school vacations in my father's company, seeing the country by train. He traveled on business, and, when lucky, I tagged along. We would leave New York either from Pennsylvania Station, on dingy tracks far below the procession of columns and the guardian eagles, or from Grand Central, after passing under the man-made galaxy in the terminal heavens. A week or so later we would end up in Wyoming, Virginia, or Texas—or, more precisely, Rocks Springs, Petersburg, or Beaumont. America became a reel of fast-moving images, framed by the Pullman car window.

My first trip, at age five, was to Philadelphia, Reading, and Tamaqua—a fitting start for someone who would come to Lewisburg in 1972. I remember being carried, half-asleep, off the coach at Franklin Street in Philadelphia, the cab ride to a commercial hotel, the bucket of ice from the hallway, the angled parked cars in Reading, and the serpent of steam under which we traveled through the coal fields to Tamaqua.

On later trips we rode the Twentieth Century along the Hudson River to Chicago and the Southern Crescent past the Capitol to Atlanta. Black men in starched white coats would serve dinner in the dining cars, but often a white mâitre d' would collect money for the bill. After dinner I would prowl through the train or read in the observation car. Sometimes a train in the West would have a dome car, and we would watch thunderstorms sweep across the plains. From my berth, always the upper, I would listen for the bells of the grade crossings or watch lights on the prairie wink like beacons at sea. Sunrise would unveil the farmland of Indiana or the red clay of Georgia.

I think of those trains, with names like the General, the Super Chief, and the Zephyr, and wonder why America turned its back on the pleasures of travel. Now a trip to Chicago means a dash to the airport, a wait in line at security, a frozen dinner and a warm beer, and then a night in a hotel watching reruns of "Miami Vice." I have flown Hong Kong to San Francisco and never glimpsed the Pacific Ocean and driven from New York to Bangor, Maine, and seen nothing beyond the interstate. It used to be that we traveled some-where. Now everyone is faxed to a final destination.

Is the age of travel over? Although I despair at the collapse of American railways, the paucity of ocean liners to France, and what the automobile has done to the cities, I still believe it is a wonderful time to be a traveler. A day in the air and you can go anywhere: Faletti's Hotel in Lahore, Pakistan; the Paul Gauguin house in Tahiti; or the Charles Bridge in Prague.

Compared to the costly addiction of home ownership, fares are a bargain, at least internationally. Today's newspaper lists roundtrip to Cairo for $499, Bangkok $839. Beyond Havana and Rangoon, little travel need be with tours.

An active retired couple can see more of the world than did Columbus. Phileas Fogg and Passepartout could easily go around the world in eighteen days and still linger in Benares. You don't need to be Charles Darwin to visit Patagonia or Ernest Hemingway to see big game in Kenya and revolution in Latin America.

What's lost is not the ability to travel, which exists as never before, so much as a sense of what travel offers. On billboards and brochures, it is packaged as downtime—a week at Disney World, an excursion to Paris, a getaway to the Caribbean. For sale is a utopia where the world will never intrude. The best journeys are made out to be sentimental— to Venice on a restored Orient Express or down the Mississippi on a paddlewheel steamer, implying that the only memorable travel took place in the past.

I love idling at the beach as much as anyone, but my most rewarding trips are when I have a reason to travel—be it to explore a particular museum, to meet people on business, to walk on a battlefield like Waterloo or Anzio, to learn more about a political question that I know only from the newspapers.

During my junior year abroad, like the others in my program, I was content to wander aimlessly, to "hit Germany," to poke around cathedrals with all the enthusiasm of someone waiting for a train. Friends would spend a weekend in Athens and then talk about having "done Greece." It drew the distinction in my mind between travel, which needs a purpose, which seeks to engage the world, and tourism, for which the destination is always a theme park. George Bush, with his dashes around the world, is a tourist; Alexis de Tocqueville was a traveler.

A friend once said to me that if I ever took a Rorschach test all I would ever see in the inkblots would be the outlines of countries. I am afraid she was right. My house seems to have atlases the way a hotel has Gideon Bibles. My taste in art is an old street plan of lower Manhattan or a chart of the Caribbean. I can sort wash looking at Cape Agulhas, Africa's literal southern tip, or peel potatoes studying the vineyards of France. Over my desk at work is a map of Australia; my top drawer is crammed with schedules.

To me one of the great pleasures of travel is simply to think about it. I run itineraries through my mind the way a computer sorts data. *The Official Airline Guide* tells me about flights. (Qantas, not United, has a flight from Honolulu to Cairns.) Thomas Cook's *Overseas Timetable* gets me on trains. (The Bombay Mail departs Calcutta at 19:45 with air-conditioned first-class cars and a diner.) I even have an old copy of Russell's *Official National Motor Coach Guide* (Wilderness Transit Co. has morning service from Craig, Colorado, to Grand Junction, with an 8:20 stop in Rifle), but I consult it only in desperation.

Guidebooks that list restaurants and hotels leave me cold— when has a hotel ever resembled its write-up in *Fodor's?*— but I find offbeat guides a delight. *Ferries of America* lists every one still in service, like the Millersburg ferry that crosses the Susquehanna to Liverpool. *The March to Victory* guides visitors to the World War II battlefields in Europe (for Omaha Beach, follow D 514 west 6 km to Colleville-sur-Mer, then turn north 1.5 km to the American Military Cemetery). *Literary New York* points out that Arthur Miller imagined

Willy Loman living at 1350 East Third Street in Brooklyn—a bit too close to my house for comfort.

If I want the unvarnished truth about a place, I turn to the *Traveller's Dictionary of Quotation*, a voluminous anthology, with excerpts arranged by city and country. In 1939, John Gunther wrote, "Japan has never been sweet sixteen." S. J. Perelman noted that Philadelphia wasn't the City of Brotherly Love so much as the "City of Bleak November Afternoons," although Alexander Mackay thought it "a great flat, over-baked brick-field." Hong Kong is described anonymously as "A borrowed place living on borrowed time." Will Rogers is quoted on Americans: "We don't know what we want, but we are ready to bite someone to get it."

Books are often the reason I travel. After reading the novels of Alan Paton, I decided I wanted to see South Africa. *August 1914* by Alexandr Solzhenitsyn lured me to the Lake District in Poland. How can anyone resist Alaska after reading John McPhee? A collection of Ernie Pyle's war correspondence is pushing me to Kasserine Pass.

A good trip also needs good reading. I take delight in matching the perfect book to the landscape: to read Boswell while in London, Maugham in Singapore, or Steinbeck in California. To take me through Louisiana, I want Robert Penn Warren, or, at Gettysburg, *The Killer Angels* by Michael Shaara. There is no better guide to Auschwitz than the memoirs of Primo Levi. *Recollections of a Life* by Alger Hiss has a melancholic remembrance of the Lewisburg penitentiary.

Such sentiment should make me a fan of travel writing, although I rarely make it through accounts of trekking in the Himalayas or hitchhiking across Mexico. What I often find missing is a connection to history or literature. Politics are rarely discussed. Wisdom is discerned through a haphazard parade of strangers. The landscape blurs. I want *The Innocents Abroad*, not simply innocence.

Of course, I have discovered wonderful exceptions to my bias. I have affection for the writing of Paul Theroux (*The Great Railway Bazaar*), especially *Riding the Iron Rooster*. He turned compartments of the Chinese railways into confessionals and produced not just a book about trains but a series of dialogues on the everyday dreams, fears, and idiosyncrasies of the Chinese.

My friend Simon Winchester, a British author and journalist, visited the fifteen surviving colonies of the British Empire—if you're trying to remember them, don't forget St. Helena, Ascension, Pitcairn, or the Falklands—and published in *Outposts* not only a graceful narrative of his trip but also a vivid indictment of Britain's colonial attitudes.

In a few instances I have followed in the footsteps of another English friend, Geoffrey Moorhouse (*Calcutta, To the Frontier, Imperial City*), and found his impressions of India, Pakistan, or New York to be mine—a personal acid test few writers pass.

I don't warm to much travel writing because I read most books as dispatches or letters from a frontier. Ideally, if I ever get that mythical free Saturday afternoon, I would arrange my library geographically, with no distinction made between fiction and nonfiction. For example, Maine would have the *Letters of E. B. White* and the stories of Sarah Orne Jewett. Italy would have both the wartime memoirs of Raleigh Trevelyan, *Rome 44*, and the speeches of Cicero. On the Prague shelf you might find Kafka and *Too Strong for Fantasy* by Marcia Davenport. My Lewisburg collection would have the novels of John Wheatcroft and *The Facts* by Philip Roth.

As much as I enjoy reading about the world—Emily Dickinson wrote "There is no frigate like a book"—until I have actually visited a country, I don't feel entitled to an opinion on its politics. It embarrasses me that I had passionate views on the Panama Canal before I set foot in the Canal Zone or that I still can hold forth at dinner parties on Iran, which I have only seen from the dubious perch of 35,000 feet.

For a trip to be successful it need not entail a drive from Cape Town to Cairo or six weeks in the Ukraine. Some of the best trips I have taken have been a day in the midst of a longer, sometimes uneventful journey.

Last fall, for example, I ended up in Thailand after a month of business in Australia and New Zealand. My meetings finished late on a Wednesday night. I was homesick, tired, and missing the presidential election and the World Series. A flight via Tokyo in the morning would get me home for Halloween.

Instead I got up in time to catch the 6:00 A.M. train to Aranyaprathet, a small town on the Thai-Cambodian border. A friend in New York had made it possible for me to visit the Cambodian refugee camps. All I had to do was get to what everyone calls Aran.

My ticket for the five-hour train trip was 48 Baht, about $1.95, and I took a seat beside an open window in a car that resembled one on the Philadelphia subway. Only third class was available, but the train was clean and departed on time.

Dawn broke in the Bangkok suburbs as the local ran a gauntlet of makeshift housing. In the foreground women were hauling water to open fires; in the distance lights flicked on at random in the modern high-rise apartments. Neatly dressed school children clamored into the car. On the opposite seat, two monks in saffron robes smoked cigarettes impassively.

Out of the city, the train ran briskly through expansive, irrigated fields, as if in a tropical Holland. Farmers navigated their crops in small wooden motorboats. Lotus leaves lined the shoulders of the canals.

This day was my first in the countryside of Indochina, and

I thought only of Vietnam, which is several hundred miles to the east. Why did the U.S., with a mechanized army, want to fight a war in a bog? What was it like for soldiers to hump knapsacks in this sun or to fight a war-in-the-round, imagining the enemy behind each line of trees?

After getting a pass from the military police, I spent the day at Khao I Dang, a refugee camp several miles from the border. My guides were young American volunteers, who took me to schools, the camp library, a clinic for children, and a special center where amputees—from the minefields along the border—learn to use their new limbs.

The camp supports several thousand Cambodians, not in relief agency tents, but in well-constructed thatched houses. The paths and streets are red clay, which in many spots is swept clean. I had expected the holding pens of *The Killing Fields* and was relieved to find a well-cared-for Indochinese village, albeit one established in no-man's-land.

These Cambodian refugees are a people without a country. The continuing civil war has driven many into Thailand, which, however, is no longer willing to grant them immigrant status. Earlier refugees were resettled in third countries, including the United States, but those windows are now closed.

The choice for those now fleeing is to return to Cambodia and possibly submit to the Khmer Rouge, which occupies western parts of the country, or to linger in the camps, which is why many of the men spend their days idling, as if outside a Depression-era soup kitchen.

The Americans and the Thais oppose the Vietnamese occupation of Cambodia and speak hopefully of a future coalition government that would exclude the participation of the Khmer Rouge and its leaders, notably the genocidal Pol Pot. Nevertheless, what is clear from conversations in the camps is that the Khmer Rouge is the strongest member of the opposition—it utilizes some refugee camps as military bases—and will fill any vacuum left by a Vietnamese withdrawal. It leaves the United States with the prospect of supporting the Vietnamese occupation or a Khmer Rouge return to power— a dilemma avoided in our political discussions.

If we do nothing at all, Pol Pot will be back.

On my trips I learn the most through conversation. As eager as I am to tour ruins or track down museums, my delight is talking politics—be it with writers or economists, business-men or strangers. But the best conversations cannot be left to chance. Before any trip I send out letters for appointments. Some never get answered. One resulted in a meeting with Alan Paton.

On arrival, I work the phones. It has always delighted me that so many people I have contacted have been eager to meet a traveling American. The notion that we're hated overseas never extends to the personal level. I have had generous receptions from Arabs and Jews, Indians and Pakistanis, Afghanis and Russians, white and black South Africans.

I take greatest pleasure in meeting friends of democ-racy, especially when their opposition is a dictatorial or well-fortified state. Horacio Mendez Carreras opposed the junta in Argentina even when it was killing those in opposition. Henryk Wozniakowski, a publisher of books and magazines in Cracow, works for freer speech in Poland. Each has con-victions to match his courage and the sense, which de Tocqueville had, that American democracy could, by example more than by rhetoric, help those living under suppression.

A love of travel comes naturally to me. But how to travel was something I learned, especially from Peter Kresl, an associate professor of economics. In January 1974—my sophomore year—he led six students on a trip across Canada to study U.S.–Canadian relations. What initially drew me to the trip,

I confess, wasn't a passion to understand the economy of Saskatchewan, but the plan to travel by rail. How would it hurt, as we rode "the impossible railway," to have a few seminars on tariffs?

The day after New Year's, 1974, seven of us met at Windsor Station in Montreal. A coach ticket to Vancouver cost $55. Peter Kresl had arranged interviews with prominent Canadians along the transcontinental route. Even more astounding, they had agreed to see us—a rag-tag crew that devoted long hours in the club cars debating the merits of Molson and Labatt.

We met French separatists in Montreal, a former prime minister in Ottawa, a publisher in Winnipeg, and the energy czar of Alberta. We ended up in Vancouver—wearing our familiar blue jeans and flannel shirts—in the expansive board room of a forestry company. How refreshing it was to learn without having to write a paper on Karl Marx or Sigmund Freud's *The Future of an Illusion*.

January 1974 was high noon of the first energy crisis. Because Canada had ample petroleum reserves, many of those we interviewed seemed to adopt the bearing of a desert sheik. Canada finally had something the Americans needed. Perhaps it would join OPEC? A number referred to themselves as "Arabs with blue eyes." Maybe now Canada would emerge from the shadow cast by the 49th parallel? Americans would finally look north with some respect.

While thinking about this article, I decided to make a trip to Lewisburg. I wanted to speak with students majoring in international relations and to attend several classes and, in effect, to remember how I saw the world when I was graduating from college.

I spent a day on campus, most of it in the lounge of the political science department. Students came and went as their schedules permitted. I asked them about their classes, and they asked me about opportunities to use their degrees in international relations.

I saw a lot of myself in the students who came through the door. They had been majors in English, history, languages, or political science. Now as majors in international relations, they loved their course variety and their professors, but they dreaded graduation.

Many spent their junior year abroad and looked forward, as they said, to "doing something international." But they weren't biologists on their way to medical school or engineers heading for construction. Is there such a thing as a career in international relations? Where is the personnel office anyway?

No two students I saw that afternoon were pursuing the same dream. Among them they wanted to work in finance in London, with refugees in the U.S., in political geography at a university, in foreign countries teaching English. They spoke of hitchhiking to Seattle and catching a charter flight to Japan. I suppose they were no different from other groups of undergraduates—a mixture of eagerness and uncertainty—but, as was written of Stuart Little, they struck me as somehow "headed in the right direction."

These students would not be accidental tourists, Macon Learys searching Paris for a cheeseburger or London for American-style plumbing. Their ideal world would never be a drip-dry cocoon, nor would they use a book simply to fend off strangers. To my mind they were travelers. It might take them time to find a career, but already they knew the life they wanted to lead.

I spent that evening with some of the professors from the political science department—Tom Travis, Charles Longley, and Harry Blair—all of whom teach students in international relations. The evening had aspects of *Back to the Future*, as each was a professor while I attended Bucknell.

Although we didn't realize it at the time, many of the professors in the early 1970s were young themselves, fresh from graduate school and starting their careers. I think we assumed that, because they knew everything, they had to be at least middle-aged. Talking to them that night, I was struck by how much ground they had covered.

Tom Travis had studied and taught for a year in India. Harry Blair was consulting relief agencies on development in Bangladesh. Charles Longley had observations on American political life that provided a context for the Reagan years beyond the sound bites of the Sunday talk shows.

We spent the evening swapping travelers' tales. It was a pleasure once again to hear the precision of their language and the range of their minds. Clearly the ideals of the professors had nurtured those of their students.

I decided to take the coal road home—south along the Susquehanna to Sunbury, east on Route 61 through Shamokin, Mount Carmel, and Pottsville. Interstate 80 is to travel what fast food is to regional cooking. The road to Reading is one de Tocqueville would have traveled.

I hadn't remembered the prosperity of Sunbury, the stately homes along the river, the rich farmland of the valley. Aluminum siding has replaced soot as the façade of Shamokin. Edward Hopper might still be drawn to Mt. Carmel, its forlorn streets, its anthracite past, its specter of black lung. But how would he paint the greenhouses filling in some of the coal pits? Pottsville appeared newer and brighter—suddenly part of the neon, video economy. But from the hill in town, the state prison still casts its shadow—part crusader fortress, part gothic nightmare.

Up ahead lay Amish country and the brewery, now run by Stroh. Soon I would join the trickle of rushing traffic that, as I drew closer to New York, would widen like the Amazon basin. But my mind lingered on another verse from "American Names."

> Rue des Martyrs and Bleeding-Heart Yard,
> Senlis, Pisa, and Blindman's Oast,
> It is a magic ghost you guard
> But I am sick for a newer ghost,
> Harrisburg, Spartanburg, Painted Post.

Guadalcanal

(1990)

Like many people now in their thirties, I grew up in the long shadow cast by the Second World War. A green wool uniform hung in our cedar closet, and accounts of the Pacific island campaigns were part of the casual family conversations during Saturday errands or cleanings of the garage.

At an early age I knew my father had served with the Marines, that the fighting had taken place on remote Pacific islands, and that the destruction of Hiroshima had saved American forces from a deadly assault on the Japanese mainland.

Legends, or so they seemed, were woven around distant places like the Solomon Islands, Espíritu Santo, and New Britain. In other families, similar stories must have been told about the Normandy beaches, Cassino, and night flights over Ploesti. These war stories were vivid scenes in the tableau that explained, not just something about my father, but what it was to fight in a war.

In the early 1960s television made it easy to imagine the war. On a nightly basis it was possible to track small units on their way to either Berlin or Tokyo. German and Japanese soldiers died by the hundreds, in a manner that portrayed war as no more difficult than a cattle roundup or, in the case of snipers, a fox hunt. By that time John Wayne was devoting

less effort to the defeat of the Japanese. But other actors, such
as Cliff Robertson in *PT 109*, portrayed the Pacific campaigns
as updated versions of chivalrous quests. Armies were never
depicted as faceless, industrial machines or as capable of such
blunders as Tarawa or Peleliu. Instead they were squads or
torpedo boats, like that skippered by Lt. John Kennedy, which
inevitably survived tough scrapes behind enemy lines. No
wonder Vietnam proved such a disappointment. Didn't the
North Vietnamese realize their role in the epic of Americans
at arms?

Although I warmed to Hollywood's romance of the war
won with errant knights, I noticed my father gave it a cool
reception. As I now recollect, he never took me to war pictures, nor did he express anything but derisive humor for
movie-lot combat. But he did talk freely about the war. And
from our conversations about what it was like to survive an air
raid or lead an assault, I inferred that the best way to fathom
war was to read about it.

Even my father's answers to my boyish questions about
bombs and bullets contained allusions to literature. Before I
was able to finish full-length books, I knew that the key to
understanding jungle warfare lay in *The Thin Red Line* by
James Jones or that Erich M. Remarque's *All Quiet on the
Western Front* applied to trenches on Okinawa as well as to
those in France. The memoirs of generals were written by
publicists and were probably unreliable. The only way to
understand what had happened was to hear it from someone
who was there. Truth, it seemed, could be picked up from a
radiant that grew weaker the farther you got from the front
lines.

Just as our conversations of war touched on its literature,
so did they usually return to Guadalcanal. My father landed
there on D-Day and led a rifle company through four months
of the campaign, which included a bayonet charge on the banks
of the Tenaru River. But he refused either to romanticize the

fighting or to wallow in self-pity for having been sent there. If anything, his narratives were, and still are, laced with ironic detachment, as if survival—then and now—required a separation from the brutality of the warfare or the misery of the conditions.

Because Guadalcanal in our family acquired the position of a mythological site, it never occurred to me that I might go there. Not only was it a dark land of giants, but it lay in the South Pacific, among the far-flung archipelago that stretched from Honolulu to Australia. I never included it even in my travel daydreams until I was given William Manchester's *Goodbye, Darkness*. The inscription from my father read: "Someday you will travel among these islands and form your own memories of the distant battle sites."

I found the Manchester memoirs a revelation. Passages evoked qualities I had admired in the autobiographies of Siegfried Sassoon and Robert Graves. But Manchester was remembering not the trenches along the Somme, but the island warfare that had loomed so large in my childhood imagination. He also retraced the steps taken by the Marines on their way from New Guinea to Okinawa.

Until Manchester proved otherwise, I had thought Gog and Magog more accessible than Guadalcanal, Cape Gloucester, or the Palaus. But with relative ease he had flown to Honiara, the capital of The Solomons, and hiked across the battlefield as if he were visiting Bull Run or Spotsylvania. His writing mixed a travel account with a wartime memoir and a history of the Pacific campaign such that it takes a careful reader to figure out that Manchester wasn't the only Marine to have seen action in all the campaigns. But I chose to overlook such narrative liberties. Manchester had given me confidence that someday I might "travel among these islands."

My chance to visit Guadalcanal came after a business trip to Australia that ended with several meetings in Papua New Guinea. Its capital, Port Moresby, is seven hundred miles west of Guadalcanal, although the flights between them tend to be on island-hoppers. I finished my work late on a Tuesday. The next morning, instead of starting the slow trip home to New York, I put in a 4:00 A.M. wake-up call, in time to catch a 6:00 A.M. flight to Guadalcanal.

The only taxi in front of the Port Moresby Travelodge needed a roll-start for the engine to engage. In the pre-dawn blackness, the driver coaxed his Holden sedan around hairpin, coastal turns and through yellow lights. Port Moresby has little to recommend it, especially in the middle of the night. Downtown is a disjointed mix of high-rise apartments, suburban office blocks, and open-front stores that attract midday idlers. Like Juneau, Alaska, it is a landlocked capital surrounded by jagged, forbidding mountains. The landscape is dry and dusty, and the one beach in town is avoided because crime is endemic. The inner harbor, with some rusting hulks and a yacht club, evokes a Somerset Maugham short story. The plot would involve the alcoholism of a diplomat's wife, who would be unable to escape the confines of the club, let alone the city or the country.

I had some doubts about leaving myself, as the driver nursed the engine at lonely streetlights. But we made the airport with time to spare. Air Niugini flight number 82 climbed to cruising altitude above the Owen Stanley Range, where low-level clouds whisked among labyrinthine valleys. Among those ridges, at the start of the Second World War, Australian troops had defeated the Japanese in bitter jungle fighting along the Kokoda Trail. The day before in Moresby I had driven to the Bomana War Cemetery that lies in the foothills of the Owen Stanleys. The cemetery was the familiar symmetrical pattern of white headstones set against neatly tended grass. All had engraved poetic inscriptions or simple family farewells, suggesting an orderly end. But the hills in the distance, where most of the men had died in the hand-to-hand fighting, had the look of a tropical Appalachia.

It takes fifty minutes to fly from Bougainville down The Slot to Guadalcanal. On either side of the plane were small clusters of tropical islands whose names form a roster of Second World War battles: Vella Lavella, New Georgia, the Russells, Savo Island, and Tulagi. At its simplest, the campaign in the Solomons was to control this turquoise corridor that came to represent the left flank of the Japanese march to New Zealand and Australia. Nowhere in the world did the U.S. suffer the naval defeats that it sustained off Guadalcanal, in waters that came to be known as Iron Bottom Sound. Eventually American firepower exhausted the enemy. But with a few twists of fate, the Japanese fleets in The Slot could easily have crossed the T on the idea of the American century.

Guadalcanal is one of those places, at least in literature, that rarely makes a good impression. Jack London, who sailed there on the ketch *Snark*, wrote: "If I were a king, the worst punishment I could inflict upon my enemies would be to banish them to the Solomons." William Manchester remembers his first emotions as mixed: "I thought of Baudelaire: *fleurs du mal*. It was a vision of beauty, but of evil beauty. . . . In between were thick, steamy, matted, almost impenetrable screens of cassia, liana vines, and twisted creepers, masked here and there by mangrove swamps and clumps of bamboo. . . . The forest seemed almost faunal: arrogant, malevolent, cruel." My father described his first impression in an account of the battle that was published in *American Heritage*: "At first light we stood along the rail and looked out across the calm, violet water. There lay the island, dark and impassively sinister, shrouded in an early morning haze pinpricked by bright orange flashes of shell fire from our ships."

For me Guadalcanal appeared as rocky jungle, whose inhospitable mountaintops were encased in clouds. We made landfall over Cape Esperance, the northwestern tip of the island, and flew parallel to the coastal road. From a map in a history I was reading, I recognized Point Cruz, the Matanikau River, Lunga Point, and the mouth of the Ilu—places of battle that I previously imagined as remote, in many ways, as Cold Harbor, Ypres, or Kasserine Pass. I was also struck by the island's colors: the warmth of an azure sea against a stark green jungle. In my mind Guadalcanal was a black-and-white photograph that showed men coming ashore or hiking jungle trails. The sea and the underbrush were always gray.

I cleared customs at Henderson International Airport, a name that tickles my father, who knew it only as Henderson Field, a muddy landing strip that was the prize of battle. In the waiting room was a brass plaque that listed the winners at Guadalcanal of the Congressional Medal of Honor. Names such as Archer Vandegrift, who was the commanding general, or Merritt Edson, a battalion commander, I knew well from my reading, but to the other passengers, who filed out carrying scuba gear and tennis rackets, this might have been an intersection in a New England town and they might well have been walking past a faint inscription about deeds accomplished at the Wilderness.

On the bus ride into town, I was seated next to an American I judged to be in his early seventies. He wore khakis, a sun hat, and betrayed none of the hesitance of a first-time visitor. He had been on Guadalcanal during the war, although after the fighting, and pointed out such landmarks as the original control tower at Henderson Field, Kukurn airstrip, and the Lunga River, which you cross on the twenty-minute ride into Honiara. To see the battlefields he said I would need both a car and a driver. To get around, he added, I should buy some topographical maps from the Ministry of Agriculture and Lands, which was a short walk from the hotel.

Honiara looks like one of those Caribbean towns that travel guides recommend for a half-day's shopping. It has schools, a few oil tanks, government buildings, lots of little boys riding in the back of pickup trucks, and the Mendana Hotel. The veranda bar, overlooking Point Cruz, is divided between local businessmen, with briefcases at their ankles, and American veterans, on trips of remembrance. Many of the Americans wore Hawaiian shirts, gimme caps, and name tags that bore the insignia of their travel brigades. I found it difficult to recognize these men as the dashing soldiers of my childhood imagination, as I am sure it is hard for many of them to fit together their lives then and now. Chatting with some of them in the lobby and at the bar made me remember meeting a World War I veteran in a Yugoslavian village in 1976. He spoke no English, but we were trying to understand each other when he abruptly left the conversation, only to return moments later, carrying a large framed picture. It showed the same man in his early twenties, with dark hair, a thin mustache, and military trim. "You see," his melancholic expression conveyed, "I haven't always been what you're seeing today."

After lunch I bought the maps and picked up the car and driver, whose name was Paul. I wondered why I needed a driver at all until we crossed the Lunga River and plunged into a coconut plantation on small dirt trails. I have always thought of Guadalcanal as Gettysburg in the Pacific—an improbable place for the collision of two industrial armies. At Gettysburg today it is hard to see the battlefields for the monuments. But Guadalcanal, as my friend on the bus had pointed out, is unmarked. I had my topographical surveys, a military history, a guide, and a rented car, and still it was difficult to navigate through the Lever Brothers plantation, which was the original perimeter. The island doesn't have a visitors' center, driving tours, battlefield signs, or gift shops. Hence, unlike the geometric symmetry of Civil War history as presented by the Department of the Interior, what remains vivid at Guadalcanal, even at midday, is the fog of war.

On one of these cart trails near Henderson Field, we came

across another car full of Americans. On the edge of the thick underbrush, a man about my age said that his father was out in the thicket looking for his foxhole. Before long the father emerged, breathless, to declare that he had found the foxhole where he had lived for the worst six months of the campaign. I asked a few questions about the island then and now, but instead of an answer, what I got was a monologue. The father recounted landing on the island, his part in the campaign, how he survived, the importance of air power, the sweep of the Pacific campaign, and on and on. Great interest on my part turned to tedium until, after twenty minutes, I walked back to my car. Paul, the driver, was more polite and got another five minutes on what General MacArthur had been up to in New Guinea. I am sure the father had spent a conventional life and functioned normally. But either the heat or his return to Guadalcanal had moved the plates along some dormant emotional fault line. I regretted my impatience, but now I understood my own father's phrase when he would talk of the war's effect and how, for some, it had scrambled their brains.

We threaded our way through the coconut plantation to Henderson Field, now a long asphalt runway, and then drove east to Red Beach, where the Marines, and among them my father, first landed. The popular image of amphibious landings in the Pacific has Marines hitting beaches edged with thick jungle. Forty-eight years ago that might have been Red Beach, but now it is a thin strip of sand that gives way to scrubby grass, the occasional palm tree, and a saw mill. I had expected a marker, a few plaques, maybe a map with arrows showing what had happened, which is typical of the American battlefields in Europe, but instead we parked near a rubbish heap and walked to the beach through the yard of a seaside house.

To reconstruct events meant spreading the topographical maps in the sand and digging through the books and articles

I had jammed into a shoulder bag. It was easy to retrace my father's steps because he has written two accounts of the battle. Immediately after the campaign, probably in January of 1943, he wrote his company's report. It was forgotten until the summer of 1989, when one of his men sent him a copy with a note: "I was cleaning out an old footlocker recently and ran across the enclosed documents. . . . Thank you for the good example you set for this 18-year-old country boy from Alabama." Before my trip my father handed me a copy, but added a critique of his own literary style. "This is written," he said, as if to place the writing along the spectrum of Guadalcanal prose, "in that dry military style. It has all the usual battlefield clichés about achieving objectives and engaging the enemy." But I know it pleased him that the report had resurfaced.

I also had my father's article from *American Heritage*, which he wrote in the summer of 1983, at the prompting of John Keegan, the military historian and a friend, who had heard his account of the battle and urged him to set it down on paper.

The narrator of the company report is a young first lieutenant, who records the action in a style now preferred in corporate memos. For example, he describes the landing: "We penetrated from the beach to a distance of 500 yards inland and crossed a tributary of the Ilu without opposition. . . . Darkness found the company deep in the jungle at the headwaters of the Ilu. . . . At 0500 firing broke out on the left flank which was answered ineffectively. Pfc Oscar Grover was killed."

The writer in *American Heritage*, by contrast, speaks in the voice I know to be my father's, and the detachment of forty years gives the narrative what Paul Fussell has described as the irony of war. Guadalcanal is not sixty minutes of well-played football, but an unending series of long days' journeys that are followed by terrifying nights. The landing and the move inland are not previews of John Wayne at Iwo Jima, but an introduction to the aspects of war that are confusing, illogical, random, and fatal:

> No orders came until just before nightfall, when we were told to move on again. We followed the company to our right, leaving the high grass and pushing through the jungle single file. Darkness came swiftly, and I thought this was an extraordinary way to be going anywhere, toward a possible enemy position, in the dead of night. When the command came to halt, the men flopped down on either side of the trail. Shortly thereafter, as we lay together in the blackness, came our first experience of pure terror. Without warning, a cacophony of small arms fire enveloped us. A Japanese ambush? But the shots were coming at point-blank range. Too close! We were firing at each other. I don't know how I made my voice heard above the din, but the platoon leaders and noncoms took up the cry, "Cease fire." Shaken and exhausted, we lay silent until the dawn, which disclosed one man dead and one wounded—the first installment of the price we were to pay.

From Red Beach, where I was standing, it took my father's company two days to advance through the jungle and seize the airstrip. Then the company took a position on the perimeter, about a mile inland, and prepared for the Japanese counterattack. His company report indicates that "outposts were manned along the east end of the air field." But writing forty years later he remembers: "There were gaps of hundreds of yards between the fortified positions of our units. . . . The only thing that enabled us to survive the battles that were to come was the incredible luck that inspired the Japanese always to attack at those points where we were dug in instead of the vast empty spaces where we were not."

Back in the car, Paul and I wandered among some of these

empty spaces, looking for the site of the Battle of the Tenaru. It actually occurred on a spit of the Ilu, a nearby river, but early military maps errantly transposed the river names. The confusion continues fifty years later. Paul knew Red Beach and Henderson Field, but not the Battle of the Tenaru. Nor did his knowledge of jungle streams match that of the topographical maps. Again I was angered that our Pentagon dollars had never included signs to remember a pivotal battle in the Pacific. Belleau Wood along the Marne is decorated with monuments and maps of the World War I Marine victory, but part of Red Beach is a junkyard, and the only way to find the Ilu spit is with topographical surveys.

I was eager to find it because that is where Americans first defeated Japanese infantry and where my father led a bayonet charge into enemy lines. Many times I had heard the story of how the Japanese had sent the Ichiki Battalion along the beach to attack and, they thought, destroy the U.S. defensive positions around the airfield. Instead it was unable to ford the so-called Tenaru and was enveloped by a battalion that included my father's company. Of the bayonet charge, he later wrote: "Marines and Japanese fought face-to-face in the swirling gunsmoke, lunging, stabbing, and smashing with bayonets and rifle butts." In the battle the entire Japanese battalion, about nine hundred men, died. A famous Second World War photograph of the Tenaru shows rows of dead Japanese soldiers pressed into the sand, as if they have washed ashore in a deadly tide. It echoes "A Harvest of Death," Timothy O'Sullivan's photograph of Union dead in a misty Gettysburg field.

After a long walk through dense shoreline bush, I finally stood at the mouth of the Tenaru and recalled the disturbing end to this familiar story. After the fighting had ceased, a Japanese soldier, playing dead, threw a hand grenade at several American soldiers, including my father, who later wrote:

"Miraculously we were unhurt by the blast; we rushed at him, and as d'Errico covered him with his rifle, I placed my .45 automatic pistol to his head and pulled the trigger."

Although such action was the ingredient of the movies I enjoyed as a child, I found it uncomfortable to visit a place where my father had killed a man. Casualties in war are easier to fathom when they come in broad engagements and end up in body counts. To contribute to my unease, whenever my father tells this story he adds that he went through the man's wallet and found a snapshot of his wife and two children smiling before a lacquered screen. Even when I was young, such a postscript changed the account from a gung ho war story to one that saw, in every one of the war dead, a distant family. For my father, the wallet picture may have been the only time on Guadalcanal that he saw the Japanese as something other than a hated foe, capable of every treachery. As he later wrote: "Hacking our way through the jungle, we tended to think of the enemy as wily Orientals at home in this nightmarish terrain. We forgot that they were young men from crowded cities like Tokyo and farmland like Kyushu, just as we were city boys from Boston or country lads from Georgia."

Both my father's company report and the magazine article are remarkable for the way they describe death in individual terms. The fighting on Guadalcanal lasted six months. Thirty thousand men on both sides were killed. Under such conditions, I would expect a battlefield report to describe casualties just as Nathaniel Hawthorne had described the death of the stranger in "The Ambitious Guest": "His name and person utterly unknown; his history, his way of life, his plans, a mystery never to be solved." Instead each death or wounding is treated with an empathy I never imagined to be part of troop movements in the Second World War. As a result, the report reads like a log from a beleaguered clipper ship or Daniel Defoe's *Journal from a Plague Year*:

At 0500 a low level bombing attack was sustained in which Private Dan R. Hunt was killed and Private Andrew J. Thomason wounded. . . . Subsequently dysentery heavily affected the health of the Company. Private Thomas J. Knichel died of the disease August 27. . . . Corp. Zoli T. Almasi was wounded by shrapnel. . . . In the ensuing fire fight Private John C. Green was killed.

The idea of war as the sum of specific deaths was also a recurring theme among the early war stories that I can remember. It formed the antidote to my favorable impression of war as a variation on professional football. In particular, the death that seared my conscience was that of Bob Fowler, who served as lieutenant with my father on Guadalcanal. Millions died in the Second World War, but his death was the only one that seemed like the loss of a family member.

By the age of seven, I knew that my father's closest friend, Bob Fowler, had died, as it was put, "on the last day of the war." I remember wondering, in a childish way, why he had not known the war was about to end and laid low. His picture in the family album shows a boyish man, in his early twenties, with sharp, exuberant features and straight blond hair, not unlike a lead actor in a British documentary on East Africa. My father always referred to him by his nickname "Swifty," which added to the legend.

In the report, Bob Fowler often gets singled out for special mention, as if he were a favorite son or brother: "The enemy was compelled to retire upon receiving fire from the light machine guns in the weapons platoon, commanded by Lt. Fowler. . . . After capturing Mahile, Lt. Fowler was ordered to move east and investigate a small native mission. . . . Lt. Fowler made a three day combat patrol to wipe out an enemy field piece which had been registering in the sector. He personally accounted for a Japanese officer." But the Bob Fowler described often to my sisters and me was not a ferocious warrior or grizzled Marine so much as a cheerful, warm-hearted friend who somehow had the ability to endure the horrors of war and maintain a genial disposition.

Although I knew Bob Fowler had died mythically "on the last day of the war," I never knew exactly how. Nor did my father, to my knowledge. Bob Fowler had left the First Marines after the campaign on New Britain, returned to the United States to take command of his own company, and died while fighting on Okinawa. More than once I heard my father say: "I always felt that if he had stayed with me I could have gotten him through." Anyone who comes home from any war returns with many regrets, and for my father they focused on the death of Bob Fowler. It was as if the war had a purpose and meaning until that point, after which all the fighting became a variation on the senselessness that destroyed the Warsaw ghetto.

The story ended there until I discovered in *Goodbye, Darkness* that the company Bob Fowler had commanded was William Manchester's. And in Manchester's book is an account of how Fowler died. Manchester includes it in a passage that elaborates on James Jones's belief of how easy it is in war to slip over "the thin red line between the sane and the mad":

> My father had warned me that war is grisly beyond imagining. Now I believed him. Bob Fowler, F Company's popular, towheaded commander, had bled to death after being hit in the spleen. His orderly, who adored him, snatched up a submachine gun and unforgivably massacred a line of unarmed Japanese soldiers who had just surrendered.

I actually read the passage to my father, strangely enough, at a Memorial Day family barbecue. He was eager to hear what had happened, and I simply started reading aloud. When I finished the passage, he flushed red and swore sharply and uncharacteristically in front of the group, "God damn it to hell," while stinging the seat cushion with his palm. Obviously he had never heard the story, and it was painful to think of his friend bleeding to death helplessly. Nor did he want to hear that Bob Fowler's death had been the cause of an atrocity. The cry was a brief scream of reason that recoiled at so many lonely, needless deaths in the war.

During the Italian campaign, Ernie Pyle wrote a celebrated newspaper column about the death of another company commander, Henry Waskow. In *Wartime*, Paul Fussell uses that column to deflate Pyle as a sentimental propagandist, who never let too many facts of war get in the way of his messages to the American heartland. But that column described to me the numbing agony of what it was like to lose a friend in the war. It could just as easily, I sensed, have been written about the death of Bob Fowler. E. B. Sledge, a memoirist Fussell much admires, wrote similarly about the death of his Marine captain: "Our company commander represented stability and direction in a world of violence, death, and destruction. Now his life had been snuffed out. We felt forlorn and lost. It was the worst grief I endured during the entire war. The intervening years haven't lessened it any." Or as Pyle quotes one of the soldiers passing the corpse of Captain Waskow: "God damn it to hell anyway."

My driver Paul and I left the mouth of the Ilu and drove south of Henderson Field to see Edson's Bloody Ridge and the terrain of the upper Lunga River. From this savage no-man's land, the Japanese had launched repeated attacks against the airstrip. Edson's Ridge, a whaleshaped hillcrest, was another of the fortified positions that the Japanese were unlucky to strike. Even though a few of the enemy broke through to the airfield, most were killed or turned away in hand-to-hand night combat that my father remembers as a distant, flare-lit rumble in which, to his great relief, his company was spared any action.

Edson's Ridge overlooks the airfield and the expanse of Iron Bottom Sound. If Guadalcanal was Gettysburg in the Pacific, this was Little Round Top. It is capped with one of the few historical markers on the island, a white obelisk as modest as the rock in the Pennsylvania woods that remembers the 20th Maine. But the rest of Guadalcanal that we saw, except for the Japanese war memorials on Mount Austen, was uncharted, at least historically. The only way to imagine what happened, even with a guide, was to evoke the books written about the island. It turned a trip to a battlefield into one of those walking tours that visits the houses of great writers.

Guadalcanal has inspired a small library of fiction and nonfiction, much of which lined the shelves where I grew up. In early 1943, almost before the fighting had ended, *Guadalcanal Diary* by Richard Tregaskis and *Into the Valley* by John Hersey were published, helping to fuel the legend that was growing. Samuel Eliot Morison devoted a volume to the importance of its sea battles in his naval history of the war. James Jones used Guadalcanal as the setting for *The Thin Red Line*, although he created a fictional landscape. As he wrote in the foreword: "To have used a completely made up island would have been to lose all of these special qualities which the name Guadalcanal evoked for my generation."

I understand why my father holds James Jones in high regard. He writes about a rifle company—even a C Company—during the early months of the campaign. "He got it right" is the phrase that conveys the adulation. He describes the company with the clinical, pinpoint accuracy that Herman Melville uses to convey life aboard a whaler. Men foul themselves in fear, laugh at ghastly wounds inflicted on the enemy, learn to fight as if this were one of the Indian wars, and, when they least expect to, show courage or cowardice. And Jones writes in the crisp, purposeful language that is the best expression of the clarity of American thought at mid-century. The prose is brutal, sardonic, pessimistic, witty, and always to the point. The intervening years may have softened the tone, but the voice I hear in Jones is one that, at times, I can recognize in my father's accounts of the war.

Unfortunately, I came to Jones after reading a number of Vietnam novels that he inspired. As a result, the graphic descriptions of combat and the absence of heroes were familiar. Incompetent command is a given in Vietnam novels, hardly the revelation that it must have been in Jones. I had expected *The Thin Red Line* to be the definitive book on Guadalcanal. Instead I found it dated. I could appreciate Jones as one of the masters of war fiction and that this was a novel about more than a South Pacific battle. But it belonged to a generation that was not mine.

Mostly I am drawn to the books that in some way tell me literally what it was like for my father on the island. Often these are memoirs, like that by Manchester or another by Herbert Merillat, whose diary of the fighting, published in *Gaudalcanal Remembered*, fleshed out incidents of the battle that I only knew in fragments. Of the Henderson Field shelling on the night of October 13–14, Merillat wrote: "The shelter shook as if set in jelly." Although *With the Old Breed* is not about Guadalcanal, E. B. Sledge's recollections of fighting with the First Marine Division in subsequent campaigns on Peleliu and Okinawa are so vivid that they encompass the earlier battle as Siegfried Sassoon's remembrances of the Somme stand also for Passchendaele and Verdun.

But it is not only memoirs and novels that can explain to a son his father's war. *Acts of War* by the Sandhurst historian Richard Holmes describes the sociology of battle, with each chapter covering a subject such as what it is like to endure artillery fire, alcohol and combat, why men desert, or what it is to be wounded. The writing is a lively juxtaposition of literary allusions and eyewitness accounts. In explaining that men fight, not out of hatred of the enemy, but to maintain the respect of their peers, Holmes marshals evidence from Vietnam, the Falklands, the Civil War, and even the holy wars. He writes that the death of a friend is often what ignites an atrocity and quotes, among his examples, the passage from Manchester on the death of Bob Fowler.

That there were bad books about Guadalcanal was another early lesson. The one always mentioned was *Guadalcanal Diary*, written by Richard Tregaskis, a newspaperman. He landed with the Marines in the early waves, spent almost two months on the island, and then returned home to write what became a best-seller and a popular movie. Tregaskis's shortcoming was that, as a reporter, he was free to leave the island at any time. Everyone else had to stick around until they were killed, wounded, taken prisoner, or relieved. In a stock story about Tregaskis, my father recalls seeing him once, from a distance, riding in a general's jeep. That was strike two: how could a general understand anything about the front lines? After a while, Tregaskis evolved into a cautionary tale. He inhabited one world, interviewing generals and riding around in jeeps; in the other were the men of my father's company, some being shot and others dying of dysentery. The fable divided the world between observers and participants. "We had no choice; we had to stay" was the refrain that defined the participant world. It also laid bare one of the great paradoxes of the war. I am sure my father hated the miseries of Guadalcanal and longed to leave the place. But if leaving meant letting down his men or departing the arena for the box seats, then he was happy to stay.

Ironically, another correspondent, John Hersey, wrote a book that my father praises as the finest on the fighting along the Matanikau River, where Paul and I ended our drive. The subtitle of *Into the Valley* is *A Skirmish of the Marines*, and it is to war what *The Elements of Style* is to writing—a concise primer.

The Matanikau flows into the Sealark Channel through

what is now Honiara. But during the war it marked the western edge of the wild frontier between the Americans and the Japanese. My father still shudders ever so slightly when discussing it. He likes to quote Daniel Boone's phrase about Kentucky, "a dark and bloody land." Merillat calls it "sinister." Hersey writes that it was like "diving into a dark, stagnant pool," and that it was "a maze of ridges fringed with scallops of jungle."

The Matanikau does not have the jungle look of a rain forest, but it does look like an angry sea where the waves have petrified into sharp hills. Such a landscape offered each side wonderful opportunities for ambushes, and *Into the Valley* describes one that engulfs a company of Marines. Pinned down and bloodied, the men retreat, perhaps not with the haste of those in *The Red Badge of Courage*, but in the same direction.

During a lull Hersey asks a group of soldiers what they are fighting for. No one really wants to answer the question. Nor does anyone advance any theories on the geopolitical balance in Asia. Finally one whispers, "Jesus, what I'd give for a piece of blueberry pie." Hersey does his best to extrapolate that what the men are really fighting for is "to get the goddamn thing over and get home." But when *Into the Valley* was reissued in 1989, Hersey returns to this passage: "If you ask how a nation could win a war whose soldiers would opt for apple pie rather than a chance for heroic death, I would be inclined to answer that this is one of the main reasons why our side won. There was a lifesaving skepticism and irony embedded in the confused courage of men bred to free choice."

In his own writing, my father never says why he is fighting. Like many, he was drafted and decided to enlist in the Marines as an officer before being swept into the Army as a private. He talks about getting it over, about getting home, as if he is on an extended business trip. But he also often draws a connection between his enlistment and two childhood summers spent on a bicycle in Germany. By chance he saw Hitler beside the illuminated columns at Nuremburg and Jesse Owens win at the Olympics. He also saw from one year to the next the rise of anti-Semitism in the towns where they were riding, and he would speak about how he believed war was inevitable—and, given what he was seeing, probably necessary.

Almost stronger than my father's reasons for joining are his impulses to speak about what happened during the fighting. Over the years we have had numerous conversations about the war. They come up at odd times and go into great detail about this action or that officer. Part of his eagerness to talk must be to keep alive memories of those like Bob Fowler or to make sense of events—like the fighting along the Matanikau—that at the time must have seemed senseless. But it also seems akin to the need among Holocaust survivors to bear witness, to make it clear what all wars are about. Hersey, who saw not only Guadalcanal, but the ruins of Hiroshima and Warsaw, reflected in the foreword of *Into the Valley*: "One of the things I learned was that war makes no national or racial or ideological distinctions as it degrades human beings."

I have always felt grateful that my father was willing to talk about his war experiences. Paul Fussell writes that many veterans were numb after the war and reluctant to tell the truth about what happened to them. Fussell believes that a consequence of such silence is a national illusion about the reality of combat. "Now, fifty years later," he writes in *Wartime*, "there has been so much talk about 'The Good War,' the Justified War, the Necessary War, and the like, that the young and the innocent could get the impression that it was really not such a bad thing after all. It's thus necessary to observe that it was a war and nothing else, and thus stupid and sadistic." Ironically, it was my father's war stories that first created and later took away a most cherished childhood illusion, that of the Good War.

That evening at the Mendana Hotel I was conscious of how my time on Guadalcanal had differed from that of my father. Tired from the long, hot day, I could take a swim, have a beer with dinner, and sleep in an air-conditioned room. I did not have to flop alongside a trail or wonder if an artillery shell would find me in an inadequate foxhole. I had even greater admiration for anyone who spent time on the island, even the maligned Tregaskis.

Darkness spread quickly after sunset, as did the mosquitoes that followed me on an after-dinner walk I took to a bridge over the Matanikau. Looking along the cavernous riverbank, I was reminded of the last sentence in *Wuthering Heights*, when the narrator, standing over a grave site in the moor, wonders "how anyone could ever imagine unquiet slumbers for the sleepers in that quiet earth." On the way back I passed a few pieces of rusting artillery in front of municipal buildings. Otherwise nothing is a reminder of the battles or makes the connection between this stream and a similar one at Antietam. In the semi-official history of monuments and driving tours, it appears a blank slate. Only books such as Manchester's and Hersey's, or the stories of the many fathers who served here, keep it alive.

Russian Rublette

(1998)

Watching the collapse of the Russian economy, I have decided that many in the West were more comfortable when the country was locked away in the prison yard of the Soviet Union. At least when the Politburo ran things, you could get someone on the hot line with the power to release hostages or break off an invasion.

On talk shows and the evening news, I hear expert after expert conclude that Russia is dying of an overdose of market forces. Commentators use the same tones of sorrow and delight in which Bob Woodward described the last temptations of John Belushi. The descriptions of Russia's market excess are as familiar as the empty pill vials on the bathroom floor at the Beverly Hills Hotel.

Yet in my seven years of Russian travel, I have seen few signs of free enterprise. To be sure, it is possible to trade shares on Moscow's exchange, and competition has spawned both new restaurants and software companies. But shareholders no more decide the fate of their companies than did the electorate invest Prime Minister Yevgeny Primakov with authoritarian powers. Nor does supply and demand matter when the state's chief source of revenue is defaulting every few years on its loans.

Instead of a market economy, what Russia has is

Communism with a consumerist face. On loan applications to the International Monetary Fund or in pitches to foreign investors, the government promotes the classless society of stock exchanges and market equilibrium. But when it comes to paying dividends or interest due, the Russian economy, rather than wiring cash, offers up variations on the five-year plan. The dictators of the proletariat still control the means of production.

I started traveling to Russia in the winter of 1991–92, after the aborted coup against Mikhail Gorbachev had the unintended effect of putting the Soviet Union into receivership. Then, as now, there were reports in the Western press about Russia "not lasting through the winter," as if the entire country were huddled in tents on the German front. Western governments were sending aid packages to Russia, and on one of my early trips to Moscow, I hoped to arrange a deal in which a Western country would give large quantities of meat to the Russians.

Riding in a taxi from Sheremetyevo Airport into Moscow, on one of the city's broad boulevards that suggest an empire of tenement housing, I fancied myself part of the relief effort, maybe a spiritual heir of Herbert Hoover, whose American Relief Administration resupplied a hungry Europe after World War I. I was not visiting the Soviet Union that had killed the kulaks or executed Polish officers in the woods at Katyn, but the Russia that, as America's ally, had unloaded Liberty ships in Murmansk and driven the trucks of the Marshall Plan north from Tehran.

I decided that the best chance to give away the food was to establish a connection with the newly formed government of Boris Yeltsin. Business contacts had arranged a meeting with a deputy minister of economics, and, after several days in Moscow, I found myself in a taxi heading toward the Russian White House, a figure in one of those diplomatic memoirs that inevitably have a chapter entitled "Mission to Moscow."

Needless to say, I got no closer to meeting Boris Yeltsin than would a Russian visitor to the American White House get the chance to give beets to President Clinton.

The so-called Russian White House is actually a towering federal building, admittedly white, that would look more at home in Fritz Lang's *Metropolis* than in Mr. Smith's Washington. In 1991, Boris Yeltsin defended it from a Communist restoration. Two years later he turned his own guns on the Duma, housed within, and set it ablaze as if it were a rebel stronghold in a breakaway Caucasus republic.

The conscript at the front door, not more than eighteen years old and thinking only of his next cigarette, flipped through my passport back to front, as if it were in Arabic. A secretary collected me from the lobby, and I ascended the monolith in a creaking elevator. Our meeting took place in a cavernous conference room where it was easy to imagine a subcommittee of the 5th Party Congress voting on production quotas. But the delegation gathered there was not made up of gray party men with flat shoes and Andrey Gromyko hats. Instead there huddled before me at one end of the plenum-sized table what looked like a university seminar. The minister, who wore a flannel shirt and hiking boots, reminded me of a teaching assistant. Around him sat a group of young men, all in their early twenties, whose idea of a collective probably was to pass around a copy of *Policy Review*.

I knew the Russian people were suffering food shortages and believed that my offering of government surplus meat would be welcome. It had sat too long in freezers to rate a spot on the counters of Zabar's or Covent Garden, and it contained more fat than Martha Stewart would approve of, but they could do with it as they wished and pay in the future with a surplus of their own. I assumed that all we would discuss was freight forwarding and cold storage. To my surprise, the minister answered my offer with a lecture on price and concluded that food relief was not compatible with the doctrines of Friedrich von Hayek.

My first thought was that the Russians were again to starve in the interests of ideology. The minister and his acolytes, however, lacked the fervor of either commissars or penny-stock investors. In their judgment, Russia was better off trying to make a go of market economics than cultivating a dependence on Western assistance. As if reading from Jack Kemp's playbook, they made the point that Russia had survived hard winters before, that state intervention had failed for seventy years, and that, sooner or later, only the markets could set Russian tables with meat and potatoes.

I had come thinking I was bringing food to a church supper. Instead I had walked into a symposium in which Laffer curves had replaced the tired fare of Marx and Lenin. Although I left with my meat unsold, I was comforted to learn that Russia wanted to get along without handouts. It cheered me to think the country would open itself to market ideas. But in our optimism, both the minister and I failed to notice that the Party wasn't over.

In 1992, despite the market optimism of certain cells within the Yeltsin government, central planning economy still had a bear hold on the economy. Delegations from ministries, such as those of shipbuilding and telecommunications, roamed the West, looking for orders to replace those no longer issuing from Moscow. The market was another word for the budget allocation that would pay workers or keep the sanitariums open on the Black Sea. In meeting after meeting, I heard plant managers plead for clothes for their workers.

Most confusing of all, with state holding companies in liquidation after 1992, was determining who owned what. Officially the Moscow bureaucracy had title to the oil in western Siberia, the diamonds of Yakutia, and the gas in the Barents Sea. But regional governments treated these claims like the demands of czarist bondholders. Assets in the ground and production in the mills were declared local property. As in America, management treated itself to stock options and divided what was left as if it were a sewer contract in Baltimore.

The government pumped trillions of rubles into inefficient state enterprises while working on market plans to put them in the hands of ordinary citizens, much the way that American corporations occasionally reward their shareholders with a nonprofitable division, dressed up as a special dividend. To play lotto with Russian industry, the government issued to every citizen a voucher that could be redeemed for shares of Russia, Inc. These coupons had nominal values of about $20 in 1993, more than a monthly wage for most Russians who, rather than buy shares, bartered their scrip for Marlboro cigarettes and Georgian champagne. Crafty merchants sent minions into the streets to acquire voucher positions that were exchanged for blocks in privatized ventures.

The program succeeded in redistributing state assets, but not the wealth. Voucher shareholdings contributed no capital to enterprises that needed equity in the amounts that Michael Milken once trafficked. But voucher trading established the rudiments of a stock exchange. Companies began issuing stocks and bonds, and the Russians embraced speculation as if losses were covered by the Federal Deposit Insurance Corporation. Certain mutual funds even began advertising on television, and their collapse became as inevitable as the cancellation of daytime serials. When MMM, an early fund, went down with the savings of widows and orphans, its promoter sought not the protection of bankruptcy court but the immunity of elective office.

After 1994, returns on the stock exchange routinely exceeded 100 percent. Certain industries, such as oil, telecommunications, and financial services, attracted strategic Western partners, who saw values at a fraction of their Western prices. A barrel of Lukoil's proven oil reserves cost

$0.25 in 1995, while the same barrel, valued in the common stock of Shell, cost $5. In 1996, Arco completed the purchase of 8.8 percent of Lukoil for $340 million.

Those gambling in the Russian stock market overlooked that they were drawing from a house of cards. One ignored quirk was that share registries—the list of shareholders—were kept at the companies themselves, not at banks or with independent third parties. Consequently, unfriendly shareholders could be struck from the ledger, like dissidents once dispatched to Siberia. Another problem was the financial statements, which painted pictures of robust companies in the spirit of socialist realism. On most balance sheets, assets were overvalued, while the liabilities were stubbornly real, such as salaries for workers who otherwise would starve.

Even the presence of Western auditors preparing statements provided little comfort. Before it failed, Tokobank, which had the European Bank for Reconstruction and Development among its shareholders, received a clean bill of accounts from Coopers & Lybrand. When the Russian stock market collapsed, beginning in November 1997, shares gave up most of their gains from the market era. The Moscow Times Index fell from 500 to 50. In less than a year, Lukoil's market capitalization fell from $20 billion to $2 billion, even though its proven reserves are more than those of Mobil and Chevron combined. As Marx and Engels wrote in the *Communist Manifesto*: "Pauperism develops more rapidly than population and wealth."

What triggered the panic of 1998 was the collapse in the market for Russian government bonds, which in turn brought down the banking system, one of the government's largest creditors. In the aftermath, large bank holding companies, such as Oneximbank, Most-Bank, and Menatep, merged operations, perhaps in the hope of confusing the lines of depositors that lined up outside their respective headquarters.

Other large banks, such as Inkombank, closed, as did a golden era of banking speculation.

Between Lenin's arrival at the Finland Station and Gorbachev's departure for Sochi, the Soviets used banks to distribute the state budget. Big banks were established around various industries, such as petrochemicals and aviation. Ruble credits were transferred from the central government to the banks and then to state enterprises. Loans were repaid, not from profits, but from an allocation from the successive budget or by a Soviet insurance fund. In America, the analogy would have involved the loans of a Tobacco Bank repaid from next year's subsidies to the growers.

Just as Aeroflot dissolved into hundreds of regional carriers after the Communist collapse, so did the banks spin into the hands of their local directorates. For example, Promstroy Bank, with a branch in every city to lend money for Stalin's industrial dreams, broke into more than two hundred pieces, as if all the branches of the Chase Manhattan Bank were to declare themselves independent.

In the last seven years, I have visited many of these new banks, including one in Ufa, near the Urals, with potatoes for sale in its lobby. In the early years, most bank buildings looked like Brooklyn warehouses or empty subway stations, down to the faded marble and worn tiles. Accounts were often kept by hand, and the filing was stacked in corners. At a major bank in Moscow, I had to step over two sleeping dogs to enter the elevator.

In the liberalized economy, especially after 1993, new Russian banks flourished because they paid little if any interest on deposits, thus prompting a large transfer of wealth from the industrial sector to the banks. Large ruble fortunes were made on these interest-free deposits, which attracted factories, unions, and even nightclubs to apply for banking licenses. Soon Russia had more than three thousand banks, some even in glass-tower headquarters, although I remember one that set up shop in the back of a Mexican restaurant. A few banks practiced the habits of thrift and provided their customers with automatic teller machines and MasterCards. But many paid interest by raising new deposits, a system of asset and liability management perfected by Mr. Charles Ponzi. The unscrupulous washed dirty money or skipped town with depositors' money. Shareholders in banks routinely borrowed more than the capital they had invested.

Beginning in 1994—when interbank rates in rubles reached 200 percent per year, and 25 percent in U.S. dollars—Russian banks moved their deposits to the gaming tables of government securities, known locally as GKO. The government became the banks' biggest borrower, issuing paper that allowed investors to double their money in a year.

Not content simply to risk local depositors' money in these get-rich-quick schemes, the Russian banks raised additional money from syndicates of Western banks. On the assumption that the ruble was a stable currency and that the Russian government would make good on its obligations, ruble assets were funded with dollar liabilities, which made both Western creditors and Russian debtors hostage to the ruble's fortune.

Western banks and investment funds also threw dice in the direction of Russian markets. Financiers invested in GKO or Russian shares, or issued letters of credit against goods still in country, with the confidence that Russia was now an emerging market, one where, it was hoped, they paid more dividends than bribes.

When the Russian government defaulted on its loans and the banking system failed, Western creditors were left holding a bag they had hoped was worth $70 billion. Add previous unpaid debt, some dating to Soviet times, and the amount of the Russian default approaches $200 billion. Among the banks, Credit Suisse had exposures that exceeded $1 billion. Bankers Trust and Smith Barney, among the U.S. investors, counted their losses at $350 million each. German banks had more than $30 billion on the table, although most of its was insured by their government.

Not counted in the initial loan losses were open foreign exchange contracts, estimated at another $10 billion, or certain syndicated loans yet to mature. Nor is it known if Western banks will be allowed to seize collateral that includes, in one case, a strategic interest in AO Yukos, a large oil company.

Even if the amount of the Russian default reaches $200 billion, Western governments and financial institutions will be able to cover their losses, if not their pride. But such provisions will virtually sate most of their appetites for Russian investment, denying capital to markets that had their previous dose before 1917. For a while anyway, Russia will live in a hermetically sealed financial world, with barter again the preferred method of payment. Even the International Monetary Fund, despite its habit of dumping billions into lost economic causes, recently held back $4 billion in committed loans to Russia, perhaps wondering whether to demand steel or vodka in return.

An irony of the Russian economic collapse is that it has tied the country's fortunes yet again to the ruble, a currency that should circulate only among collectors, much like postage stamps from Pacific islands. During the reform era, all large transactions were measured in U.S. dollars, hordes of which can literally be found under mattresses in $100 bills. But the policy of the recently reorganized central bank is to break this dollar standard, the effect of which can only be to keep Russia in the gulag of nations with non-convertible currencies.

In the Soviet era, the ruble was scrip, accepted at the company store but having no value on world exchanges. Little of the country's wealth was stored in the currency. By paying its workers with near-worthless money, the Party maintained all the options. Following the fall of the Soviets, the government printed rubles to subsidize industry and pay workers. The ruble turned into Monopoly money. During the great inflation that followed, those in the ruble world stayed on Baltic Avenue, while anyone with dollars advanced to Marvin Gardens.

In 1992 the Russian government organized a Moscow currency exchange, at which a few banks could trade rubles for dollars. In a limited way, the ruble became a convertible currency. But nearly every day from 1992 into 1995, the ruble depreciated against the dollar by the amount of the prevailing rate of inflation, falling from R85 = $1 in 1992 to R5,000 = $1 in 1995.

To support the ruble, the Russian government did its best to restrict the money supply, even if that meant using monetary smoke and mirrors. The central bank canceled older ruble notes. Executive orders were issued to mandate the conversion of oil profits into rubles. More recently, new bank notes were issued without the last three zeros, to give the currency an air of respectability.

For more than two years, the ruble was hailed as a stable currency. The government used hard currency reserves to maintain its value. The stock market soared, and the government stoked its budget deficit with dollars from oil exported at $20 per barrel and industries privatized at lofty multiples. By 1998, however, the government's money had vanished. The price of crude oil had fallen to $12. The country was importing grain. Taxes were uncollectible. Reserves had dwindled to $11 billion. The crack in Asian markets made further privatization impossible and forced hedge funds in the West to bail out of their Russian positions.

To raise revenue, the government had few options: it could print money or renege on its obligations. It decided to do both. In August 1997 it defaulted on its public debt and declared a moratorium on the country's corporate borrowings,

hoping to hoard cash for the long winter. Nor could it continue to use hard currency to defend the ruble, which fell by
half against Western currencies. Those who needed to convert rubles to pay off dollar loans suddenly found that their
debts had doubled. To stabilize the banking system and meet
payrolls, the government decided to print new money. For
the third time in ten years, those holding the ruble found
their assets, in effect, nationalized. Ruble gold had been spun
into straw.

With the ruble's recent collapse, logic would suggest making the dollar legal tender, much as South American coins circulated in post-revolutionary America, when there was little
confidence in the Articles of Confederation. With at least a
stable currency, Russia could avoid the instability of inflation
and trade more easily in the community of Western nations.
Instead, the Yeltsin government has discouraged the circulation of dollars and bet the bank on the ruble, ignoring that its
value is pegged to political confidence.

Those successful today in Russia used to be the life of the
Party, which gave them the chance to travel, learn English
or French, and to have the contacts that now let them deliver
oil products or Scotch as once they delivered reports *On
the Solidarity and Fraternal Relations of the Peoples of
Tadzhikistan.*

Just like Wharton and Stanford MBAs, graduates of the
workers' paradise learned little about contract law or warehouse operations, but a lot about how to reach a certain minister on the phone. A generation that expected to stoke the
furnaces of the central plan now controls banks and nightclubs
and pays in cash for vacations in the south of France. Are these
new men a mafia? The appellation is one of choice today
in Russia. To many older Russians, anyone making money
selling used cars or running a hardware store is mafia. The
word also describes muggers, bodyguards, political officials,

and conglomerates as diversified as Time Warner.

The mafia in Russia is billed as one of capitalism's mutant genes, but its origins lie in the paralysis of the dying Communist system. Distribution networks were spawned in the Brezhnev era when the central economy failed to plan for such items as sugar, flour, shoes, and blue jeans. Some of these groups drifted into extortion, drugs, money laundering, and drive-by shootings, while others used their talents for overnight delivery to set up supermarkets or distribute the ornaments of the duty-free lifestyle.

On the streets, especially in Moscow and St. Petersburg, the mafia plays a Russian version of numbers and protection. Even Western businessmen operating locally whisper about guardian angels and godfathers as if they were investment tax credits. In his book about the Russian mafia, *Comrade Criminal*, Stephen Handelman makes the point that Russia need not fear a counter-revolution from the Communist Party because so many of its former members are now millionaires. Heard in the market are apocryphal stories of this minister's links to gas or that group's stranglehold on liquor. Several years ago the personal guards of Boris Yeltsin donned ski masks and beat up security agents in the lobby of Most-Bank. The American equivalent would involve the Secret Service, in disguise, roughing up the guards of Citibank or J. P. Morgan.

Aside from extortionists and racketeers, the Russian mafia consists of trusts: combinations of political, military, and economic interests that control this mining region or that bank. Wealth is concentrated in the hands of members of parliament, oil chiefs, or regional governors who manage their spheres of influence as Huey Long ran Louisiana. For example, during privatization, banks such as Menatep and Oneximbank leveraged their influence to buy, at steep discounts, blocks of shares in the largest oil companies. In these incarnations Russian capitalism has less in common with the thought of John Stuart Mill than with Mussolini's Italy. The economy is the province of oligarchs, who use a combination of state power, violence, and industrial strength to control votes in parliament or the distribution of Heineken beer. As Machiavelli advised his prince: "It cannot be called talent to slay fellow citizens, to deceive friends, to be without faith, without mercy, without religion; such methods may gain empire, but not glory."

Oligarchy is not new to the Russian experience. In the nineteenth and early twentieth centuries, Russia failed to develop either a constitutional monarchy or a broad middle class. The ruling nobility shared the wealth of the nation only with itself. A hundred years later, the country's assets are as closely guarded as the jewels in the Kremlin. The market economy has proved little more than a Potemkim village, set up in Western conference rooms to coax easy money from such unsuspecting lenders as hedge funds or the International Monetary Fund.

Nor have the lessons of market illusion been lost on the commissars. When Gennady Zyoganov assumed the leadership of the Communist Party several years ago, he was asked if he planned to change its name. Maybe the old brand name had lost its appeal in the market? Maybe a new one referring to Labor or Social Democracy might find more customers? But with little hesitation, the new chief executive officer answered: "If you bought Coca-Cola, would you change its name?"

Abroad

(1995)

The past is another country: they do things differently there.
—L. P. Hartley, *The Go-Between*

Three years ago at midsummer, when shimmering waves of grain in the Swiss countryside give it aspects of Kansas, I moved with my family from a row house in Brooklyn to a farming village outside Geneva. Out the back door, instead of the New York neighbor who paved his yard and then painted it the colors of the Jamaican flag, were fields "buried in wheat and corn," as Willa Cather described those of her prairie childhood. Farther on in the summer haze were vineyards whose wine was selling in nearby cellars and the first ring of the Alps that glimmered either with snowcaps or the fireworks of Bastille Day.

Like many moves abroad, this one was unexpected. I left New York for Switzerland on a routine trip, with several suits and a sweater. Six weeks later I called home with the proposition of a move to Europe. We weighed our family and friends in America against the echo of small-arms fire in the Brooklyn night and decided to try what the French call the provincial life.

Geneva is the old world, with a graceful lakefront and a huge small-poodle population, that survives without clusters of motels or car washes on its perimeter. As with any city in the world, it also has its expatriate ghettos: tree-lined suburbs where the language is English, the bridge club meets Thursdays, and cable television makes it possible to shave by the newscasts of Dan Rather. The coffee may be espresso, but the caffeine is all American.

By chance I found a house off the information superhighway. I answered an ad on a bulletin board and, one Saturday morning, I biked seven miles west of the city. Once clear of the congestion, I rode through springtime fields, feeling like a character in *Escape from New York* who crosses the 59th Street Bridge and ends up in *Heidi*.

Struck by the view and the landlord's eloquence on village life, I rented the house without counting the bedrooms or investigating the bus schedule. We spent the summer unpacking boxes, looking for French classes, and adjusting to the incomprehension that goes with foreign life. The first night, when I arrived home from work, my wife reported a strange chirping sound that we later discovered was the telephone.

In the three years since moving to the village, we have tried our best to mix locally. Our two daughters attend the local schools. We go to all the village *fêtes*—holidays celebrated with town suppers—and we buy bread each morning in the small *boulangerie*.

In turn, the village has been gracious in accepting us, even if our American taste for gadgets marks us as distinctly non-Swiss. When our son was born, the postlady, whom we know only at the mailbox, knitted him a sweater. Others in town invited us to their mountain chalet, and we have danced at a local wedding reception. In Spain or Greece, all this would happen before the moving van pulled away from the driveway. But in Switzerland, we could live in the village for three generations, take up farming, drive a small four-cylinder Renault, and still we would be known as the newcomers, or perhaps *Les Americains*.

As much as we want to assimilate locally, our neighbors are correct in always thinking of us as Americans. We buy all of our clothes from the Lands' End catalogue and live on a steady diet of strange food. Whenever guests come from the United States, they are instructed to bring Cheerios, chocolate chips, peanut butter, and maple syrup. We decorate the house on Halloween, and, on the fourth Thursday in November, we perplex the local butcher with an order for a fresh turkey.

We also spend a lot of time struggling with French. My wife and I both studied it in school and thus arrived knowing that verb conjugations were in our future. We acquired dictionaries and enrolled in classes. I speak some French at the bank where I work and thus know the language of bankruptcy and goodwill. My wife spends most of her time chatting with small children, so she knows the words for *sandbox*, *wading pool*, and "be nice to your brother." We speak French with the neighbors, but usually the subjects are lost dogs and the weather.

Not to have fluency and slang in a language is to inhabit one of those cloistered worlds so often described by Charlotte Brontë. Although after three years we can now have dinners in French and speak on the telephone, most of the time we still feel like Lucy Snowe, the heroine of *Villette*, whom Brontë dispatches to a life of homesickness in Belgium: "I had no flow," she confesses of learning French, "only a hesitating trickle of language."

My father describes teaching his father to drive in the 1930s and says of my grandfather that he would never shift out of first gear, finding it sufficient for his purposes. I feel the same way about my French and steer most sentences away from the subjunctive, as though it were a New York City pothole.

My wife is prone to Franglais—the insertion of English words when the needed French is missing. Often the French word is similar to the English, but sometimes the connection is less apparent. At one dinner, she launched into an account of a trip we made to Prague and from that started describing the wonders of Czech beer. No, she explained to those at the dinner, it didn't have all the chemicals Americans inject into their Budweis. The guests didn't follow, so she switched to Franglais, and announced that Czech beer was "sans preservatives," which unfortunately in French means: "without condoms."

No matter how long I live abroad, one of my internal clocks will always be set on American time. On holidays, family birthdays, and distant family gatherings, I think of myself as stranded in the Emerald City and want nothing more than to petition the great Oz for a trip home.

Come Sunday afternoons in the autumn, I long for professional football in a way that suggests it is a chemical dependence. And like James Joyce in Trieste, tracing the steps of his imagination around Dublin, I find that a lot of my daydreaming is spent on walks along Flatbush Avenue or on Mulberry Street heading from Little Italy to Greenwich Village.

We worry that the kids are missing an American childhood, that one day we'll wake up to discover three Swiss in their bunks. They spend summers in America, visiting relatives, but speak French at school and know little about Niagara Falls or the Statue of Liberty. One of our daughters announced one evening that she had learned a new letter at school and then pronounced something that sounded like "airrrrr," a perfectly rolled French r.

Most people think young children can learn a foreign language in the amount of time advertised for taped lessons. But our oldest daughter spent a miserable year in kindergarten, sucking her thumb and understanding little. We fretted, in parent fashion, until one afternoon, about a year after we arrived, she started speaking the most perfect French—the same kind that is so difficult for us to understand.

Having children fluent in the local language makes us feel all the more like immigrant parents, speaking in thick accents and being something of an oddity to their friends. On the bus to work in the morning, I feel very much like a Russian emigrant on the F train in Brooklyn. I'm wearing a foreign-cut suit with foreign shoes and reading a foreign newspaper.

Another Brooklyn subway rider, Willy Loman, reflected: "I still feel—kind of temporary about myself." That also describes the uncertainty of much life abroad. Many expatriates do not know if they're going to finish their days in Flanders fields or be called home at the end of June.

We came for two years, like most Americans we know—even those now applying for permanent residence. Some days we imagine our children here in high school; at other times, when the weather is grim and friends seem faraway, we look aloft at the jets banking west above the Jura mountains on a course for America, and there isn't one we don't wish we were on.

The pleasure of Switzerland is that it rarely lives up to its reputation for stale predictability. In three years of work in a bank, I have never seen a suitcase of cash. A few shops by the railroad station sell noisy clocks, but most of the production run is hustled off to Japan. And I suspect more chocolate is consumed in an American mall than anywhere in Switzerland.

Most surprising is the country's devotion to Athenian democracy. Important decisions are made in town and village elections, as was true in America when Tocqueville wrote that "the township was organized before the county, the county before the state, the state before the union." A stock journalistic story about Switzerland involves a chance meeting of two men at a cocktail party. After considerable conversation, one discovers that the other is president of the country. The cantons—equivalent to American counties—decide school hours, tax rates, budget items, and unemployment compensation. To become a naturalized Swiss citizen, you need a character reference from your town and its agreement to support you in your old age.

At a time when the rest of Europe is moving toward political union, and even Russia is weighing membership in the North Atlantic Treaty Organization, Switzerland is retreating into its historic neutrality and isolation. Led by the German-speaking cantons, the country voted against a first step toward European confederation. And the same voting bloc is opposing more truck routes through the Alps, deciding instead that the containers can piggyback on trains.

Income from banking, tourism, and watchmaking allows the Swiss to subsidize the dairy farmers whose cows are so splendidly belled. The same is true of the *viticulteurs* in our village whose wine is protected from the flood of French imports. European union would end these subsidies, and without them the small farms and vineyards would wither, and the fields around every village would be sold to subdevelopers.

Nor are the Swiss relaxing their defenses, even though most invaders these days carry ice cream cones or strap skis to their cars. The Genevois fought their last war in 1602, when Savoyards, from neighboring French Savoie, attacked Geneva on a cold December night. An old woman walking the city ramparts spotted the French placing ladders against the city walls and, after sounding the alarm, doused the invaders with boiling soup—presumably a defensive capability then allowed under Geneva convention.

No one knows if the Savoyards would have made it if threatened only with raclette or fondue, but since then the Swiss have preferred to prepare for wars rather than actually fight them. All Swiss men serve in the army until age forty, and most spend a month of each year playing soldier. They shoot mortars in the wilderness, fly F-18s through alpine crevices, inspect the defenses near Zermatt, and enjoy time off from work at nearly full salary. It all seems like national summer camp, until you consider that Adolph Hitler bypassed Switzerland, having decided the cost of an Alpine invasion too high.

Whether Hitler needed Switzerland to launder stolen gold or purchase ball bearings is one of those historical questions that still arouse passion on both sides. But a military friend told us that the German invasion plans called for eighteen divisions and that there were great fears that they would bog down in the mountains. During the war, the Swiss army went on alert several times, expecting an attack, and mobilized its army to patrol the borders, including the one with France that we see from our backyard.

We often try to imagine the frontier during the war. Vichy France, in particular the jurisdiction of those such as Klaus Barbie, was less than a mile from our house. In the little towns that we can see while we sip coffee or enjoy a barbeque, Jews were rounded up for final destinations. But the war never touched our village or its inhabitants.

Civil defense is understandably a passion of the Swiss, and nearly all underground garages and tunnels double as bomb shelters. Similarly, new houses must be built with a shelter, although John McPhee, in his book about the Swiss army, noted that they tend to fill up with ski boots and wine. Our shelter has mothballed long-playing records to get us through the nuclear winter. Nevertheless, how many houses in Bosnia have bomb shelters, or how many Bosnians wish they did?

The durability of Switzerland was an early lesson. In the summer of 1991, the confederation celebrated its seven hundredth anniversary. In America such an occasion would merit William Tell impersonators and fireworks like those over

Dresden. But although Geneva and Zurich each lit up the night sky, the main celebration took place in towns and villages.

On August 1, the date of the original cantonal pact, our village and a neighboring one erected a white tent and served a dinner of soup, sausage, cheese, bread, and wine. The local parliamentarian made a speech, only parts of which we understood. But we did get his allusions to Yugoslavia and the message of Switzerland's stability amidst the turmoil of Europe. A few couples danced to accordion music, and when the sun set, a bonfire was lit on a nearby field. Across the valley between the Alps and the Jura, and then north along Lake Geneva, similar bonfires connected one village to another, as if part of a tribal ritual. After the glow faded, everyone walked home, with the children carrying small paper lanterns, which bobbed along the vineyard paths like spirits from an ancient world.

One consequence of our move to Switzerland was that we gave up television. American sets do not work in Europe, and a decent television in Geneva can cost more than a thousand dollars, before all the cable charges that bring Australian Rules Football into your life. But we balked at more than the price. Our daughters, then four and almost two, were reaching the age when we would have had to offer rudimentary explanations about the war in the Balkans or the reason for so many rub outs in prime time.

We decided to follow the advice of the Oompa-Loompas, Roald Dahl's creations, who told Charlie and Mr. Willy Wonka:

> The most important thing we've learned,
> As far as children are concerned,
> Is never, never, NEVER let
> Them near your television set . . .

It rots the senses in the head!
It kills imagination dead!
It clogs and clutters up the mind!
It makes a child so dull and blind
He can no longer understand
A fantasy or fairyland!

The children have filled the void with books on tape and a host of imaginary friends, some of whom seem indistinquishable from the stars of daytime televsion. We don't miss the French talk shows, which feature men in striped shirts, smoking cigarettes and chatting to women wearing scarves. Nor is it a hardship to pass up dubbed American programs such as *Hawaii, police d'Etat*. But it is a dislocation not to see the news clippings of the presidential election or the effects of the Los Angeles earthquake.

Aside from phone calls, letters, and travelers' tales, our connection to the dark continent is with the *International Herald Tribune*, which washes ashore every day as if a series of notes in a bottle. I look forward to it all day and read it only in the evenings, turning first to the sports pages and afterward to the scandal updates from Washington and the train wrecks in India. The essence of the *Washington Post* and the *New York Times*, and once the voice of Americans in Paris, it is dutiful in recording wars and deficits. The progress of the New York Yankees can be tracked like that of IBM. But as a letter from home, it is as disappointing as finding an envelope from a friend that contains one of those computer-printed Christmas letters that tells about Uncle Karl's colostomy.

Seeing America through the prism of the *Herald Tribune* is like watching a silent movie. I know that President Clinton likes jogging, the occasional hamburger, and night riding with state troopers, but the sound of his voice or his instincts for war and peace are as hard to fathom as the images in the cabinets of Dr. Caligari.

Nor does the *Herald Tribune* choose columnists who can provide the sound track. Most could write about my own children, and I don't think I would be interested. The political commentators speak the Esperanto of Washington, for which local television is the only dictionary. Only in the humor columns and the comics—Doonesbury, Calvin and Hobbes, Art Buchwald, and Russell Baker—do I hear voices of the friends we miss in Brooklyn.

As best as we can, we try to stay current with American writing. We subscribe to *The New Yorker*, but, as with so many other magazines, we get the feeling that we have come late to a cocktail party where everybody knows everybody and no one knows us. On my trips to the States, I try to fill a bag with new books. Occasionally in the carpetbag we discover a new writer—at least to us—such as Barbara Kingsolver, but mostly it is easier to replay the classics, especially those that describe Americans abroad.

In the past year I have read all the novels of F. Scott Fitzgerald as if they were a box of old letters. Stories of undergraduate pretensions or first jobs in New York free memories that a life abroad can often store away with the luggage. Waking up every morning to the Swiss countryside, I need to be reminded of Nassau Street in Princeton or the way that the late-afternoon sun dapples the waters of Long Island Sound on whose shores I grew up.

Fitzgerald is also the columnist that I long to find in the *Herald Tribune*. When I read that "Jay Gatsby of West Egg, Long Island sprang from his Platonic conception of himself," I think of Ronald Reagan or Bill Clinton and their invented lives. What better describes America's dependency on celebrity than his observation, in *The Beautiful and Damned*, that "there was nothing, it seemed, that grew stale so soon as pleasure."

Without the interruption of television, we assumed that we would spend our evenings improving our French or perhaps

developing a stamp collection, In fact, after children are cor-
ralled, branded with toothpaste, and lassoed to bed, there is
neither the time nor the inclination to read Balzac with a dictionary or study postmarks from the Solomon Islands.

We fill the evenings reading newspapers or chatting at the
dining-room table, flipping through L.L. Bean or IKEA
catalogues as though they were family albums, or reading out
loud passages from Dave Barry. But many nights, when
otherwise we would be watching *Hawaii, police d'Etat*, we
retreat into familiar passages, much the way frontier families
huddled with the Bible.

My wife prefers the proverbs of Peter Mayle, whose
provincial life is not unlike our own, except that he has better
access to truffles. My texts are a series of bicycling histories by
Samuel Abt, a talented writer whose day job is editing the
Herald Tribune, which—to be fair—is superb in its coverage of
Paris-Roubaix or the Giro d'Italia. Without access to baseball,
football, and ice hockey, which I get only as box scores, I have
filled the sports fix with cycling, and Abt is the Marlow of professional racing, as well as the hagiographer of Greg LeMond,
the American who is the three-time winner of the Tour de
France.

I have admiration for LeMond, not just for his accomplishments, but because he is an American—with three children, no less, and undoubtedly relatives who wonder what's he
up to in Europe—who has triumphed in a foreign culture. He
races with a French team, speaks what sounds to me like good
French (I borrow a television for the Tour), and has succeeded
not just in sport but in overcoming the attitude that
Americans abroad are *domestiques* not *patrons*.

Among the many pleasures of biking is that it comes with
a rich vocabulary, well recorded by Abt, that can be dragged
into conversations that require a sports analogy. Riders never
tire in the mountains—they "blow up in the hills"; nor are

they left behind—they're "dropped." Football and baseball analogies find an audience with some Americans, but no one ends a meeting in Europe saying, "I think we oughta punt." At least with the language of cycling, I have small talk for taxis and trains. The other sports, such as European soccer, I will never understand, especially the impulse of British fans to treat every match as if it were a prison riot.

Not only do I read about cycling to take the chill off a long day, but on evenings and weekends, in true Walter Mitty fashion, I pull on a Brooklyn jersey and Italian racing shoes and head for the hills. Although I sometimes ride with a local *vélo* club or friends at exhausting speeds, the rides more suited to my age and temperament are long loops through the ancient French towns that hug the hillsides of the Jura or the slopes that lead to the Alps.

What is unexpected on these tours is the forlorness of French villages, even on Saturdays. Lace curtains with pastoral designs cover the windows of houses on narrow, worn streets; and barns, with their rusting equipment and crumbling, weathered cement, suggest paintings by Edward Hopper rather than Claude Monet.

These rides evoke not just the timeless insularity of rural French life, but also the only novel of Alain-Fournier, a writer killed in the First World War, titled *Le Grand Meaulnes*, which was published in English as *The Wanderer*. As with many of my rides, especially in spring when the roads are a mixed metaphor of flowering fruit trees and snow-covered Alps, the book is a flight of fantasy through the French landscape that ends with the discovery of a mystical chateau, not unlike the manor houses that surround Geneva.

What I appreciate about *Le Grand Meaulnes*, especially when living in Europe and far from New York, is that it is also an account of the difficult journey that we all make away from home. Not unlike Dorothy in Oz, Meaulnes discovers an enchanted world that is at once terrifying because it is unfamiliar and exotic because of its romance. The novel ends with Meaulnes on his bicycle:

> As he rode away from the town, charming farmhouses appeared here and there on either side of the valley near the banks of the river, their pointed gables covered with green trellises showing through the trees. On their lawns no doubt girls were gravely exchanging love secrets. It was a setting for people with hearts and souls—innocent souls.

Often I end my rides in Présilly, a French village high enough in the hills that the churchyard commands a sweeping view of Geneva, the lake, and the surrounding mountains. On this square the town erected a monument to its own adolescents who never made the journey home from the wars. The simple obelisk reads:

ALSACE VERDUN MARNE

PRÉSILLY

A SES ENFANTS

MORTS POUR LA PATRIE

The names of the children engraved in stone, such as Fontaine, Megevand, and Naville, are also the names of classmates in our daughters' school.

The idea in Europe that war lurks around the corner from peace is most clearly felt in the similarities between Switzerland and the old Yugoslavia. Both have a mix of religions and cultures. Each has citizens that do not speak the same language. And each evolved from a defensive pact of rural cantons to thwart neighboring imperial designs.

On my rides around Geneva, I am reminded constantly of Balkan villages and especially of a lazy summer spent in

Yugoslavia. During my senior year in college I studied Serbo-Croatian, read the Bosnian novels of Ivo Andrić and, after graduation, spent several weeks swimming in mountain streams and exploring the villages and towns of Old Serbia, which, like those in Switzerland, are a mixture of wheat, orchards, dairy barns, and softness in the late-afternoon sunlight. I had been accepted at graduate school in the fall, and this was the summer of my Grand Tour, although instead of Paris and St. Tropez, I was footloose in Sofia and Sarajevo.

The journey had elements of danger and burlesque, hallmarks of any trip behind the Iron Curtain. On the train to Nish from Bulgaria, I shared a compartment with four Turkish students, who hated everything American and, at that particular moment, America's only representative on the train. In Nish, it was impossible for me ever to be alone. On those quiet evenings when it appeared I might retire early with a book, my host would show up to serenade me with his accordion.

After several weeks, and not a few evenings with the accordion, I decided to travel to Sarajevo and southwest to the coast. In particular, I wanted to see the bridge on the Drina, which is also the title of the Andrić novel that recounts the history of a Bosnian town, Višegrad, during successive periods of Turkish occupation.

To get to Višegrad and Sarajevo, I had to take a narrow-gauge train across eastern Bosnia, through towns that now have been ethnically fouled. Andrić opens his novel by writing "The river Drina flows through narrow gorges between steep mountains or through deep ravines with precipitous banks," and the same was true of the miniature train that took all day to reach the minarets of Sarajevo.

The novel ends at the start of the First World War with the bridge's destruction—"This terrible blow which seemed to destroy, break up and suffocate everything down to man's very thought"—and so too the destruction of the balance in Bosnia between Serbs, Moslems, gypsies, Austrians, and Jews that the bridge had come to symbolize. The book was written in 1959, but the story continues.

With Andrić as a guide, it was easy to see Bosnia as Daniel Boone saw Kentucky, "a dark and bloody land." But, as the Swiss well understand, Europe is many bridges across many Drinas, and as I ride on my bicycle around Geneva or take trains across the Continent, I wonder which idyllic towns in twenty years may become the wraiths of Gorazde or Mostar.

When you live abroad, the days that are hardest are the American holidays. To be sure, Christmas, Easter, and New Year's Day are celebrated as in the United States, but Memorial Day, the Fourth of July, and Labor Day are just routine days at the office. And Swiss holidays, some of which are a delight because of their elegant simplicity, do not evoke the childhood reminiscences that are the pleasures of such days off.

Nevertheless, a year ago, I found myself flying to Washington, D.C., on the Fourth of July. It was a business trip, and I was arriving on a late flight from Amsterdam. But I had decided to go immediately in a rented car to the Mall to watch whatever fireworks or spectacle would be in progress.

Any trip to America raises my spirits. I see family and friends, browse in bookstores, eat familiar food, and slip into old habits, such as reading the *New York Times*, as if they were slippers I'd left at the outbound airport.

But trips to the States also emphasize how difficult it is to go home again. The worst is the sense of not quite belonging. My home is now Switzerland, not Midwood Street in Brooklyn. It depresses me to stay in hotels or to feel like a tourist in New York, the city where I was born. And sometimes it is hard even with old friends to pick up where we left off.

Nor do I always recognize the United States, especially

on a short trip. I am not current with the latest political strategy or movies making a run in the theaters. New Yorkers seem indifferent to the guns on their streets, and the importance of Tonya Harding is lost in translation.

On this particular evening in Washington, however, I had none of these mixed emotions. I collected my bag and, in that trance of the long-haul traveler, presented my passport at customs. Like everyone else, I usually get a question or two, or sometimes a ball score or a "Welcome home." But in this instance I was taken to a corner of the arrival hall and surrounded by several agents. They searched my suitcase and then my briefcase and wallet, item by item.

All I had to declare were Swiss chocolates and a model KLM airplane for my son—hardly the stuff of big-time smuggling. But I resented it when the agents opened my passport and started asking sarcastic questions. Was I still in contact with anyone in Argentina? Why had I been to Thailand? Was this stamp not Russian?

What stung the most were the questions about the Solomon Islands. I had visited the battlefields on Guadalcanal where my father and many others like him had fought so that we could have more Fourths of July. But it all seemed un-American, as did having curiosity about the world.

Mercifully, the inquisition was short-lived. I supplied my social security number, which was inserted into the computer, at which point the agents apologized for their suspicions. I passed into the humid Washington night and drove to the Mall.

The fireworks were over, and all that I saw of Washington, besides a silhouette of the Lincoln Memorial, was a traffic jam seemingly the size of Switzerland. I had wanted to find the capital and the Fourth of July as magical as they were in the sixth grade. Instead, shaken by the rude arrival and distracted with jet lag, I wandered through some grim slums, yet another European lost in a rented car. When I finally got to my hotel room—with its molded plastic and central air conditioning instead of the screened windows and crickets of my childhood summers—it was easy to recall the way *The Great Gatsby* ends: "So we beat on, boats against the current, borne back ceaselessly into the past."

For me nothing better expresses the mixed emotions of an expatriate—the longings of homesickness and adventure—than Willa Cather's *Death Comes for the Archbishop*, which starts in a villa in the Sabine hills, overlooking Rome, and ends with the bells tolling in Santa Fe. It is the story of French missionaries sent to New Mexico in the late nineteenth century, although it could easily describe anyone dispatched abroad for business or a cause.

"That parting was not a parting," Willa Cather writes of those who left their small French towns for the American Southwest, "but an escape—a running away, a betrayal of family trust for the sake of a higher trust." Father Latour, the archbishop, carves his diocese from the red, parched landscape around Albuquerque, even though he longs for his native Auvergne in France, "the comeliness of the villages, the cleanness of the country-side, the beautiful lines and cloisters of his own college." Nevertheless, as Willa Cather notes, "in the Old World he found himself homesick for the New." For me these emotions are strongest whenever family, especially my parents, come for a visit. Saying good-bye at the Geneva airport, I know well the feelings of the young vicar, "torn in two before his eyes by the desire to go and the necessity to stay."

Going for the Gold

(1997)

As tried and convicted in the American press, the Swiss are guilty of collaboration with Nazi Germany, embezzling the savings of Holocaust victims, and lying about both. Further charges have been brought by New York Senator Alfonse D'Amato, who convened the Senate banking committee to document the misconduct of the Swiss in World War II and to chronicle the more recent Swiss refusal to return the savings of Holocaust victims to rightful heirs or worthy causes.

The *New York Times* published the indictments in the guise of an editorial:

> A lingering mystery of the Nazi era is what happened to the gold, money and other valuables deposited in Swiss banks by Jews throughout Europe who were fearful their assets would be seized by Gemany.

The editorial musters the requisite indignation in concluding that "for decades the Swiss banking industry arrogantly thwarted inquiries about its role in the Nazi period."

The Washington Post editorial hinted of damages yet to be awarded:

> The surge of declassified documents after the end of the Cold War shows that in World War II some Swiss banks

79

swallowed depositors' funds, at the moment when tens of thousands of Germans seeking refuge were being turned away at the Swiss border. It also appears that the Swiss laundered substantial assets looted by the Nazis; in short, they helped finance the German war effort—and this while their government was avowing a wartime "neutrality" whose full price has yet to be revealed.

The Swiss responded to the charges by agreeing with the World Jewish Congress and the Jewish Agency to convene what is called an Independent Committee of Eminent Persons, with Paul Volcker as chairman, to audit the records of Swiss banks for the money of Holocaust victims.

Jewish organizations, looking to create a trust fund for survivors, have staked a claim on as much as $74 billion that they maintain the Swiss either laundered for the Nazis or stole from Holocaust victims. And several lawsuits have been filed, one claiming as much as $20 billion from Swiss banks, which in their searches since 1985 have found only $29 million in unclaimed funds. When the retiring president of the Swiss federal council described these demands as "ransom" and "blackmail," a spokesman for various Jewish groups threatened to organize a boycott against Swiss financial institutions.

In response, after a series of public blunders, the Swiss banks created a $70 million fund to assist victims of the Holocaust, and the Swiss government proposed revaluing its gold reserves and dedicating at least 3 billion Swiss francs to endow a trust fund to aid those who suffered under Nazi aggression. But at that point the Swiss were branded collaborators, and, at least in the press, the right to appeal was denied.

Most press accounts about the markets in Nazi gold conclude that Switzerland's neutrality during World War II was nothing more than a guise to cloak war profiteering and collaboration with the Germans. Like a Reuters piece that ran with the headline, "Swiss Reject Calls for Nazi 'Truth Commission,'" they depict Switzerland as indistinguishable from the French government in Vichy, and those unfamiliar with Swiss history might assume that the Germans occupied Switzerland during the war, as they did Austria and most other European countries.

Militarily, Nazi Germany never conquered Switzerland. After Germany invaded Poland, in September 1939, the Swiss army mobilized up to 10 percent of the population and throughout the war went through long periods when it expected attack from the Germans. That Hitler wanted Switzerland as he wanted the rest of Europe for his Thousand-Year Reich is well documented. As Gerhard Weinberg writes in his history of the Second World War:

> At 1:35 a.m. on June 25, 1940, the armistice between Germany and France went into effect; a few hours later orders went out of the high command of the German army to prepare an invasion of Switzerland. . . .The plan was to crush Swiss resistance quickly . . . it was never launched as more important projects came to the fore in German planning. The end of Switzerland, that pimple on the face of Europe as Hitler described it in August 1942, would have to wait until Germany had defeated her European enemies.

Operation *Tannenbaum* was the code name for the invasion of Switzerland. That it was never implemented is to the credit—aside from the sacrifices of the Red Army—of Swiss generals, who conceded the lowlands between Zurich and Geneva for a fortress strategy that entrenched the Swiss army in the high mountain passes. The estimate among Hitler's generals was that at least eighteen divisions were needed to dislodge the Swiss from their redoubts, and after the failures to defeat Britain and the Soviet Union, the cost of a Swiss invasion became a mountain too far.

At the same time, however, that the Swiss army was protecting the high ground, the Swiss economy was quietly surrendering to the Germans. In exchange for food and basic raw materials, the Swiss traded with the Axis powers. As a friend of mine who lived through the war says bluntly: "They had us by the throat."

With words like "Holocaust victims," "Nazis," "looted gold," and "justice" in the refrain of each article about Swiss banking during World War II, it is an easy leap of faith to assume that Switzerland played an active part in the extermination of the Jews. In a *Time* essay, Lance Morrow writes: "The case of the Swiss and the Holocaust plays interesting variations on the theme of remembering and forgetting."

But unlike the three countries on its borders—France, Germany, and Italy—Switzerland protected its citizens, including 18,000 Jews, from deportation and, before and during the war, accepted refugees fleeing Europe's cauldrons.

Nevertheless, during the 1930s and throughout the war, the Swiss adopted policies that reacted to the German threat against the Jews in contradictory ways. In 1934 it passed its laws on banking secrecy to prevent the German government from investigating the foreign accounts of Jewish citizens. As the Nazi pressures increased, Switzerland accepted more Jewish refugees than any other country, when measured as a percentage of population. More than 14,000 Jews escaped Germany to Switzerland during the same period that 55,000 left for the United States and 15,000 went to France. But it was the Swiss, not wanting to be flooded with more refugees, who concurred when the Germans marked passports with the odious "J" to prevent more Jews from slipping into Switzerland undetected.

After the outbreak of war on the western front, in the spring of 1940, Switzerland accepted 6,000 Jews who fled before the *Blitzkrieg* launched against Belgium and France. After that, it continued to admit other refugees, including 50,000 French and Polish soldiers. But in 1942 the Swiss government issued a decree stating that "refugees on the grounds of race alone are not political refugees."

The effect of the ruling was to deny perhaps as many as 30,000 refugees entry to Switzerland; most were Jews, some of whom committed suicide on the Swiss border rather than return to Hitler's inferno. An eyewitness to this disgrace is quoted in Martin Gilbert's history of the Holocaust:

> Two of these poor wretched creatures slit their wrists on the bridge on the same day, while a woman (whom we had seen being hunted down in L'Haut de Morge) threw herself from the fourth story of the hotel in Saint-Gingolph where she was staying.

In 1944, the Swiss National Assembly voted to admit up to 14,000 Jews who were trapped in Hungary and who were the charge of the Swedish diplomat, Raoul Wallenberg. But Adolf Eichmann only allowed 1,600 to leave for Switzerland, and those denied safe passage as "Swiss-protected persons" were deported not to Palestine but to the gas chambers.

The Swiss assistance to Jews trapped in the Holocaust may appear both insignificant and hypocritical when compared to the total numbers who vanished. The Swiss no more comprehended the sweeping tragedy of the Holocaust than did the Allies. But during the war Switzerland absorbed more than 10 percent of its population as refugees. To put such numbers in perspective, David S. Wyman writes in *The Abandonment of the Jews: America and the Holocaust 1941–1945* that during the war the United States admitted only 21,000 Jewish refugees, and describes how Britain did all it could to prevent Jews fleeing the Holocaust from settling in Palestine.

Because few American reporters speak French or German, much of the case against the Swiss and the Swiss banks has been assembled from secondary sources, beginning with the hearings of the Senate Banking Committee. "U.S. Senate Panel Probes Holocaust Survivors' Missing Money," is a headline typical of many that condemn Swiss bankers of embezzlement. Under the leadership of Senator D'Amato, who recognized in the Swiss banks what President Theodore Roosevelt called "a good, safe menace," the hearings provided the press the irresistible combination of personal narratives of the Holocaust along with the dark shadows of financial scandal—Whitewater on the Rhine. And few Swiss bankers vote in New York senatorial elections.*

Another source in the case against the Swiss banks, and one that so far seeks only an "accounting" of dormant accounts for ten years after the war, is a lawsuit filed in U.S. federal court on behalf of all victims of what is called the "Nazi Regime." Although the defendants in the lawsuit are the three large Swiss banks—Union Bank of Switzerland, Swiss Bank Corporation, and Credit Suisse—the conspiratorial language of the allegations is such as to incorporate the government of Switzerland, all Swiss banks, and the conduct of the Swiss during World War II, and, as such, reads like the transcript of a Berkeley teach-in.

In the narrow confines of the claim, the plaintiffs allege that they are heirs to bank accounts lodged with the defendant Swiss banks that have refused to turn over funds that were first deposited prior to World War II by persons who

---

*When I wrote to the Senate Banking Committee requesting a copy of the hearing transcript, the response was a constituent form letter from Senator D'Amato: "Thank you for writing and sending me your claim for possible accounts in Swiss banks. . . . "

later died in the Holocaust. The individuals testify that they approached the Swiss banks to recover the missing funds of their forebears, only to have doors slammed in their faces.

Were the suit only about recovering money lost in the Swiss banking system, presumably it would have been lodged in Switzerland, in the canton where the bank in question was hiding the funds. But this suit was filed in New York, and as such is a political document, not unlike an editorial in the *Washington Post* or a press release issued by a re-election campaign, perhaps that of Senator D'Amato.

As for its politics, it reduces history to the level of "Hard Copy" or "Geraldo," and tries to redress the sufferings of World War II as if they were caused by a negligent airline or the Tobacco Institute. As the suit inveighs:

> From 1933 through at least 1946, the Swiss collaborated and acted in complicity with and aided and abetted the activities of the Nazi Regime in furtherance of the commission of war crimes, crimes against humanity, crimes against peace, slavery and slave labor, and genocide. Specifically, the actions and conduct of the Swiss Banks exceeded the obligation of a neutral country and actively assisted the war objectives of the Nazi Regime.

Whatever the lawsuit lacks in specifics about which bank may have taken what money, it does speak volumes for the quality of the work that is now produced at the country's leading law firms. Apparently the best legal team money could rent does not include anyone who can read German, French, or Italian, the three major languages in Switzerland, as all the sources cited in the lawsuit are in English, and most come from Washington archives, which, as in the Senate hearings or the forthcoming report of Stuart Eisenstadt, are assumed to be the Rosetta Stone of Swiss history.

Nor does the lawsuit display even rudimentary knowledge of Swiss banking. To wit "Defendant Swiss Bank Corporation is a banking institution organized under the laws of Switzerland. Its main office is in Zurich, Switzerland." In fact, Swiss Bank Corporation (SBC) has its headquarters in Basel. There is a section boldly entitled "Factual Allegations: the Nazi Regime and Swiss Neutrality: 1933–1946" that incorrectly dates the fall of Hitler's government and states that Switzerland supplied Germany with "raw materials," when, in fact, the county has no mineral deposits.

To substantiate the claim that Swiss banks collaborated with the German war effort, the suit quotes at length, not from Swiss sources or one of the many books published on this question, but from a U.S. Treasury Department internal memorandum, drafted in Washington during the war:

> In general the Swiss Bank Corporation officials have served the German [sic] and Italians in the field of chemicals and pharmaceuticals, foodstuffs, electricity, and metal products. The principal firms served are: Pirelli, Farbe, Shering, Ciba, Lonza, Franck La Roche, Brown-Boveri, Atlantic, Alliance Aluminum, and Mannesmann . . .

Such a claim may fool a jury in Brooklyn, and produce a judgment like those against asbestos manufacturers, but any Swiss would recognize that half of the listed companies are Swiss, not German or Italian, and thus traditional clients of SBC.

Although the editorial board at the *New York Times* considers the economic relations between Switzerland and Germany—specifically the trade in gold bars—during World War II a "lingering mystery," the record has been available to anyone in Switzerland with a library card and the ability to read either French or German. Even the paper's "News of the Week in

Review" asked: "Why has the known suddenly become news?" and quotes the author of a 1989 book, *Hitler's Gold*: "The basic outline of all this has been known for many years. . . . "

Both the Swiss and German national banks, which handled the large gold transactions, accounted for their purchases and sales in the way that so much suffering in World War II was recorded—with an accountant's pencil. The ledgers, long in the public domain, are now being recycled in the guise of sensational revelations.

According to the records of the Swiss National Bank—not to be confused, as it is in another lawsuit, with SBC—it purchased from the German Reichsbank the equivalent of 1.2 billion Swiss francs' worth of gold during the years 1939–45. During the war, the U.S. dollar exchange rate was $1 = 4.20 Swiss francs, which values all Swiss gold purchases at U.S. $285 million. Gold in the war years was pegged to a value of $35 an ounce, which means the Swiss National Bank purchased 255 tons from the German Reichsbank. The profit on this trade has been estimated at $20 million, in the dollars of that period.

As Germany began the war with an estimated $200 million in gold reserves (which includes those of Austria and Czechoslovakia), what is clear from the ledgers is that the Germans used looted gold to balance their trade accounts. Only by selling gold could the Germans acquire either U.S. dollars or Swiss francs, which were the only wartime convertible currencies and thus necessary if Germany were to trade outside the Reich, for example, with Spain, Portugal, or Argentina.

The Germans supplemented their reserves either with gold taken from the banks of occupied countries—the gold of the Belgium central bank was dragged through Africa to Berlin, and finally sold in Switzerland—or from the private holdings of vanquished populations. The Swiss National Bank has denied knowing the source of the gold that it accepted from the Reichsbank in exchange for Swiss currency. More likely it suspected the origins of this bullion—if not from death camps, then vandalized bank vaults—and subscribed to the adage, if not the international convention, that to the victor belongs the spoils.

Tracing the source of looted gold is, unfortunately, impossible from the records of the Swiss banks alone. It awaits the release of central bank records throughout Europe and in the United States, which until recently has refused to release documents pertinent to these questions under the Freedom of Information Act. Ironically, only the Swiss government has appointed historians to reconstruct its wartime dealings even though much of the flight capital that Switzerland attracted in the late 1930s was sent on to the United States or South America when it appeared that Switzerland would fall to Nazi expansion.

Never mentioned in a *Time* cover story, illustrated with a swastika of gold bars, is that in the years 1939–45 the Swiss National Bank purchased almost twice as much gold from the United States as it did from the Germans. For both Allied and Axis powers, Switzerland was a clearing house for gold trades, in lieu of a functioning foreign exchange market. Deserving further research, perhaps by the editors of the *Washington Post*, is the statistic that the Swiss National Bank sold to the Americans the same amount of gold that it purchased from the Reichsbank, raising the strong possibility that the U.S. also funded the German war effort.

Published accounts routinely imply that the Germans hid looted gold in secret Swiss accounts. One Associated Press report states: "During World War II, the Nazis looted at least $550 million in gold—now worth more than $6 billion—from German-occupied countries and stashed most of it in Swiss banks," the implication being that some of it might turn up in dusty vaults. But as Thomas Maissen of the University of

Potsdam concludes: "The gold delivered to Switzerland—it should be remembered in the current debate—was not hidden at the behest of a criminal state and war criminals; it was payment for Swiss currency and military goods, which were also sold to other countries during the war."

Most press accounts assume that without Swiss trade the Nazi war machine might have ground to a halt. But what sustained the German war effort was not gold sales to the Swiss, or receipt of their ball bearings, so much as having its armies on the ground in Belgium, the Netherlands, France, Austria, Italy, Yugoslavia, Hungary, Czechoslovakia, Greece, Romania, Poland, the Baltic states, Ukraine, large tracts of Russia, Norway, Bulgaria, Finland, parts of the Caucasus and North Africa—places in which the Germans did not need to exchange gold for war supplies.

Historian Gordon A. Craig describes Nazi economics:

> The conquerors regarded these lands, without exception, as legitimate objects of economic exploitation. The methods varied, and there was a decided difference between the style of the bland representatives of the Deutsche Bank who cheated French and Belgian industrialists out of their holdings by quasi-legal methods and that of Herman Goering greedily egging his associates on "to plunder and plunder copiously"; but the result was much the same.

No one who fell victim to or opposed Nazi fascism in the years 1933–45 can easily accept the trade that existed between the Swiss and the Germans. Only on October 1, 1944, did the Swiss end their arms trade with Germany. Toward the end of the war, the Allies blacklisted Swiss companies that traded with the enemy. But countermeasures were always tempered because the Swiss were useful to the Allied cause.

The importance of Switzerland to the Allied war effort

can be measured in a 1943 memorandum sent by the British high command to the American Joint Chiefs of Staff:

> The British Chiefs of Staff attach considerable importance to the military advantages they now derive from Swiss neutrality and are anxious that our policy towards Switzerland should aim at ensuring that these advantages are neither discontinued nor curtailed.

Switzerland was also a listening post for the Office of Strategic Services (OSS) and during the war provided a safe haven for 1,600 American pilots shot down in raids against Germany. In the 1944 attack up the Rhone valley, it was a neutral wedge into the Axis powers that protected the Allies' flank.

After the war Switzerland found itself economically isolated. Central Europe lay in ruins, and the Swiss were shunned by the West for their dealings with Germany. In 1946, to settle the claims of war profiteering and to rejoin the bloc of Western trading nations, the Swiss agreed to pay the Allies reparations of 250 million Swiss francs ($60 million, or 6 percent of that year's federal budget). The Washington Agreement settled all outstanding claims that the Allies had against the Swiss government.

There remains the question of the savings of Holocaust victims locked away in Swiss banks—a separate issue from the gold traded by the Swiss and German national banks. Before the Senate Banking Committee and in numerous press articles, survivors of the Holocaust or their heirs have made claims to funds presumably deposited in Switzerland. Stories have circulated of heirs being turned away from Swiss banks for lack of a death certificate of parents or relatives lost in the Holocaust. In the cover story of its European edition, "Called to Account," *Time* extrapolates

from one woman's disappointment with Swiss banking to
allege systematic fraud:

> What happened, Sapir and other Jewish survivors of the
> Holocaust charge, is that Swiss banks implacably refused to
> hand over to the survivors of death camps or their heirs the
> money deposited in secret, numbered accounts before
> World War II engulfed Europe.

All of the allegations against the Swiss banks assume that
a lot of money was deposited in Swiss banks in the 1930s
and that after these accounts became dormant the banks
quietly conspired to defraud the rightful heirs of their funds.
Few believe the Swiss when banks are questioned for dormant accounts from that era and only small amounts—in
one recent search it was eleven accounts worth $21,000—are
found.

Unfortunately, no reliable study exists, nor can one be
undertaken sixty years later, even by eminent persons, that
can verify from where and how money came into Switzerland
during the 1930s. At the start of World War II, no central
authority collected information on accounts any more than
the banks themselves asked those depositing money to supply
addresses or any personal information. Nor was there regula-
tion of lawyers, accountants, and fiduciaries who held funds
on behalf of clients, often in escrow accounts with fictitious
names. And money found its way to Switzerland in the bags
of traveling salesmen who may have lost track of their friends
as the populations of Eastern Europe started to drift like
ocean sands.

Nor are those claiming funds always specific in their allegations. The class action suit, filed in New York, describes
one claim as follows:

> To Lewis Salton's best recollection, he knew his parents had

traveled to Switzerland, he knew his father conducted stamp transactions with Edelman in Zurich, and he overheard his father's telephone calls discussing stamp-related banking transactions occurring in Switzerland; therefore, he believes his father had a Swiss bank account.

Not only is it not known how much money was deposited in Swiss banks in the 1930s, or by whom, it is not known in which currency or what instruments these deposits may have been made. A deposit made in 1938 in Reichsmarks would have been worthless at the war's end, as would have bonds issued by a Romanian industrial company or the obligations of the Czech government. And the records of settlements with Holocaust survivors after the war are as impossible to trace as are the exchange rates of European currencies that no longer exist.

In 1962, the Swiss banks formally investigated the dormant accounts of persons who may have died in the war, but all that surfaced was 10 million Swiss francs (then $2.5 million), which was paid to survivors and Jewish causes. Current claims of $7 billion and the like, however, do not represent amounts of lost savings that Holocaust survivors are hoping to uncover in Swiss banks. These amounts relate—give or take a few billion—to the current market value of the gold that the Swiss National Bank purchased from the German Reichsbank.

Auditors addressing the matter of dormant accounts again today will confront numerous bank mergers that have reduced the number of Swiss banks from 1,051 in the early 1940s to 413 at the end of 1995, plus the obligation only to maintain banking records for ten years. Could American banks find an account that became dormant in 1945 and make a judgment as to who today might be entitled to such funds? Would they even begin to look?

Dormant accounts in New York, after five years, are

turned over to the state, after an obligatory ad in the newspaper. After the war, undoubtedly the accounts of Holocaust victims were swept up in such a system, just as the U.S. government foreclosed on $100 million in frozen Swiss assets that were thought to belong to the Nazis or their collaborators. The forces of General George Patton found 100 tons of gold in a German salt mine, but these spoils of war were distributed to Allied central banks, not to individual victims.

In Switzerland, legitimate claims to assets in a bank never expire, but problems arise when accounts are opened without proper instructions on the management or disposition of assets in the event the money goes unclaimed. Even in Switzerland, banks are ineffective probate judges, and aside from the intervening tragedy of World War II, the distribution of family assets would be problematic enough.

The most accurate reporting on the problems of matching Holocaust victims with accounts dormant in Swiss banks and on the separate issue of Nazi gold has been published in the German language *Neue Zürcher Zeitung*, which has reconstructed the accounts of the Swiss National Bank during the war and explained the problems of trying to locate "a Swiss account" sixty years after it might have been opened.

On July 12,1996, it also published a letter from Dr. H. R. Voegeli, who after World War II worked as a lawyer in London and Zurich trying to trace the Swiss accounts of Holocaust survivors:

> After 1952, I was once again involved in this depressing— because of the sad circumstances—area, this time in the legal department of a big bank in Zurich. This time I had to advise the claimants of "unclaimed assets" on how to obtain access to their "heritage" and what sort of proof was necessary. . . . In my experience, banks and insurance companies paid claims without making a lot of fuss when the claimant could provide reasonably sufficient proof. . . .

> I must point out that a not inconsiderable number of claimants hadn't the least bit of evidence or proof to sub-stantiate their claim. . . . A father's occasional trip to Switzerland could certainly arouse the hope that there are assets to be found in banks there; however, it is not a plausible reason for a bank to acknowledge such vague claims. . . . It is certainly not a reason to accuse Swiss banks of an improper and uncaring attitude.

Unlike the rest of Europe, Switzerland survived the war intact, with neither its population nor its cities in ruins. Despite being surrounded on all sides by fascism, it preserved a nation that could easily have disintegrated along the lines of its French, German, and Italian speaking communities. The cost was a policy of self-defense that allowed it to abet the war effort of the Nazis. After the war, Switzerland paid war repa-rations to the Allies, as compensation for its fortunes of neu-trality.

If it is easy to criticize the apparent collaboration of the Swiss, how does the rest of Europe fare?

Ireland was neutral as well, if not openly sympathetic with the Germans. Franco's Spain maintained membership in the Axis club throughout the war. Unlike the Swiss army, the French army fell to the Germans in a number of weeks, and the Vichy government, as shown by its treatment of the Jews, was as cruel as that of its masters in Germany. Austria, like Switzerland, a predominantly German-speaking country, warmly embraced the *Anschluss* and its integration into the Third Reich. Russia's non-aggression pact with Germany allowed for the partition of Poland and its attendant final solu-tions. Italy surrendered itself to the public pleasures of fascism. Its client, Croatia, enthusiastically carried out policies of exter-mination. Czechoslovakia, Hungary, and Romania lacked the military preparedness to oppose the German onslaught, and many of their soldiers were impressed into German divisions or the mechanics of the Holocaust.

Only Britain can say it opposed fascism unequivocally from the war's beginning. But after the war even the British repatriated thousands of Russian prisoners to Stalin's death camps. The United States remained neutral for the war's critical first two years, during which time its merchants traded with the Nazis. Both the U.S. and Britain suppressed clear evidence that Germany had declared a war of annihilation against the Jews. Even when the facts were clearer, the Allies adjusted neither their military strategies nor immigration policies to address this reality.

That most countries in Europe during World War II committed atrocities does not mean that Switzerland's conduct should go unexamined. Like individuals and other nations that faced the war, it was capable of simultaneous acts of cowardice and courage. Nevertheless, alone among the countries of central Europe, Switzerland protected its citizens from the ravages of war, much as it had armed itself across the centuries to protect its democracy from the encroachments of the Hapsburgs, the lances of Napoleon, or Europe's periodic ritual suicides, like those practiced before the trenches of Verdun.

If the measure of a nation is its defense of "life, liberty, and the pursuit of happiness," Switzerland deserves a hearing based on the facts—not just petitions of lawyers—when it confronted what Thomas Jefferson called, in that same declaration, "absolute Despotism."

Life with Father

(1996)

Like many who drive cars the size of bread vans, I looked up one Sunday at lunch to discover four children. From various facial resemblances, not to mention the names chalked into the rug, I knew these children to be mine. But such are the tricks of memory that in the instant I looked up, I had the illusion that all four had arrived that afternoon—perhaps on order from L.L.Bean—and that, when the meal began, my wife and I had had no children and had been contemplating a lazy afternoon reading books or getting ready to go to the movies.

Although the lunch was sandwiches, my wife and I had a glass of wine and hopes of turning the meal into one of those happy family gatherings recommended in *Parents* magazine, even if at such times, instead of discussing Greek history, we express astonishment about the stickers needed to fill a Barbie album.

No sooner were we settled at the table than there came forth the demand for "more juice" . . . "no, juice with water" . . . "no, Daddy, juice with warm water, and don't forget to dry off the top." Obedient busboys, we scurried to and from the kitchen until the thread of conversation was lost, the two older children had been excused, and the toddler, dressed as a cowboy, had filled his chaps.

Were I a with-it modern dad—the kind so often profiled in *Esquire*—I would have taken all this routine chaos in stride. I might even have changed the diaper without a death threat. I might have joined in the postprandial game of scattering the sofa cushions and pretending I was on Dr. Dolittle's ship to Africa where—as the rules in our family dictate—on arrival one succumbs to cholera. Instead I retreated to the cocoon of a nearby *International Herald Tribune*. When it came time to stand up and be counted for diaper changing, I was checking the standings in Japanese baseball. And when the ship mutinied over the issue of which captain would invite Curious George to the messroom, I was deep into an article about the Clintons' holiday in Grand Teton.

All this isn't to say that I put myself in the negligent-father category. I am happily married to my wife, the mother of all my children, I spend my weekends inhaling chlorine at indoor swimming pools, I roller blade to keep pace with training wheels, and, in heroic dad fashion, I sometimes remove dead birds from the driveway.

On the other hand, I do not work the cough-medicine night shift, clean the rabbits' cages, or tackle the finer points of toilet training. To use the analogy of professional football, which I have watched while childhood unfolds around me, I reluctantly see my position as that of a backup quarterback—pacing the sidelines with a clipboard or calling in a play from the press box or, more realistically, the office. On most downs, my wife takes the snaps from center, sending the children around end to school or marching the family downfield to IKEA.

Something too close to home strikes a chord in *The New Yorker* cartoon that shows a light-footed executive coming through the front door, briefcase in hand, raincoat over his arm. His wife is waiting expectantly with two drinks in the living room, where, in the opposite corner, a baby is in a playpen. Smiling to his wife, the executive says: "Be there in a sec, darling. I just want to touch base with Tiffany."

Even when I trot onto the field as the backup quarterback, plays have a way of getting broken. One evening my wife badly sprained her ankle, and during the night, when one of the children was coughing, she asked if I could give the child a dose of cough medicine. Knocking about the bathroom in the stupor of an addict preparing a fix, I measured the dose, propped up my sleepy daughter, poured the syrup down, and went back to bed—feeling as virtuous as Clara Barton. In the morning, when my wife heard the dispatch from the front, she could only sigh: "You gave Helen the medicine? . . . but it was Laura who was coughing."

However harshly I might judge my performance on the playing fields of fatherhood, I have relished the role ever since my first Lamaze class. I continue to bore colleagues at work with stories of the children's witticisms. As the weekend impresario, I lead circus expeditions with the pride of General de Gaulle retaking Paris, or swimming expeditions as if we were to cross the Channel and not simply the long hours of a Saturday afternoon. And I never miss the chance to tell any of their birth stories.

As a rule, fathers do not have the serial rights to childbirth stories. Mothers retain the copyright to these epics, which mostly are told during dinner parties, to other mothers, when the men excuse themselves to "check the score" in the 49ers game. Our oldest daughter, who is now eight, was born in New York City, and as it now appears in memory, we started Lamaze childbirth classes several years before we decided to have children. Lamaze is, of course, the name of the doctor who championed natural childbirth, including the participation of the father in the delivery. The class was held in a lounge at New York University Hospital, and by the second session the fathers who had not deserted their wives had at least abandoned the class.

I made it to the last class, which featured a visit to the hospital birthing room of John McEnroe and Tatum O'Neal and the Movie, the gynecological equivalent of those fatalistic films shown in high school drivers' ed classes. Lamaze, the movie, ends with a birth, not a teenage road accident, but otherwise it features the same couple from the 1960s: he in a paisley shirt and bowl haircut; she looking and sounding like Janis Joplin, especially at the end.

Sadly, Buster Keaton never starred in a Lamaze movie. Ours featured this earnest young couple sharing the experience of labor. The with-it father-to-be leads his wife on tension-easing walks, packs the famed overnight bag, times contractions as if they were Olympic trials, and during the worst of labor, utters the psalm of all expectant fathers, "You're doing great, honey," which to a woman in transitional labor is as comforting as reading aloud a chapter from Joe Namath's memoirs.*

Although I was a Lamaze graduate, during our first encounter with labor I was not able to time the contractions because at that moment someone decided to break into our house. We were living in Brooklyn, where burglaries are even more natural than childbirth, and when my wife awoke at 3:00 A.M. in labor, she heard someone moving about downstairs. She timed contractions while I looked for the intruder. Wanting to confront neither the burglar nor impending fatherhood, I drew on my Lamaze training to feed the cats and relock the back door. Finally, I loaded my wife into a friend's car for the trip into Manhattan, leaving the house to the mercy of burglars. In Brooklyn, you only call the police when the break-ins are five minutes apart.

At the hospital we were put in a labor room with what Monty Python in *The Meaning of Life* called "the machine that goes ping." A cross between a seismograph and a Wall Street ticker, it recorded the peaks and valleys of each contraction. I

* *"I Can't Wait Until Tomorrow . . . 'Cause I Get Better Looking Every Day."*

fed my wife ice chips and hoped that John Cleese wasn't the doctor on call.

Lamaze had prepped us to "Just say no" to painkilling drugs. When the doctor arrived and said that my wife had "that epidural look in her eye," I gave a speech that sounded like the text of a Nancy Reagan address to Young Republican mothers. The doctor cut me off to say that Lamaze was there to get us to the hospital, as if it were a New York car service. Soon the room filled up with cheerful anesthesiologists from the Indian subcontinent who connected the epidural as if they were stringing up Christmas lights at an office party.

When the dripping painkiller took effect, the birth passed into the eye of the hurricane. My wife stopped shaking. I could massage the fingernail marks in my arm. As it was no longer necessary to comfort my wife with stories of Joe Namath at the Orange Bowl, the doctor and I could spend the next hour, before the final pushing, discussing the effects of higher interest rates on her real estate portfolio. No longer was I Joseph at the manger. Now I was at a funky Soho cocktail party where one of the guests had decided to give birth.

I credit Mick Jagger with getting me through the birth of our second child. When it came time to renew our Lamaze vows, the coach waived the requirement of the breathing exercises and put us through a one-session refresher course that was taught by an obstetrical nurse who, for her fifteen minutes of fame, had delivered one of the children of Mick Jagger and Jerry Hall.

After the nurse checked our breathing skills and reminded us of the essentials, such as how to find hospital parking, she settled into a two-hour description of the Jagger-Hall nativity. As might be expected of the lyricist of "Mother's Little Helper," Mick failed to grasp some Lamaze principles and passed the birth of his child at the side of his bodyguards, who were breathing in hamburgers at a neighborhood tavern. Obviously something had gone wrong in his childbirth class, and *This Is Spinal Tap* was the feature film.

With such a precedent, it did not surprise me that, close to my wife's due date, I accepted an invitation from a customer to attend a Rolling Stones concert at Shea Stadium. "Forty-year-old guys dancing to fifty-year-old guys," is how my friend, Tom Leonard, describes the modern Stones' concerts, although in this case we mixed in some thirty-year-old secretaries from Australia, as our host was a Sydney bank. Sensitive to the needs of my wife, I called home from the skybox several times, even leaving the line open during "Jumpin' Jack Flash" so that we could share the experience.

The next afternoon, while I was humming "Satisfaction" at my desk, my wife sensed the early stages of labor. She was in Manhattan, about a mile from the hospital, actually leaving the doctor's office. But a nesting instinct put her on the subway home to Brooklyn, where I arrived breathlessly an hour later. We timed contractions, talked with the doctor, and decided it was better to be early at the hospital than to have a baby born out of gridlock.

The attending physician deduced that it might be a false alarm and made us wait in a room better suited to Argentine police interrogations. As there was little labor, the machine hardly went ping. After fifteen minutes, an intern came in to ask some questions for the admitting forms.

"Have you ever had malaria . . . rheumatic fever . . . small pox . . . jaundice?" went her questions. "Rubella, scarlet fever . . . mumps . . . heart disease . . . ?" The intern looked the age of Doogie Howser and read the list of questions with a tone of nervous embarrassment, as if maybe this was all part of a high school prank.

We were working our way through, "kidney stones . . . anthrax . . . cholera . . . ?" when labor hit with the sudden force of a California earthquake. Tremor after tremor washed through the dim room. At each contraction, I would hold my wife while the intern would pause, politely standing aside until the destruction of Los Angeles was complete. Once the contraction subsided, the list would continue: "asthma . . . rickets . . . neuritis . . . ?" Maybe Buster Keaton had made that Lamaze film after all.

Finally, I interrupted her. "Maybe you should try to find a doctor?" I suggested.

The doctor who arrived was also a young woman, wearing an embroidered sweater and Top-Siders, who looked as if she had opened the wrong door and, instead of finding the skybox at Shea Stadium, had walked in on a birth. To her astonishment, she discovered the breached head of the baby. We each grabbed one end of the rolling bed on which my wife lay and rocked our way to a delivery room. The doctor scrubbed frantically. Nurses prepared the bedside. I put on the surgical whites of the standard attending-dad uniform. Within minutes, our second daughter was born, as the Stones might say, under my thumb.

Our third child, a son, was born in Maine, for the same price as the epidural in New York. By that time we were living abroad in Switzerland, but decided to return to the States for the birth, an even longer drive than that from Brooklyn to Manhattan.

Swiss hospitals assume all patients to be related to the Shah of Iran. Routinely a woman delivering a baby spends ten days in a clinic overlooking Lake Geneva, where she learns to grapple with her new responsibilities over pedicures and Bordeaux wines. But as our son's birth in August was coinciding with a wedding and my wife's summer trip with the children to visit our families in the United States, we gambled that I would arrive in time from Europe to get my wife to the hospital. I was sure that at least Mick would feel that time was on my side.

Two days before the due date, which is rarely accurate, I flew from Geneva to Frankfurt, then to Boston, and finally to Bangor, Maine, a trip that started out feeling like the Orient Express and ended as if on Greyhound. The next evening we ate lobster and drank French champagne—births need to be celebrated ahead of time if the mother is to enjoy the party. That night, in the dark hours before dawn, a bat flew into our room about the same time that my wife went into labor. Numb with jet lag, I woke up feeling as if Goya had scripted the Lamaze film and chosen Alfred Hitchcock as the director.

At 4:00 A.M. we backed out of the driveway and set off for the hospital through pine forests and fields edged with stone walls. As experienced Lamaze parents, instead of timing contractions, we argued about names and whether there was time for me to stop at Dunkin' Donuts for coffee. We finally agreed on the names but not the coffee stop and thus, uninterrupted, checked into the hospital by telling the nurse at reception my wife's first name. In New York, before one birth, I was told at the admitting desk to come across with $12,000 in cash, until an insurance voucher was found.

The delivery room overlooked the Penobscot River and the first flickering rays of the sun to touch the United States. It felt like a camping trip, not the Fawlty Towers of New York University Hospital. The attending nurse was named Bunny, and she changed sheets, heated blankets, and comforted my wife with Maine chatter ("Don't worry, honey, I ain't goin' to frig with you"), while the obstetrician settled into a chair at the end of the bed with his mail and what I think was a fishing magazine. This episode of Lamaze featured 4077 MASH's Colonel Henry Blake practicing fly casting before surgery.

At the last possible moment, or perhaps at the end of an

article on trout, the doctor waded into the white water of birth and pulled in the catch, who was squirming and flipping about at the shock of his new life on land.

Why would anyone have a fourth child in an age in which the World Population Organization recommends quitting after 2.3 have been born? It was a question we asked ourselves. Against the fourth was all the rigamarole of a baby—the diaper bag that never leaves your side, the feedings at 2:30 A.M., the anxiety of pregnancy and the fear of birth defects, not to mention the projected cost of a college education in twenty years, which, as my father likes to remind us, will be the same as Ghana's gross national product.

What pushed us toward the fourth—aside from wanting another child and, more important, having room in the bread van—was the closed shop of a three-child family. Although they meant no lasting harm, the two older girls treated their younger brother as if he were always trying to cross a picket line. On most days he would wake up with the dream of acquiring a union card and playing in their imaginary games or with their boxes of toys. Inevitably, a union heavy would suggest that playing with those Barbies "wasn't such a good idea." His first words were "No, Henry," chanted even to himself when the little teamsters were off at school.

When the die was cast, we decided to have the baby in a Swiss hospital. This time there was no social occasion to call us back to America, and we had exchanged our American health insurance for Swiss coverage. We also wanted a chance to try some of the recent white burgundies.

My wife selected a local doctor on the sound medical grounds that her office had unlimited parking. Wanting to meet the new doctor before the big event, I tagged along to one of the appointments to review the results of a sonogram. With the assurance of a briefing officer for the National Aeronautics and Space Administration, the doctor picked out lungs, fingers, and backbone on the negatives, while all I saw was the silhouette of a tiny astronaut and the shadowy confines of the mother ship.

During the last months of the pregnancy, I kept nagging my wife about the lack of a Lamaze refresher course. My claim had a long list of particulars: I had forgotten the breathing exercises; I didn't know if anyone in Switzerland had even heard of Joe Namath; lastly, I had no idea where to park. My case, however, was dismissed on the grounds that I was an experienced father and that, with a fourth baby due, all we needed to know was how to get to the hospital on time.

When my wife went into labor, it was a Sunday evening in November, and, just to make things interesting, I was at the office. I wasn't shirking responsibilities so much as joining the chairman of our bank for a meeting with out-of-town guests. When I called home during a lull in the flip charts, she suggested I skip the business dinner, which is how a woman from Maine says "It's time."

I have always enjoyed the drive to the hospital. For the first two births we drove at a safe parental speed through the back streets of Brooklyn—slow enough for me to time contractions and point out such landmarks as the storefront of the Reverend Al Sharpton's hair impresario. But this evening, playing with the fire of a fourth baby, we were roaring through the small farming villages that surround Geneva at chicken-scattering speeds, which went against my view that the official film for transport to the maternity hospital should be *Driving Miss Daisy* instead of *The French Connection*.

It was Sunday night, and the hospital was a ghost town, at least figuratively, save for one unlucky wraith who sat behind a desk in the emergency room. By now we were running, the bag was waving around like a flag, and when I shouted "Maternité!" to the night man, I'm sure he thought I was shouting "Fraternité!" as if this Lamaze film featured a storming of the Bastille.

Had we been refreshed with Lamaze, we would have known that the delivery rooms were on the third floor. Instead we rushed headlong down empty corridors that now echoed the accented French of two Americans hoping to deliver a baby on the other side of the ramparts. A heroine of the revolution, dressed in a nurse's gown, rescued us from our labyrinth of panic and led us to the tranquility of the *salle accouchement*. In New York the delivery room always looked like Kojak's office, but here there was a bed by a large picture window, a view of the mountains, subdued lighting, interesting art, and a jacuzzi suitable for Plato's Retreat. It made me wonder: If this is a delivery room, what do the rooms look like in the fertility clinic?

Before we could have the baby—this was Switzerland, after all—we had to produce our passports and work permits, and various insurance vouchers, much as if we were on vacation with a package tour. And with labor in full force, a nurse started asking my wife for her medical history. ("Here we go again, *encore*," as Yogi Berra might have quipped in French.)

Not being a licensed obstetrician, our doctor brought with her a card-carrying specialist—the kind whose rates usually include valet parking. His arrival in the delivery room reminded me of the way late-inning relief pitchers hop the fence of the bullpen and walk slowly to the mound. As the room filled up with doctors, nurses, and a midwife, for what was clearly going to be a rapid delivery, I tried to console my wife with a damp washcloth and anecdotes from Super Bowl III. Thirty-five minutes after parking the car, our fourth child and second son was born.

With newborn babies my wife is the head coach and general manager. Occasionally she sends me in from the bench to go off-tackle with a diaper or to pick up the blitz that is the nightly bath. But mostly I'm a man in motion, backing the car out of the driveway or folding the stroller into the trunk.

The job I take seriously, however, is reading bedtime stories. Even on nights when I am diverted to a business dinner, I try to dart home to read, for example, *It Happened in Pinsk* ("Ah, Pinsk, could there be a lovelier city?") or to make way for ducklings on their ramble through Beacon Hill.

Even with squirming toddlers, I have spent countless hours wondering if Spot is under the stairs or in the piano (he's in the basket), although my favorite first book is *Goodnight Moon* by Margaret Wise Brown, the story of a small rabbit saying goodnight, with the melodious harmony of Ogden Nash, to the things in his room:

> Goodnight comb
> And goodnight brush
>
> Goodnight nobody
> Goodnight mush

Who can tire of Dr. Seuss?

> Sometimes
> I feel quite CERTAIN
> there's a JERTAIN
> in the CURTAIN

But the same is also true of anything by James Marshall (*Miss Nelson Is Missing*) or Arnold Lobel, the author and illustrator of nature's odd couple, Frog and Toad.

Mostly my reading list for the children is stuck in *The New Yorker* magazine, from the era that precedes S. I. Newhouse and his editors' weakness for words and images not suitable for children. We have, for example, a near-complete collection of the books of William Steig, whose illustrated classics are also a reason to have a fourth baby.

Steig is the cartoonist of such emotions as Greed or Folly

with near-pointilist caricature. But to me he is the genius of *Rotten Island* ("They loved their rotten life. They loved hating and hissing . . . screaming, roaring, caterwauling. . . . Rotten Island was their Paradise."); *Doctor De Soto*, a mouse of a dentist who outwits a fox ("The fox, still woozy, said goodbye and left. On his way home, he wondered if it would be shabby of him to eat the De Sotos when the job was done."); *Amos and Boris*, the friendship at sea of a mouse and a whale ("They knew they might never meet again. They knew they would never forget each other."); *Dominic*, a beagle errant who bests the Doomsday Gang (" . . . four foxes, three weasels, eight ferrets, a wildcat, a wolf, six tomcats, two dingoes, and a parcel of rats. . ."); and *Brave Irene*, Mrs. Bobbin's daughter, who delivers the duchess her ballgown through a blizzard ("The wind wrestled her for the package—walloped it, twisted it, shook it, snatched at it. But Irene would not yield. 'It's my mother's work!' she screamed.").

Steig uses mice, whales, foxes, and wandering beagles the way Chekhov does overcoats and bus rides—to illustrate cowardice, love, jealousy, and temptation. And not the least of Steig's virtues is that his books can be read quickly in that low moment between a late homecoming and dinner from the microwave oven.

On many evenings, after I give up, our kids fall asleep listening to E. B. White reading on tape *Charlotte's Web* or *The Trumpet of the Swan*. I had never heard White's resonant, New York voice until my friend Bill Rodgers mailed us the tapes. I find it a magical connection across place and time that my daughters can go to sleep in bedrooms that overlook the Swiss Alps and listen to White tell the story of a pig and a spider at a New England county fair. He starts with these words: "This is the story of the barn. I wrote it for children and to amuse myself. It is called *Charlotte's Web*, and I will read it to you."

When I was a magazine editor, and before I had children, I edited an article by Alison Lurie that made the point that "the lasting works of juvenile literature are thoroughly subversive" and that children prefer books, like *Alice's Adventures in Wonderland* or *Peter Pan*, that deflate the pretentions of the bourgeois world. I admire Ms. Lurie's essay and often try to apply her thesis as I make my way with the kids through *The BFG* or *Black Beauty*. Unfortunately, I think it better explains why adults love children's books. Children, I've noticed, just like hearing the sound of their parents' voices.

Like other parents of small children, I find myself at the headwaters of a slow-moving river of gifts. I tend toward earnest presents: picture books about Burma or folk art from Russia, although what the children love most is shampoo from hotel bathrooms or toothbrushes from airplanes. Around Christmas, my wife and I—even in Switzerland—stroll the aisles of Toys R Us, pushing a flatbed truck.

Nevertheless, everyone has limits with his indulgence, and I have drawn mine offshore, near the consumer mooring of Barbie's boat. In the time between my younger sister's collection and the birth of our daughters, Barbie cashed in stock options and acquired a yacht. Roughly the size of *PT 109*, and just as easy to cut in half, the boat makes every list for Christmas and birthdays. Neighborhood children who have it are held up as examples of happiness and objects of parental devotion.

The sell is in the box, which depicts Barbie and her friends in mid-cruise, probably somewhere near Bimini. Ken's expression hasn't changed since 1966, and here he appears on deck, dressed in a white suit with a gold anchor chain, raising the possibility of an Elvis sighting on board. Barbie, with that dental hygenist's smile, has cruise wear suitable for a czarina. Together on the yacht they look like friends of the British duchess Sarah Ferguson, who once out of camera range are capable of compromising each other's toes.

Although we have managed to keep the yacht in dry dock, we have started on The American Girls Collection of dolls, which are only slightly cheaper than adopting babies in Romania. Each doll comes with a six-volume history of trial and tribulation in American mythology—one girl escapes from slavery; another emigrates from Sweden to the great plains—and the idea is to hook parents on the books and little girls on the accessories and outfits, which in price and variety conjure images of Ivana Trump on the Underground Railroad.

When I learned the price of the American dolls, at the time of the first pleas, I lowered my voice to Ward Cleaver tones and announced that the girls, then ages six and four, would have to earn money to help pay for them. A lemonade outlet was decided upon, and shortly thereafter the first franchise opened on a rocky Maine beach where the water is usually the temperature of German beer and sunbathers arrive in sweatshirts. I provided the working capital—for ice, cups, and raw materials—and the price list was established on cardboard taped to an ancient folding table.

Our daughters, who can be shy with grandparents for the first half hour, took to sales with the enthusiasm of Fran Tarkenton on cable television. Immediately they started using phrases like: "I'll collect from that one," and "Get those two guys on the motorcycle." I thought I was teaching the values of thrift and hard work. Instead I had created The Force, which devoted the rest of the vacation to reviewing product lines and cutting jackpots.

A lot of being a father reduces to what Juvenal called bread and circuses. During the week I'm at the office, spinning memos into gold. But come the weekends, almost like a mythical divorced father, I lead skating parties, coach bike riding, and set strategy to visit snake vivariums.

Most decisions about children's entertainment, be they afternoon excursions or, for us, summer trips to America, can be filed under the notion of trying to do the right thing. Although most days the children are content to play with the sofa cushions or mix poison in the bathtub, we walk them through museums, cram them onto airplanes, and rent hotel rooms for them in strange cities.

In a moment of weakness, we also decided to take them to the mountains. The idea behind renting an apartment in the Swiss Alps was to escape Geneva's winter fog and expose the children to clear air and the delights of skiing. In hindsight, what we showed them is that their parents would only survive Outward Bound if they were dropped in Central Park, preferably not far from a delicatessen.

For the five winters preceding our rental, the Alps had had little snow. Neighbors talked of global warming, and how there was more snow when they were children. We set off on Christmas afternoon, expecting to find brown slopes and idle ski lifts. As we had decided to stay through New Year's Day, the girls filled the car with their Christmas presents. Because no one could be found to feed either the cat or the rabbits, they were also packed into the car. Food stores were laid in, as were enough Barbie outfits to amuse Princess Diana.

Halfway to the village in the Alps above Montreux, we began to think we might find snow at higher altitudes. But when we arrived in the town, we found four feet of new snow, and the road to our chalet impassable. Having dieted on stories of the greenhouse effect, we had neglected to purchase either snow tires or chains, and thus we had to abandon the car in the village and hike the last kilometer to the chalet.

Over the next three hours, with darkness falling and snow swirling, I dragged a small sled between the car and the chalet, hauling stuffed animals, bottles of wine, puzzles, and kitty litter. Thrashing about in snow drifts on Christmas Day, I felt like the only member of the Donner party who was traveling with dwarf rabbits.

For the next week of vacation, the snow came down sideways, I tried to buy chains for the car, and the children huddled inside the chalet, as if they were in the federal witness protection program. No amount of coaxing could convince them, at least for long, of winter's magic. Meanwhile I searched for chains and, when needing exercise, shoveled the car out of snow drifts.

The last two days of the holiday were spent reloading the car for the trip home. The children huddled in the safe house while I played Sherpa with sacks of new games and the cat carrier. The car was parked near the chalet on a lonely alpine road. All around were the snowy spires of mountain peaks. On the last trip to the car, I dragged the rabbits in their cage as if part of a sled race in Alice's Wonderland. When I got to the car, I found a Swiss policeman writing out a parking ticket. On a remote road in an empty countryside, he said I was in a No Parking zone, as though I were loading skis in front of the Capitol.

All French deserts me when I'm angry, so I reverted to being a mad Brooklynite and demanded to know the policeman's badge number. Puzzled with the request in a town of 250, which has one policeman, he gave me his name, his rank (chief of police), and the ticket, and then carefully and slowly backed away from the raving New Yorker who had come to the Alps with his rabbits.

If there is anything bittersweet about having children, aside from emotional meltdowns in supermarkets, it is knowing that one day, sooner than we think, the house will begin to empty with the same tidal swings that now have it filling up.

Some evenings we read *Rascal*, Sterling North's memoir of

raising a raccoon in the Wisconsin woods. After a year with Rascal, the twelve-year-old Sterling must let his pet answer the call of the wild, and he packs Rascal in his canoe for the short trip to freedom. I know that one day, like frisky raccoons, my children will want to be taken to the far end of the lake and set free, as North writes of his last trip with Rascal, "straining to see through the moonlight and shadow, sniffing the air, and asking questions." He ends the book with words that can mist my eyes:

> I left the pecans on a stump near the waterline hoping Rascal would find them. And I paddled swiftly and desperately away from the place where we had parted.

Whether it comes in front of a freshman dorm or the Gare Cornavin in Geneva, I do not look forward to telling my own raccoons, "Do as you please. . . . It's your life." For now, maybe until they are teenagers, I prefer to keep my raccoons closer to home.

Cleaning Up
After the Dirty War

(1998)

No doubt because I first saw Buenos Aires on my honeymoon, it lingers in my mind as a city of dreams.

In the 1980s we flew down from Rio, after what seemed like five days in a Brazilian rain forest. We took a room in the Hotel Dora, where it was said the author Jorge Luis Borges took afternoon tea. We read books in grand cafes and walked the crumbling sidewalks of a city that the poet Archibald MacLeish had praised in 1928:

> [Buenos Aires] is a great city as the ancients measured great cities . . . in the sense in which Paris and London are great cities . . . a cosmopolitan, twentieth-century metropolis with all the fixings, crowds, avenues, parks, subways, visiting pianists, confusion of tongues, screaming of brakes, shining of movie theatres. . .

In 1984 Argentina had just emerged from the long shadows of the "Dirty War," the years from 1976 to 1983, when more than 30,000 people lost their lives at the hands of government death squads or urban guerrillas. Defeat in the Falklands war had toppled the military junta; and less than a year before our visit, Raul Alfonsin had been elected president. Few were optimistic that he could tame the dragons of militarism and ruinous inflation that had turned Argentina into a metaphor for national mismanagement.

Earlier this year, alas not on a second honeymoon, I went again to Buenos Aires. The angry Peronist graffiti had been scrubbed from the parliament walls, perhaps because a Peronist, Carlos Menem, was serving as president. Otherwise the city had changed as little as the design of the 1964 Ford Falcon that, under the banner of industrial self-sufficiency, was produced locally well into the 1980s.

What came as a surprise on this visit were the country's economic and political successes. The military had been mustered from politics. Large industrial corporations were privatized. The peso was pegged to the dollar, and the two currencies were freely convertible. Interest and principal was being serviced on foreign debt, and hard currency reserves exceeded $30 billion. Unemployment was down to 13 percent, and the budget deficit was less than 1 percent of gross domestic product.

True, the government was plagued with various scandals, and the president was making noises about rewriting the constitution to allow himself a third term in office. One friend said ironically: "Menem will soon become Consul Vitellius as the first step to becoming emperor." But no one suggested that the rule of law was whatever was shouted from the balcony of the Casa Rosada.

During the years of turmoil, about the only U.S. export to Argentina was advice on how to reverse the country's political decline. On a number of occasions President Jimmy Carter sent his assistant secretary of state, Patricia Derian, to preach the sermon of human rights to the military junta. In a memorable phrase, she explained the shift in American policy: "We're not going to sell thumbscrews anymore. You got it now?" She was later credited with saving lives. But the junta responded to piety as Josef Stalin might have done, and the worst government torture and killing corresponded to Carter's time in office.

In contrast, the Reagan administration's policy was to reduce pressure on the Argentine generals by explaining that they were authoritarian not totalitarian—to use the distinctions of the then U.S. ambassador to the United Nations, Jeane Kirkpatrick—and thus capable of reform. In exchange for their support in the Cold War, especially in the jungle wars of El Salvador and Nicaragua, the generals were allowed to pursue their domestic agenda, which reached the heights of folly when Argentina sensed tacit American approval for the occupation of the Falkland Islands.

"Who won Argentina?" was the question on my mind when I listened to accounts of the country's recent success. Did Jimmy Carter's confrontations with the generals, Ronald Reagan's quiet diplomacy, or Margaret Thatcher's iron fist bring about the changes? Or did the country manage to heal itself, indifferent to American prescriptions?

In the end the United States had little influence on events. Only Thatcher, in restoring a British colony, had overthrown the government of occupation in Buenos Aires.

Seeing the country at peace, I thought back to those I had met on our honeymoon. They had been on the front lines of the Dirty War. Each had risked his life speaking out against torture when few wanted to listen. All had been physically or emotionally scarred by the repression. Fifteen years ago they had been pessimistic about the country's chances for a democratic future. Yet fate had proved them wrong, and Argentina had prospered.

During the summer before our wedding, though absorbed with preparations more detailed than those for the early space shots, I had found time to write the former editor of the *Buenos Aires Herald*, Robert Cox. From my reading I knew him as a brave man who during the worst of the Dirty War had challenged the junta's campaigns of terror. After many years as a lonely voice for justice, and more than a few death threats, he had moved his family to Charleston, South Carolina, where he wrote editorials for a local paper.

Cox had generously given me the names of writers, artists, and bankers to contact, and on an old rotary phone in the Dora I tracked a number of them down. Thus my wife and I spent our honeymoon in the company of strangers who soon became friends.

First we met Hermenegildo Sabat, an illustrator, painter, and political cartoonist whose pointillist studies of tango captured both the pageantry and dark tragedy of Argentine life. He served us coffee in his studio.

When we sang the praises of Buenos Aires, Sabat said, yes, it was beautiful but also "a façade, a moving picture," and that underneath the broad boulevards like those of Barcelona and the parks like those of Paris lay the quiet brutality of Leningrad and the legal labyrinth of Kafka's Prague.

The great truism about Argentina is that early in this century it had one of the highest standards of living in the world. A country with the sixth largest land mass on earth generated wealth from its meat and grain, which moved to foreign markets on railroads and ships financed by British and French investment houses.

In the nineteenth century, Argentina adopted a constitution modeled on that of the United States, and until 1930 democratic government maintained the country's standards of living. But the preference of Argentine politicians for Tammany rather than Independence Hall, and the historic sense that the military had founded the nation always left the country vulnerable to men on horseback.

During the 1930s and '40s, Argentina flirted with fascism, maintaining links to the Axis powers though not confronting the Allies. In 1946, a popular military officer named Juan Peron won the presidency on a platform that set cabaret fascism to the music of Eugene V. Debs. As described by Martin Edwin Andersen in his *Dossier Secreto*, a definitive history of the Dirty War:

> The state and industry would march lockstep toward modernization orchestrated by a set of reciprocal relationships between nationalist, pro-industry military men; members of the local manufacturing community (many of whom had grown fat on state subsidies); and the working class, represented by a cooperative and quiescent leadership.

Peron used the country's dwindling foreign currency reserves to purchase the railroads built by the English and the French, and negotiated generous pay packages with the unions, but he balanced the budget by printing money. His state capitalism married the worst impulses of Italian Fascism and Indian self-sufficiency. At war with the Catholic Church, estranged from the middle class, and threatened by a military revolt, Peron resigned and fled the country in September 1955. For the next twenty years the armed forces and weak civilian governments ran the country along the constitutional principles of musical chairs.

Casting himself as the hero of an autobiographical romance, Peron once said: "If I had not been born Peron, I would have liked to be Peron." He got his chance to play Peron in 1973, when he returned from exile to lead a government that he hoped would keep at bay the extremes on the left and the right. But by then—through corruption and economic stagnation, and with extremists on all sides claiming to be Peronists—the political center had collapsed. Peron was ill, and he could do little more than ask his constituency not to cry.

After Peron's death in 1974, the presidency passed to his

second wife and former belly dancer, Isabel. "Imagine Jayne Mansfield as president," was Sabat's offhand remark. Unable to cope with either nascent terrorism or rampant inflation, Isabel was overthrown by a military junta that saw in the opposition, both real and imagined, the threat that Hitler perceived in the Jews. As Andersen observes:

> The military reserved for itself the power to patrol what they called Argentina's 'ideological borders.'. . . The new junta dissolved Congress, replaced the Supreme Court, and purged judges; it abolished individual legal guarantees and decreed the death penalty for political reasons. The generals baptized their rule the Orwellian-sounding National Reorganization Process, known in Spanish as el Proceso.

Thus began the Dirty War.

Until I met Horacio Mendez Carreras, the Dirty War was an abstraction to me. I had read press accounts of repression in the 1970s, but a state of siege in South America was as difficult to comprehend as the prose of the "fabulist" novelists then fashionable across Latin America.

A lawyer then in his forties, with a warm smile, thick dark hair, and Ivy League clothing, Mendez Carreras invited me to meet him at the Jockey Club, one of the parthenons of Argentina's establishment. But though he was an heir to such tradition, he also did not mind going against its grain. As we sat in the stuffed club chairs, he gave his account of the repression, which he saw both as a lawyer and as a columnist for the *Buenos Aires Herald*.

Only through the foreign press, in 1976, did he first become aware that people were disappearing. In response to several well-publicized guerrilla attacks, police and military units without search warrants or the instructions of judges were rounding up those deemed subversive. Mendez Carreras remembered how many were quietly relieved—as if it might finally end the violence—when the prominent editor Jacobo Timerman was detained in 1977. Yet only the Mothers of the Plaza de Mayo, who had lost children in the siege, and his friend Robert Cox took notice of the "disappeared." From journalists, lawyers, and judges, there was only silence.

Listening to Mendez Carreras was like hearing someone read aloud from Dante. (*"I never would have thought Death had undone so many."*) He spoke about the hundreds of teenagers rounded up by the military; of the many burial sites and detention centers around Buenos Aires; of the Naval Mechanics School on the edge of the city, converted into a medieval dungeon complete with instruments of torture. "It's terrible," was the phrase that punctuated most of his paragraphs.

In 1977, the notorious Captain Alfredo Astiz, then a junior officer in the terror, infiltrated a group campaigning for peace that included several French nuns. After a December meeting at which they prepared some publicity around the theme of a "Christmas of Peace," the nuns were abducted, tortured at the Naval Mechanics School, and "disappeared."

By 1984, when Mendez Carreras represented the French government in the matter, there was no chance that the nuns were still alive. They had either been buried in anonymous mass graves or, like many others, thrown from planes flying over the Atlantic Ocean. But as a lawyer he sought to account for those missing lives.

Speaking to me that same year, Mendez Carreras was pessimistic about the future of his country. Those who had prosecuted the terror, including Captain Astiz, remained in uniform. President Alfonsin was under enormous pressure to pardon those responsible. With the inflation rate exceeding 20 percent, the government defaulting on the national debt, and the military so firmly entrenched in Argentine culture, who had the appetite for a Nuremberg trial?

"Most of the country does not want to remember any-thing," he lamented.

With Mendez Carreras, I went to see Emilio Mignone, a lead-ing human rights activist. We climbed a dim apartment-build-ing staircase, as if behind the Iron Curtain. We listened as a man in a V-necked sweater and bedroom slippers, sitting with his wife on their living room sofa, told the story of May 14, 1976, the day their daughter Monica had disappeared.

At about 5:00 A.M., several green Ford Falcons, the chariots of death driven by the security forces, had appeared outside their building. Men in dark leather trench coats had pounded on their door. Those armed men had carried the screaming Monica away. "We lost our daughter," Mrs. Mignone recalled in a whisper.

"There was no war at all," was how Mignone remembered the period. Many of those "disappeared" were targeted for their work with social causes, but the threat from the left was exaggerated. The guerrillas were few and badly organized and faced a well-equipped army. The enemy were "children." In the notes I kept of the meeting, I found these names: "Louis 25, Claudio 23, Lela 20, followed by: "Disappeared."

Like others with whom I spoke, Mignone retold the decline and fall of democratic Argentina, emphasizing not just the many coups since 1930, but the evil that entered the coun-try's bloodstream after World War II when it accepted so many escaping Nazis. The combined effects of fascism and inflation had collapsed the political center and left the gov-ernment in the hands of "criminals using the resources of a modern state to commit crimes and cover them up. They thought themselves above the law."

For the families of the "disappeared," what was hardest was that they suffered their pain alone. Few friends acknowl-edged their loss. The effect of this silence was to indict the victims, or their families, for the crimes.

Mignone, although a Peronist, believed that Britain had saved Argentina from despotism. Only the war in the Falklands had reversed the tyranny of the generals. Echoing the sentiments of many I met, he concluded: "They should put up a statue for Margaret Thatcher."

Leaving Argentina two weeks into the marriage, we had our first argument as husband and wife. Before going to say good-bye to friends, I had given my wife the equivalent of $300 in Argentine pesos, assuming that she would go shopping. When we met later at the airport, I asked what she had purchased.

"Oh, here," she said handing me back a great wad of small bills. "I went to the café and read my book."

No bank at the airport was interested in purchasing my pesos for dollars; convertibility only went one way. Nor could we buy anything in the duty-free shops, since a general strike had been called. The good news was that I had not married a "shopper." The bad news was that Argentina's depleted foreign exchange reserves were up $300.

Argentina's non-convertible currency and its isolation from global markets were more reasons, I now believe, that it descended beyond the first circles of the civilized world. The economy that the generals seized in their 1976 coup had a rate of inflation of 500 percent, high wage demands among workers, state control of key businesses, no foreign investment, and captains of industry whose only marketing experience was from the front lines of torture. As Sabat quipped: "We had an inflation of generals."

Foreign debt had plugged the gap between revenue and expenses. Between 1976 and 1983, the debt rose from $10 billion to $39 billion. Little of this money found its way into businesses that could generate foreign exchange. For example, in 1980, spending on armaments was $8 billion—$2 billion more than the country's foreign reserves. Inflation became the only growth enterprise.

My father, a believer in the simultaneous breakdowns of monetary and political stability, visited Argentina in 1981 and wrote:

> There was the sense of being on a foundering ship while watching the crew below decks playing blackjack. The speculation I heard was financial rather than political. Thus, if one is searching for analogies to the collapse of civilian authority in Argentina, it is to the Weimar Republic, which paved the way for the kind of general totalitarianism that Timerman describes in particular, that one should turn.

To their credit, Presidents Alfonsin and Menem made the same links between civilian authority and a sound currency, and, like Margaret Thatcher, privatized state monopolies to reduce government debt and promote productivity. Parity between the peso and the dollar has restored local savings, and even those who once tucked away their investments in the United States or Switzerland are repatriating their dollars, in some cases to buy government bonds.

While driving me around Buenos Aires in 1984, friends would quietly point out this detention center or that military barracks. This time, on similar outings, all I heard was that George Soros was now the country's largest landowner, that Wal Mart had opened many stores, or that the stock market was up 9 percent. I heard exemplary tales of those who had lost jobs in privatizations and were now scrambling to open restaurants and boutiques; or of cab drivers indifferent to being paid in pesos or dollars.

Buenos Aires is now a tributary of global capitalism, in which banks and international capital markets put up the front money for mobile phone networks, chain restaurants, and one-bedroom apartment blocks. The problem with this is that those down the chain are serfs to changing consumer tastes; and those granting the franchises to democracy are not above reviewing the small points in the leases.

In *A Century of Debt Crises in Latin America*, Carlos Marichal links economic cycles in the West with the periodic debt crises south of the border:

> The phases of the loan booms generally corresponded to a period of expansion in the industrial nations that spurred a rise in world trade and the accumulation of surplus capital in international money markets . . . the waning of these phases . . . cut short the flow of funds to Latin America and led to debt crises.

Little wonder that the rise of Argentine democracy has coincided with the expansion in the global economy after 1983, or for that matter, that *The Wealth of Nations* was published the same year the Declaration of Independence was signed. As Adam Smith wrote in a 1775 essay: "Little else is requisite to carry a state to the highest degree of opulence from the lowest barbarism, but peace, easy taxes, and tolerable administration of justice."

Before leaving Argentina on this visit, I went again to the Jockey Club to meet Horacio Mendez Carreras. This time, instead of huddling near the door, we ate lunch in the dining room. But otherwise the conversation could well have been the one we had had in the large padded chairs a decade and a half before.

Although the French government had lost interest in the case of the nuns, he had persisted on his own, and that week had been in court again. The military men who had so far testified, he said, remembered few particulars. Sometimes they were present when someone was kidnapped or tortured, but they never took part nor could they recall the details. As he had said so many times when we first met: "It's terrible."

From the hearings of the Sabato commission, convened to establish a chronology of the terror, Mendez Carreras at least knew the outline of the nuns' fate, but he still did not know where they were buried or if, as he suspected, they had been thrown into the ocean. As Martin Andersen recounts part of the story in *Dossier Secreto*:

> In fact a group operating out of the Navy Mechanics School [ESMA] headed by Rear Adm. Ruben Chamorro carried out the operation. "During working lunches," recalled Miriam Lewin de Garcia, an ESMA survivor, before the Sabato commission, "Lt. Jorge Radice showed off his black humor, saying with a sneer that his task force had carried out the murders of [Argentine diplomat] Elena Holmberg, the French nuns—he called them his 'flying nuns'—and the Palotine priests."

In the newspaper that day, President Menem had alluded indirectly to Mendez Carreras, in criticizing those stirring the embers of the Dirty War. But the lawyer would carry on until he found out who was responsible and what happened. "It's my life's work," he added.

Times were better in Argentina, Mendez Carreras admitted. The military was no longer a threat. Menem had retired many generals. The economy was strong and linked to the West. But although he was one of those who had prevailed in the struggle, his tone was anything but that of a winner.

Why, he asked repeatedly, did the country want to forget its past so quickly? Chile and Uruguay had had their own dirty wars, but neither of those had matched the extent of the repression that had divided Argentina, one of the costliest civil wars in the Americas since that of the United States. Had the divisions really healed? We talked about countries—Japan after World War II, Greece after the colonels, Russia today—

that had little use of history. What, he asked, are the consequences of forgetting?

Given the numbers that disappeared in the 1970s, I asked him why he had never been arrested. Obviously the junta had despised him.

"They wanted to kill me," he said. "But I wrote a column for Bob Cox. That helped me. My father was a judge. And I had a cousin in the navy. He told them not to touch me. That's probably what saved me."

"Are you and your cousin close?" I asked.

"No," he replied. "He hates me."

But in Argentina family still means more than politics.

When we had first met in 1984, after our conversation in the Jockey Club, we had spent a day together in the countryside outside the capital. I remember it as a perfect honeymoon day: We grilled an enormous steak, met his friends and family, and toasted our new marriage. Mendez Carreras drove my wife and me to see his sister's house, built around a Spanish courtyard and graced with worn tiles, overlooking the River Plate. During the terror, bodies thrown from planes had washed up on the same shores that we now saw in the distance.

At the house, Mendez Carreras showed us some of his books, many of them on the American Revolution, the South American wars of independence, and early Argentine law—three traditions that had probably saved Argentina.

The view of water in the distance, the company of so many books, the presence of minds filled with both courage and warmth reminded me of the house on Long Island where I had grown up and where, two weeks before, we had been married. It seemed "altogether fitting" to find, on one of the walls around the patio, a bronze plaque engraved with the words of the Gettysburg Address.

A Jour with the Tour

(1997)

Ever since I described Sam Abt—the author of many books about the Tour de France—in an academic journal as the "Marlow of professional racing," he and I have been pen pals. "Which Marlow(e) of professional racing do you think I am, Christopher or Philip?" he inquired. As I had in mind neither William Shakespeare's contemporary nor Raymond Chandler's private eye, I wrote back to say the comparison was to Joseph Conrad's Marlow, the narrator of *Heart of Darkness* and other stories. In subsequent letters both of us speculated as to whether Mr. Kurtz, before leaving for Africa, had ever raced in the Tour de France.

Because I live in Switzerland, last year Sam and I made a date to spend a day with the Tour. He held out the possibility of VIP passes, and I reciprocated by showing up not only with three of my children, all under the age of eight, but also with my friend Rob and his two young sons. "The horror! The horror!" was a phrase first uttered by Mrs. Joseph Conrad after the famous writer tried to go on Tour while leaving behind his wife with four children, one of whom was a newborn.

We agreed to meet Sam "at the start, around noontime," as if this were a village race in August, not an Alpine time trial to Val d'Isère that would attract tens of thousands. Two kilometers from Bourg St. Maurice in the French Alps, we abandoned the car, despairing that we would find Sam at what looked like a state fair.

The Tour de France lasts three weeks in July, consists of twenty-two stages or one-day races, makes a big loop around France (although the route varies each year), covers about 2,000 miles, and ends in Paris on the Champs Elysées in a mad sprint finish.

Twenty-two teams start the race with nine cyclists, and the winner is the individual with the lowest cumulative time from each day's racing. It is possible to win the race without ever taking first in a stage. A typical day's racing covers 120 miles in about five hours. Champions like Greg LeMond or Miguel Indurain have "put time into their opponents" in the high Alpine stages or in time trials, like today, when riders race only against the clock.

The Tour is also famous for its carnival atmosphere—the giveaways, water bottles, and product samples that get hurled from the publicity train as it rumbles around France. But despite living in Geneva for six years, I had never seen the Tour in person. During the month of July, for several years, I was traveling on business. Our first year in Europe, my wife used the excuse of the moving van's arrival to deny me the chance to see a prologue, or opening day, in Lyon.

Hence my first taste of Tour promotion was an espresso, elegantly served by Maison du Café, which sends among the crowd waves of attractive young women adorned with small cups of coffee and little else.

Sam's emergence from the maelstrom saved me at least from a second coffee. He lifted the children over the barricades, presented us with passes and the children with souvenirs, and led us to a warm-up area where the press can interview the riders.

Conrad described his Marlow as having "sunken cheeks, a yellow complexion and with his arms dropped, the palms of hands outwards, [he] resembled an idol." By contrast, Sam Abt—while an idol to those who admire his books about the Tour—evokes the friendly qualities of Franciscan monks rather than the austerity of an Asian deity.

His day job is to edit the *International Herald Tribune*, which is published in Paris. For that paper and the *New York Times*, he writes a daily column during the Tour, which he then edits into a book. He restricted his access to the best tables in France when he described the Frenchman Laurent Fignon, the winner of two tours, as "a Parisian with Gatorade." No one minded a joke at the expense of a moody champion; but Parisians despaired the association with Gatorade.

Sam's regret when we met was that we would be on our own for the day, as he was shortly to head up the mountain. There was only one road with limited access to Val d'Isère, and a Motorola team car was his last-chance ride. In a back seat Sam disappeared into the jungle of Tour fans that lined the race course, almost as Marlow described an earlier trip to the interior: "They howled and leaped, and spun, and made faces; but what thrilled you was just the thought of your remote kinship with this wild and passionate uproar."

Left to our own devices, Rob and I decided to find lunch for the children and perhaps that second cup of coffee for ourselves. Inside the Tour's magic kingdom—a pavilion of billowing tents near the start—many of the sponsors had hospitality suites. At the far end there was even a Tour de France barber shop.

The kids had lunch—pieces from a cake the shape of the day's course—and collected freebies from the sponsors, although few lend themselves to retail promotion: Polti manufactures electrical equipment, Mapei is a chemical company, ONCE sells Spanish lottery tickets, and Gan writes insurance—hardly the things to fill a child's treasure bag. Nevertheless, at Maison du Café, I noticed that even some of the riders had stopped for a last cup, if not the ambiance.

That sponsorship also has its hearts of darkness I knew from a dinner I had with Mario Condé, now indicted but then chairman of Banesto, the Spanish bank for which Miguel Indurain rode. Throughout the meal, held at the bank's opulent headquarters, I kept wanting to ask one of the waiters for a jersey or if perhaps there was an old racing bike in the basement that no one was using. But the business conversation never climbed "beyond category" (Tourspeak for the tall mountains).

Finally as the dinner broke up, I congratulated Condé on his team's many wins in the Tour, expecting him to show me the desk where in winter Indurain made loans. Instead he feigned indifference to bike racing. Yes, he said, the bank sponsored a lot of sporting events, but for him it was just advertising—Miguel Indurain, the winner of five consecutive Tours, was media time.

"I looked at him," as Marlow remembered Kurtz, "as you peer down at a man who is lying at the bottom of a precipice where the sun never shines."

With lunch in the children, we were free to return to the pedestals of cycling's Mt. Olympus—the press area near the start where the riders were warming up. The first of the Greeks we spotted was the Englishman Chris Boardman, who holds the world record for the longest distance covered in one hour. He was peddling furiously on a wind trainer, but his heart rate monitor flashed something ridiculously calm, such as 115 beats per minute. But the day before, a shattering mountain stage through rain, fog, and hairpin descents, Boardman had, as riders say, "exploded in the hills" and finished just ahead of the barber shop.

The kids said hello, and I asked one of those hard probing questions that no doubt caught the Gan team leader/ *Cycle Sport* columnist off guard:

"Pretty tough day yesterday, Chris?"

In an isolated corner of the press area, we were the only ones watching Boardman spin. But for whatever reason—the concentration of a champion, not enough espresso—Boardman ignored both the children's greeting and my question, as if he were Roger Maris and I was badgering him about breaking Babe Ruth's record.

The Babe in Greg LeMond would have at least said "Hi, kids" or promised to win the time trial. LeMond's greatness in winning three Tours was a first-class temperament that let him draw strength from the madness of crowds. In a sport that celebrates monastic virtues, he even had his family along in a Winnebago. But Boardman preferred to sulk—Achilles getting ready for the Trojans on rollers.

Revenge, however, came quickly, as it often did for the Greeks. Rob wandered over with his son, aged four, and pointed toward Boardman.

"Look, Danny," he said. "He's the best in the world at what he does."

Danny looked up at Boardman and said, as only a child can: "You mean warming up?"

A few minutes later the greatest cyclist of all time, the Belgian Eddy Merckx, entered the pantheon, in many ways looking like the Colossus of Rhodes. Merckx won the Tour de France five times, the Giro in Italy three times, and countless one-day classics, like Paris-Roubaix, with a flair for relentless attacks.

He had handshakes and hellos for his friends, and was oblivious to the fanfare that engulfed him. As he chatted with a friend, both Rob and I took turns posing for pictures next to him, as though he were a cardboard Merckx set up on the main square in Brussels.

What gave the day drama was the sudden vulnerability of Miguel Indurain, the winner of the last five Tours. The day before, as the leaders had accelerated on the final climb to Les Arcs, he had looked like Superman feeling the effects of kryptonite.

While we were in the press area star gazing, Indurain had made several passes through the encampment. Each time he drew a crowd, except on the last occasion, when I saw an opening and took the kids over for a ceremonial picture, as though in front of the Lincoln Memorial. I got several snapshots while Miguel chatted with his *directeur sportif*—this not being the moment to go over my dinner with Mario Condé.

When Miguel turned to head for the start, he found that my son Henry, almost four, was blocking his front wheel. Henry had zigged when he should have zagged, and now he was holding up the parade.

Once after a stage of the Tour of Romandie finished near our Swiss village, my oldest daughter, Helen, then seven, got in the way of Tony Rominger on his way to the podium, and his handlers had shunted her aside as though they were Clint Eastwood protecting the President.

In this instance Miguel showed his élan. He was on the verge of losing his first Tour in six years. He had struggled in the mountains. Now his critics could say that even four-year-olds were on his wheel. But instead of getting angry with Henry, he reached down, scratched him on the top of his head, and gave a little Navarran whistle that said: "Hey, kid. I gotta Tour to win." He might well have pointed to the center-field wall.

I untangled my son from the spokes, and in a flash Miguel was gone. As Sam describes him: "In a chivalrous age Miguel

Indurain would be the parfait knight: pure, serene, untroubled by second thoughts." On this day he lost a minute in the time trial to Evgeni Berzin and subsequently the Tour. But for a little boy's father, he became the man for all seasons.

Dealing in Russia

(1993)

Before privatization became a popular Russian icon, V. I. Lenin, who was skeptical of shareholder participation, liked to boast that the West would sell him the rope that he needed to hang capitalism. Unfortunately for Russia, he found enough rope in the domestic market to keep his buyers busy for more than seventy years. And although such a strategy was useful to control the board of directors, it left the country dependent on a product that had little demand outside North Korea and Albania.

It was in the spirit of a rope salesman that I started traveling to Russia in the autumn of 1991. Before departing, I collected the names of bankers to contact on arrival, received a mandate to place credits for Western food, and departed on the Swissair flight from Zurich to Moscow that was as tightly sealed with its own revolutionary sentiments as the railcar that brought Lenin to the Finland Station.

The plane followed the narrow corridor that tracks from Warsaw and Vilnius into the Russian capital. I read the *Wall Street Journal*, glanced at a backlog of faxes, and weighed the choice of red or white wine to accompany the smoked salmon—easier rites of passage than that, as in revolutionary days, of worrying about a wig and a disguise.

The international airport, Sheremetyevo, is twenty miles northwest of Moscow, in farmland reminiscent of the lakes near Minneapolis. Small clusters of dachas mix with pine forests, and vast uncultivated fields convey a forlorn sense of neglect, as if the tractors had been repossessed with the party. On this particular December evening, the countryside was blanketed with Moscow's trademark frozen fog, and the pilot let the plane roll on landing, much as a skier avoids his edges on an icy run.

I have always been apprehensive when crossing East European borders, and remain so, even though the Berlin Wall is now nothing more than concrete fragments on sale for tourists.

Over the years I have been denied entry into Hungary for want of a picture, hassled at the Czech frontier, and searched at gunpoint in Romania. On this occasion, I had reason for concern, for I was entering Russia without a visa.

During the Cold War, such informality would have been unthinkable. But now Western businessmen are the commissars, I was traveling—of all revisionist things—business class, and the Russian consulate in Switzerland had sent instructions for the visa to be issued on my arrival at Sheremetyevo.

Teenage soldiers, as if part of a scout troop dedicated to indolence, guard Russian airports. One steered me toward the consulate. In a few minutes I was telling my story to an immigration officer, although he never looked up from the scraps of paper officialdom that once bound the Soviet Union. The consular office had the ambiance of a freight forwarder, and it was full of young men, like the one I was addressing, who gave the impression of having forgotten why they were posted to these particular gray metal desks.

The examining magistrate flipped through a sheaf of telexes, took several unrelated phone calls, and then, turning surly, said that I had violated Soviet law and would be

deported in the morning. I made the usual protests and even
called my hosts—senior Russian officials—who had arranged
for the visa. But they said nothing could be done on a Sunday
evening. I considered, but then rejected, the possibility of
extending to the consular section the capitalist notion of
incentive compensation, as my tormentor's brown suit hinted
of a man still humming union hymns.

In the manner of Herr K. in *The Trial* who was told, "I am
no longer obliged to hear you," I was asked to wait outside for
further instructions. Another adolescent soldier arrived and
signaled for me to collect my bags. I followed him down
lonely corridors at Sheremetyevo, where I knew that the last
flights to the West had departed.

Our footsteps echoed the cadence of a spy being brought
in from the cold, even though we ended up outside on the tarmac, which was thick with fog and the whine of jet engines. I
became the only passenger on a dark, freezing bus, which in
mid-winter had its doors and windows open. In the eerie
half-light of the runway, we drove along a fleet of mothballed
Aeroflot jets, now being stripped for parts. The setting was
from John Le Carré, although the skeletal remains of socialism were images from *Clockwork Orange*.

Maybe I was to be put aboard a plane and dispatched to
the frontier? Maybe they did something else with Western
businessmen who tried to sneak into the country and give
away food? We stopped in front of a tall building on the edge
of the airport, and I was led to a guarded door that only
opened with a key. Inside was a hotel, although not the kind
that has fruit baskets waiting in the rooms.

Left in the custody of the hotel staff, I was led by the
concierge to a locked wing on the ninth floor. Everything about
the hall and the room I was given reminded me of my freshman
dormitory, except that no one was chilling beer in a wastepaper
basket. Small groups of young men were huddled in several
doorways, as if reviewing *Playboy*. Undoubtedly, they were visa

scofflaws from countries such as Ethiopia, Afghanistan, Vietnam, and Angola—places where the red star was setting on the Soviet empire. They filled the hall with laughter, wall pounding, and loud voices, and after a while it became clear that what was to me the Gulag was to them Ellis Island.

The dining room, where I could go on my own, was a cavernous, dimly lit hall with the air of a Jamaican nightclub. Russian tobacco has the pungency of ganja, and a number of my fellow travelers wore braided Rastafarian hats—another lost tribe of Africa confused about the immigration requirements for Nirvana. My interest in dinner waned after the stale bread course, and I returned to my room for a supper of Swiss chocolates. I assumed I would be deported in the morning and passed an unsettled night, scanning my shortwave radio for the BBC and wondering if Susan Sontag would champion my cause in the *New York Review of Books*.

In the morning I was put back on the bus and returned to the same desk at the airport consulate, although this time it was manned by another officer. He heard my story, flipped through the telexes, found the instructions, issued the visa, and waved me away, without even the hint of an apology. I cleared customs, found a taxi for the ride into Moscow, and, eighteen hours behind schedule, finally meant business.

In the last two years I have made more than ten trips to the former Soviet Union, visited a number of the republics, shivered in unheated hotel rooms, met with presidents and finance ministers, shared overnight train compartments with strangers, walked the ruined splendors of Samarkand and Bukhara, negotiated with trade unionists, set up several Russian offices, and read authors like Boris Pasternak and Aleksandr Solzhenitsyn while waiting to be seen by one of their former tormentors.

In the right disposition, when asked what I think is Russia's future, I can easily sing its economic praises. I have set speeches on its oil in Siberia, its educated population, why the current accounts are really in surplus, or why the country's respect for literature will make the change easier from communism to democracy. But left waiting in a cold terminal for a canceled flight, betrayed in a business deal, or reminded that Russia tolerated Lenin or Joseph Stalin as leaders, I can also paint its geopolitical landscape in the images of Salvador Dalí, in which the hands on the molten clock point toward ethnic violence or where economic development is a steam engine attempting to haul freight in a world of semi-conductors.

Most of my trips are to Moscow, an imperial city although one of power instead of glory. To be sure, the Kremlin, Red Square, and St. Basil's Cathedral are ornaments of empire, even if, in their midst, the polished marble of Lenin's tomb casts a reflection of death. Moscow's boulevards are the width of parade grounds, although that has less to do with changings of the guard and more to do with thwarting barricades. The skyline is punctuated with steeples and red stars, gargoyles of central planning, that were added to hotels, office buildings, and party headquarters in the manner that Karl Marx finished most phrases with the word materialism.

Beyond the inner ring of the city, Moscow is dreary, more the Bronx than Berlin. Nearly every building in the city needs paint, plaster, and new brickwork, although the cobbled sidewalks and potholed streets make it hard to tell if the fault lines are geological or geopolitical. The better apartment buildings have the lobbies and hallways usually found outside crack dens. Most Moscovites live in vast tombstones of public housing that dot the city limits much the way, in New York, the borough of Queens has its acres of cemeteries.

Nevertheless, the sense of life on the edge—the food shortages, the political intrigues, and the constant fear of rebellion—gives Moscow the excitement of a frontier town. Rumors are its lifeblood. The talk on an average day has President Yeltsin dead, Lithuania invaded, Mikhail Gorbachev returning, Chernobyl smoldering, or Siberia voting for secession.

Nowhere is the flavor of the frontier stronger than in Moscow's new collection of five-star hotels. Although they have been given names to convey the impression of established wealth—Savoy, Metropol, Palace, etc.—in reality, they are best understood as Yukon saloons. Not only does each have a lobby bar filled with prostitutes—women smothered in fur to tempt wealthy trappers—but all the hotels project the buy-and-sell fever of a gold-rush general store. To wit:

Prospectors, who in the West are senior officials of major corporations, come and go to meetings in black Volga sedans, all of which are encrusted with mud and have the look of covered wagons, if not getaway cars.

Businessmen who would not dream of speaking to anyone in a Kansas City Sheraton find themselves in Moscow passing out their calling cards in elevators.

At breakfast one morning at the Olympic Penta, a stranger at the buffet tried to sell me an oil refinery that he said was in boxes.

During a lunch at the Metropol, I sat near a notorious swindler who conned millions from the banks in Australia but who has since opened shop in Moscow.

I have had endless dinners with middlemen offering billion-dollar oil deals, even though their annual salary is less than the cost of the wine.

As in any boomtown, speculation is rampant, and there are no small deals. Moscow is desperate for vegetable stands, restaurants, car washes, dry cleaners, and hardware stores, to name a few essentials missing from the streets. But most people in business are selling oceans of natural gas, tons of gold, timber concessions the size of Michigan, or used MIG aircraft.

The historian Hugh Seton-Watson wrote that nineteenth-century Russia failed to develop a merchant class: "There was no such bourgeoisie in Russia: even the merchants had little of the outlook of Western businessmen. They thought far too much in terms of exclusive guild privileges and favours from the government, to which they were prepared to give unreserved political obedience." Nor, to put it gently, did communism have an interest in cultivating shopkeepers.

As a result, Russian capitalism has no forebears. Its banks are not heir to the tradition of Venetian trade houses. Its farms have never calculated forward prices in Chicago. Its law firms have never searched for titles. Its financial statements missed the evolution of double-entry accounting. Yet under the current let-the-market-rule philosophy, each has to compete with German, French, and American corporations. The sports analogy would involve a Bedouin tribe that, after many years of subscribing to *Sports Illustrated*, decides to challenge the Atlanta Braves.

Having seen capitalism only in the magazines, the Russians have embraced the free market as if it were synonymous only with gold rushes. Deals are promoted feverishly, no matter how long the odds. Small ruble stakes are imagined transformed into dollar-sized fortunes. Anyone pitching business to the West boasts the coordinates of a lode and a sure-fire method of assay. All they usually lack is someone to finance the pan and the donkey.

In addition to divining rods, the Russian economy has retained its faith in what Seton-Watson calls "guild privileges." The market ends where the influencers start peddling. Inevitably they know someone who knows a minister who knows Yeltsin. Always a scarce resource is to be allocated. The business is awarded to those with the finest pedigree.

Most distracting of all is that in the collapse of the central system all sense of institutional loyalty has been lost, as if everyone on the deal side of the frontier has no need for a passport. In most meetings, it is impossible to tell if the men seated in front of you are government ministers, corporate executives, or buccaneers. Usually they have the qualities and business cards for all three professions. The only thing that is clear is that everyone at the table has come to split a jackpot.

Although much of Russian capitalism is developing along the lines of a ward meeting on Chicago's South Side, it also has antecedents in the five-year plan. In the West, business means selling a product or a service. If something develops, documents—a contract, an order, or a sales receipt—are exchanged. In Russia, however, business means negotiating protocols.

Before my travels, I had heard of protocols only in connection with news stories about the United Nations. But in the last two years, I have negotiated and signed dozens. These memoranda of agreement resemble legal contracts that are for sale in stationery stores. Usually the preamble includes a phrase such as: "Whereas the parties wish to develop certain Siberian oil fields. . . ." The required action is always: "The parties agree, within 60 days, to conduct feasibility studies. . . ." And the hard bargaining begins over the clauses that set forth "the terms of this joint-venture."

One reason that there has been so little progress with the Russian economy is that negotiating these protocols has become the end, not the means, of business, an elaborate mating ritual that rarely leads to marriage or children. All over Moscow, Western businessmen, assisted by an interpreter, are drafting these memoranda, as if their work was to set forth the articles of the Treaty of Joint Understanding for Bulgarian-Romanian Economic Exchange.

Usually the meetings are held in a grandiose ministry office, where, from above the director's desk, the scowl of Lenin still scans a vast conference table. Western and Russian delegations sit opposite each other, as in the *Life* magazine photographs of Andrey Gromyko meeting Dean Rusk. Assistants serve mineral water that tastes as if it has been drained from a swimming pool. Seating arrangements follow old party lines.

Except in a few instances, the Russians prohibit 100 percent foreign investment and require that Western companies form partnerships with a local entity. Usually the joint-venture partner is a defunct state ministry, drilled in methodology of central planning, that somehow has succeeded in taking itself private: an odd cross between a management buyout and the axiom that possession is nine-tenths of the law. Everyone grasps the possible business at hand, and the negotiations race ahead at the beginning, especially as the Russians assume that those seated in front of them are prepared to invest millions in projects where the only details available are on the back of an envelope.

Most protocol negotiations hit a snag over a problem of language and interpretation—What is goodwill? How do you calculate the prime rate?—not to mention the question over how the seller, usually a Western company, will be paid. Even when they are signed, most protocols end up in the dustbin of deals because Russia lacks the legal, financial, accounting, or banking systems around which the business can be done. Those acquiring Russian real estate cannot prove title. No reliable standards exist to verify financial statements or the contents in a warehouse.

Hence Russian business is still a mixture of barter and central planning, except where American dollars are the unit of exchange. But it is impossible to say who owns what in a collectivized free market. Is it the state, the city, the regional council, the management, or the workers? Under Lenin's formula, the Soviet Union owned everything. But with communism in liquidation, the means of production belong to anyone who can load a tanker in Odessa.

Most hindering to the economy is that the Russian ruble is not a currency—what Adam Smith once defined as "the great wheel of circulation, the great instrument of commerce"—but Monopoly money that stores none of the value of the country and is worthless in international trade. Nevertheless, Russia clings to the ruble because it is a symbol of nationalism, in the same way that islands of the Pacific continue to issue commemorative stamps.

Many that I meet, especially the hard-money men of the Central Bank, insist that Russia must support its currency, and in Moscow one hears speculation of moves to make local dollar transactions illegal. Unfortunately, many of those who are sentimental about a national currency also have a hand in its depreciation.

Under the Soviets, the ruble was less a unit of exchange and more a monetary caste system. Rather than have its value fluctuate in relation to gold, silver, or a basket of world currencies, the ruble was fixed to political expedience. Rates of exchange to the dollar, for example, varied for tourists, foreign investors, state banks, and the industrial sector. There were also two kinds of rubles: cash rubles, bank notes with etchings of the Kremlin or Lenin that workers used in the stores; and transferable rubles, bank credits issued by the government that could not be converted to cash, but which the industrial sector used to settle payments and debts. The tiered-ruble system, which is lingering, explains why Russia can have runaway inflation and a paucity of ruble notes, or why the shortage of paper and ink does not constitute the foundation of a corrective monetary policy.

Under Boris Yeltsin, the ruble became a convertible currency, in theory no different than the lira or the French franc. When I made my first trip in 1991, the tourist rate was 35 rubles to one dollar; but in official exchanges, one dollar equaled 60 kopecks or 0.60 rubles. As I write, it requires 812 rubles to purchase one dollar, although a month ago it was 650. A year ago the rate was 120. Such a drop might give the ruble status as a wheelbarrow currency, were there not in Russia a shortage of farm equipment.

The loss of confidence in the ruble is a result of

hyper-inflation, estimated in 1993 at 1400 percent. Under the Soviets, wages and prices were fixed far below world market values. Rents were $4 a month, because salaries were $20 and because the state provided most services, like education and medicine, free. Now that Russia has a market system, prices have increased—in some cases to their dollar-equivalent level—although wages reflect the low productive capacity of most Russian businesses. A meal in a Western restaurant could cost 168,000 rubles (about $200), although for a typical Russian that would amount to a salary for three years.

Adam Smith made the point that money's worth was relative to what it would acquire, and at present in Russia the ruble buys little. Hence a new Volga automobile costs 12,000,000 rubles in an era when Mikhail Gorbachev's pension was set at 4,400 rubles monthly. Another serious cause of inflation is that there is no control over government credits. Each month, the money supply expands exponentially because parliament, through the Central Bank, is pumping trillions of rubles into an economy of inefficient state enterprises, vast bureaucracy, and social welfare, all of which makes American defense spending, by comparison, look like a Japanese quality circle. Rubles are also being dumped into Russia from the former Soviet republics, such as Estonia and Ukraine, which are now issuing their own currency. In Moscow, stories circulate, perhaps apocryphal, of trains laden with small-denomination currency crossing the frontier to settle foreign exchange contracts.

The first president of Cornell University, Andrew Dickson White, delivered a lecture to Congress in 1876 that established the link between what he called fiat money in France, the circulation of worthless currency, and the terrors of the French Revolution. He could well have defined the problem with Russian democracy two hundred years later: "The main cause of these evils was tampering with the circulating medium of an entire nation: keeping all values in fluctuation; discouraging enterprise; paralyzing energy; undermining sobriety; obliterating thrift; promoting extravagance; and exciting riot by the issue of an irredeemable currency."

When traveling in Russia, I often visit banks outside of Moscow. Without giving away company secrets, our goal in Russia is to develop a network of regional banks. Toward that end I spend time with bankers from such cities as Ufa, Tomsk, Ekaterinburg, and Vladivostok.

Despite my optimism for the future of Russian finance, I acknowledge that a capitalist economy is only as strong as its banking system. And in Russia today, most banks are bankrupt. Under the old Soviet Union, banks were an extension of the budget office. Loans were advances of that year's budget allocation, and repayment came from next year's allotment or from a state insurance scheme. The credit worthiness of a borrower was immaterial, as the state was lending money to itself. When the Soviets fell, their debtors happily defaulted. Banks and state enterprises were left holding bags of worthless receivables.

To Russia's credit, the domestic banking industry is oblivious to its insolvency and has aspirations to thrive. Every company, no matter how insignificant, wants to open a bank, and more than two thousand have been chartered since the collapse of the Soviets. Often these banks are located in former party offices, which means that some of the waiting rooms have portraits of Marx and Engels, as if they were retired chairmen. Others are in dilapidated brick tenements, and the offices are rabbit warrens filled with clerks reconciling accounts, which are kept with carbon paper and stacked in corners. They conjure up images of Blanche Dubois as a branch manager.

Most banks lack dollar-denominated assets, such as gold or

foreign currency, and watch their capital deteriorate at the rate of inflation, which far surpasses what they charge on loans. But this point is lost on most bankers. I have sat through many meetings where I am told proudly that the bank under discussion earned 150 percent on its capital last year, even though inflation diminished that same equity by 2000 percent.

As difficult for the banking system has been the collapse of the Bank for Foreign Trade, known as Vnesheconombank, which collected all of the country's foreign earnings and paid interest and principal on the foreign debt. All the state organizations and banks that earned foreign currency were required to maintain accounts at Vnesheconombank, which functioned as a cross between a central bank and moonshine revenuers.

When the Soviet Union dissolved, Vnesheconombank froze most of the accounts with foreign currency, in a desperate attempt to bolster its dollar reserves. Companies and banks with dollars in the bank had, in effect, their accounts nationalized. For a while such confiscation allowed the Vnesheconombank to service the debt obligations of the defunct Soviet Union. But then the money ran out, and many of the former Soviet republics refused to contribute to pay off the Soviet debt.

The default has taken the capital out of Russian capitalism. Foreign banks refuse to lend money there, and foreign investors fear losing their equity. Thus the lender of last resort is the patchwork of foreign aid. But the West is not lending to a Third World country that is poor or lacks natural resources. Russia has the oil of Saudi Arabia, the gold of South Africa, and the wheat of Canada. It also has the unionism of Argentina, the corruption of Brazil, and the bureaucracy of China.

On one of my recent trips, I met the chairman of the Central Bank of Russia, Viktor Gerashchenko, who is often blamed for many of the country's economic problems. Directly or indirectly, he is responsible for the Russian banking system, including Vnesheconombank, the money supply, and the repayment of the foreign debt, none of which is having a record year. Not only is Gerashchenko charged with causing the great inflation, by pumping trillions of ruble credits into the economy, but there is also the accusation that his is the invisible hand behind the fall of the ruble and the plan to swap old rubles into new ones.

I found myself drawn to Gerashchenko, despite his notoriety. He gives the impression of being an independent thinker, an experienced and technically sound banker, and receptive to new ideas. Most engaging of all is his fondness for American literature. We met in his ballroom-sized office. Although he has the jowls of a party war-horse, a sparkle in his eyes leavens his appearance, and his speech is laced with allusions to F. Scott Fitzgerald and Theodore Dreiser, both of whom had few ideas about the vicissitudes of wealth.

Without searching for scapegoats, Gerashchenko let it be known that it is the Russian parliament, not the Central Bank, that controls the money supply. Although he did not draw the analogy, it would be as if members of the U.S. Congress could print money and mail it out with their constituent letters. He spoke despairingly of the dollar revenue that now avoids the tax system and thus is unavailable to support the ruble or pay the interest on foreign debt. Banks, companies, and even governmental authorities, if possible, keep their money in dollars and away from the grasp of Moscow.

One solution to which Gerashchenko alluded was foreign exchange controls, the old system of tiered rates for ruble-dollar conversion. By his reasoning it would allow Russia to defend its currency, collect taxes, and pay its debts. But it was an unconvincing argument, a remembrance of things past, and it confirmed Joseph Conrad's pessimism about the possibility of change in Russia. As Conrad wrote in *Under Western Eyes*:

> In Russia, the land of spectral ideas and disembodied aspiration, many brave minds have turned away at last from the vain and endless conflict to the one great historical fact of the land. They turned to autocracy for the peace of their patriotic conscience as a weary unbeliever, touched by grace, turns to the faith of his fathers for the blessing of spiritual rest.

Even though I disagree with a return to the monetary rest of tiered exchange rates, I found myself sympathetic to Gerashchenko's plight. He understands that Russia needs a sound currency to bolster its banking system, balance its budget, retire its debt obligations, and trade with the West. But like Dick Diver in Fitzgerald's *Tender is the Night*, he is a bystander to a collapse which is also his own.

Advice on how to solve economic problems is one of the few products the West is willing to provide Russia on open account. Salesmen, dressed up as experts from the World Bank or International Monetary Fund, besiege the president's office, parliament, and various ministries with arguments about why Russia should curb inflation, privatize its industry, repay its debt, retrain its workers, pump more oil, stabilize its currency, and convert its munitions plants into Home Depots. Sadly, the Russian government takes advice seemingly from anyone, as if each were a Siberian monk and able to prevent the young economy from hemorrhaging.

One of the more peripatetic advisers is Professor Jeffrey Sachs, from Harvard University, an economic mendicant who is counseling the Yeltsin government on privatization. Sachs's reputation is for advocating so-called shock therapy—that is, ending the subsidies for inefficient state enterprises and letting the markets rule. He is heir to the tradition of Professor Milton Friedman, who lectured to the Chileans about the sanctity of monetary restraint, or even to the Christian missionaries who preached the value of abstinence.

Conferences on the deliverance of the Russian economy are held with the frequency of golf tournaments, and Sachs is one of the touring pros. At a conference in Frankfurt, where the *Wall Street Journal* was charging $1,000 greens fees, I heard him deliver his standard lecture. Listening to him read a prepared text in a dull monotone, I could not help but think of the Great Oz's confession to Dorothy: "I found myself in the midst of a strange people, who, seeing me come from the clouds, thought I was a great Wizard."

Sachs advocates for Russia a strict adherence to market doctrine. Russia, he holds, should privatize industry, end subsidies, restrict the money supply to curb inflation, and use foreign aid to provide both companies and the country with relief from debt obligations. Large enterprises would fail, jobs would be lost, and Russia would be tested in crossing a "valley of tears," conditions much like those today in Russia but still a distance from the Emerald City.

The problem with granting Russia courage for privatization is that it conjures up the image of an inefficient defense plant, perhaps one making nerve gas, transformed into a public corporation with a line of vacuum cleaners and happy shareholders. Although it is easy to change the shareholders of a state enterprise and have it become what is known as a joint-stock company, what does not change is that the new corporation is usually as starved for capital as the old one.

I have no doubt that if Russia follows the advice of Sachs the economy will improve. At the moment it is the world's largest motor vehicle department, governed by arcane procedures, indifferent clerks, long lines, and regulations that read like eye charts. Under Sachs's mandates it would convert to a showroom or go out of business.

The political question is whether Russia has the patience to spend time in the valley of tears. For many Russians, even those who long ago gave up on Marx and Lenin, the preachings of capitalism evoke only the excesses of czars, the privileges of party officials, or the current generation of new men getting rich selling state assets for private gain. A market system brings to mind the cynicism of Fitzgerald or Dreiser, not the hardworking optimism of William Dean Howells: a businessman is Frank Cowperwood, not Silas Lapham. And not everyone in Russia wants to privatize the yellow-brick road.

As discouraged as I can get about Russia's prospect for solving its economic and political dilemmas, I never lose my affection for traveling in the country. Moscow in the snow evokes a Chekhov short story; in late summer the canals in St. Petersburg shimmer with the grandeur of Venice.

I developed a fondness for Russian travel in the summer of 1975, after I spent a junior year abroad in London and Vienna. During the Vienna semester, I took a course in dissident Soviet literature from a Professor Max Peyfuss, who spoke a number of East European languages and who edited underground magazines for distribution in the East. Often he would come to class with the story of a brief trip to Budapest to pick up a manuscript or with a firsthand account of political intrigue in Bucharest.

I had enormous respect for Peyfuss's courage and a mixture of envy and admiration for a life that always had him in correspondence with famous dissidents or translating a Solzhenitsyn short story. I remember once seeing him through an elegant café window, seated before a beer and deep in conversation, no doubt on the Polish question. It was a peek at a life that I wanted to lead, and I signed up immediately when, at the end of the term, he decided to lead a trip to the Soviet Union. Marlow himself was to take us to the heart of darkness.

Just before our departure, the Russians revoked Peyfuss's visa, which made us feel as if the Soviets would be watching our every move. The trip, however, proceeded without suspicion, although now we were just another group of students riding around Russia on a bus with worn seats and tired springs. (Bill Clinton made a similar trip during his college days, later arousing the suspicion of George Bush, who during the campaign implied that, while in Russia, his opponent had seen the future working. In fact, most American students who saw Russia under Soviet control concluded that they had seen the past and it was broken.)

Our trip, in high summer, was a series of harmless blunders, as if part of a silent movie. On arrival, we found that all our reservations had been canceled or never made. We were finally given a guide and bus and, after a while, rooms in a student hotel past the last stop on the Moscow metro. We spent the first few nights, when it was daylight until 11:00 P.M., wandering through Moscow's broad parks, eating ice cream, and drinking water from public machines that recycled the same glass for all customers.

Without reservations, we were shunted around the Soviet Union like so many lost railcars. In fact, someone in the Soviet travel hierarchy decided that we were best dealt with on the train. On many nights we were put aboard sleepers and dispatched from Moscow to a regional city, only to be returned to the capital on the train the following evening. As such, we saw little of tourist Russia. We were hustled through the Kremlin—between trains—but missed the Hermitage in Leningrad, where they put us on the night train to Tallinn. We missed Kiev, but had several days in Smolensk, idling in the Intourist hotel, waiting for the return express to Moscow.

Before arriving, I had images of Russia only from literature, for example, *The Gulag Archipelago* or the *House of the Dead*. I had expected *Darkness at Noon*, but instead encountered Charlie Chaplin in *The Great Dictator*. I saw none of the country's nastiness: its police state, its frozen winters, its taste for alcohol. I went swimming in lakes edged with birch trees, retraced the steps of Napoleon in Smolensk, and spent a delightful summer day on the Baltic coast in Estonia.

For reasons of incompetence or perhaps crafty design, I had been shown a Russia of rural markets, provincial cities, and magnificent parks where no one I met cared anything for the Cold War, destroying the West, or joining the Comintern in Angola. I also saw that the Russian economy still functioned with ox carts and abacuses, hardly the great instruments of state that were going to color the rest of the European map red.

Most of all, perhaps unavoidably, I developed a love of Russian trains. Even though we were a foreign group, we were thrown randomly into Russian compartments, each containing six berths. Some bedrooms had parties through the night, with vodka for all. Others were transient hotels. I still remember strangers shuffling into their berths, snoring heavily for several hours, and then shuffling out, as anonymous as characters passing through a Russian novel.

In the morning, we would drink hot tea from glass cups that had silver holders, stare at the vastness of the plain or the monotony of the forests, and arrive at our destination in time for breakfast, although where we were headed was usually where the train was stopping at eight o'clock that morning.

It was a short trip, not enough time to do more than look out the window, and we left by ferry from Tallinn to Helsinki on a glorious, blue summer day. We developed a fondness for Russians but decided the Soviet Union was a lost cause. As Marlow remembered his passage upstream: "We were cut off from the comprehension of our surroundings; we glided past like phantoms, wondering and secretly appalled, as sane men would before an enthusiastic outbreak in a madhouse."

Traveling in Russia has changed little in the last twenty years, except for the five-star hotels in Moscow and St. Petersburg.

Aeroflot, the state airline, is still a national lottery in which ticket holders gamble on their chances of arrival. City traffic is a great game of chicken, in which the median of any road is the line of passing cars. And the hotels are all part of the Intourist chain, which seized on the idea that travelers would be comforted to find the same dreary room and broken plumbing no matter where they are in Russia.

The trains are also as I remember them—long lines of green metallic cars, each with a red star and the embossed "CCCP" crest. Usually the ones I take now are the night trains between Moscow and St. Petersburg. There is a wonderful feeling of intrigue and romance, especially in winter when the snow swirls on the platforms, to board a sleeper at midnight in either city, to ride through the cold night on a berth piled high with heavy woolen blankets, and then to drink the same hot tea that evokes summer mornings of 1975.

One of my trips to St. Petersburg ended early on a weekend, and I had no reason to rush home to Switzerland. I decided to take the express either to Warsaw or Berlin, and then fly from there. But the cost of a ticket to Poland was five hundred dollars, so I settled on a second-class sleeper to Vilnius, the capital of the recently independent Lithuania.

The train departed at sunset, although it was nearly midnight. The others in my compartment were a family of Azeris, from Baku, who had with them vodka, chicken, bread, sausage, and pickles. I added Swiss chocolates to the picnic, and until 2:00 A.M. we communicated with sign language, pictures, and vodka shots as the train rocked through a flat landscape of scrub pine.

The train arrived in Vilnius the next morning at 10:30 A.M., although it was hard for me to read the signs to be sure I was getting off at the correct station. With only a day in the city, I decided to take a tour. But as I was the only one asking to see Vilnius that day, I was sent off with a car and driver, and also a guide, a young woman in her twenties who spoke impeccable English.

We spent most of our time walking the narrow lanes of the old city and at the university, which is one of the oldest in Europe. Loreta Raulinaityte, my guide, had studied English literature there, and she knew the writings of the Brontës, Edith Wharton, and Thomas Hardy as well as she knew the scenic walks of old Vilnius.

The wars of modern Europe spared the city, which is remarkably free also of Stalinist city planning. Nevertheless, Vilnius is a ghost town. Even today it should look like a Roman Vishniac photograph of the Jewish pale. But the Jews of Vilna, as the Polish city was then called, disappeared into the Holocaust, and where now they should be hanging wash or selling goods, there are empty cobblestone streets and vacant townhouses that suggest a stage set for a tragedy that has already been filmed, screened, and forgotten.

Over lunch in the old town, Loreta told me about the rebellion, in January 1991, that challenged Soviet rule. It was the first open defiance of Russian hegemony, and on January 12 and 13, the citizens of Vilnius, among them my guide, stood vigil in front of the parliament and the television tower to defend the emerging democracy.

Russian troops responded by storming the television tower, killing thirteen Lithuanians and occupying Vilnius until August of that year, when the failed coup against Gorbachev dissolved the Soviet empire. I asked Loreta what she did when she saw Russian armored personnel carriers move in on the parliament, where she was standing. "We started praying," she said. But they never flinched.

As we walked after lunch, we passed a truck belonging to the British Broadcasting Corporation that was parked near a central square. Inside were continuous showings of the BBC's World Service, and for a glimpse of the news, Lithuanians had formed a long line, as if for bread. Loreta explained that newspapers and English books were still hard to find in Lithuania. When I asked her what I could send, she requested a novel by Margaret Drabble, a dictionary of legal terms, and a textbook on international law—a reading list that, to my mind, sums up what the countries of the former Soviet Union need most to emerge from Lenin's tomb.

I was dropped at the airport for the flight back to Switzerland, and while I had no trouble confirming my seat reservation, I was stopped at immigration for not having a visa for Lithuania. No one on the train had stamped me out of Russia or into Lithuania, and the immigration officer wanted to know why. My blood ran cold. I had images of being taken away to another jail hotel, of meeting my tormentor in the brown suit who would want to know why I was now breaking the laws of Lithuania. For a few moments the officer and I stared at each other, as if he were the truant officer and I had escaped from school.

"You know," he said, waving my passport as if it were a teacher's ruler, "this is not good." But then he smiled, opened the passport, stamped "Lietuvos Respublika, Vilnius" on a blank page, and told me a day wasn't enough time to see Lithuania.

To Baku and Back

(1998)

Like Charlie Chaplin in *The Gold Rush*, I recently joined the list of those panning for oil in the murky waters of the Caspian Sea. In the company of other prospectors, some lined with fur and others whispering into portable phones, I flew Lufthansa from Frankfurt to Baku and checked into a frontier hotel, which, although managed by Hyatt International, had its share of Black Larsons huddled near the bar.

On the western shore of the Caspian, Baku is the capital of Azerbaijan, one of the Newly Independent States of the former Soviet Union. Set on hills that roll down to the sea, the city mixes metaphors of a bazaar, socialist provincialism, and the oil patch of east Texas. Down the alleys of the old city it is still possible to sip mint tea and haggle for carpets, while the waterfront evokes Red Square and the sea is awash with drilling rigs if not Yukon dreams.

Unlike either Belarus or Latvia, Azerbaijan had the good fortune to depart the Soviet Union with large reservoirs of oil and gas. Azeri crude oil production predates the discoveries of Colonel Edwin Drake in western Pennsylvania. Hitler invaded Russia with the dream of fueling the Thousand-Year Reich with oil from the fields around Baku, which in early days collected in puddles on the ground. Recent offshore discoveries in the Caspian have prompted a more subtle invasion

in which the assault troops come armed with lawyers and pro-
duction-sharing contracts.

"More than one billion tons of oil are in the entrails of
Azerbaijan," read one of the briefing memos in my briefcase.
Even at today's market price of $15 per barrel, that would be
worth more than $100 trillion. Other reports allude to sub-
terranean oceans of natural gas. The so-called "contract of the
century" that includes companies like BP, Exxon, and Statoil
in an off-shore field calls for $8 billion in development costs
and dreams of 500 million tons, for which the street value
runs to the trillions.

Were Azerbaijan in Scandinavia or on the North Slope of
Alaska, it would be hailed as the antidote to the Organization of
Petroleum Exporting Countries (OPEC) and lavished with
export insurance and unsecured bank loans. Unfortunately, it
straddles the fault line not just between the West and Islam, but
also the seismic plates that shift between the United States,
Russia, and Iran, without belonging to any one camp. With
coordinates inside Rudyard Kipling's Great Game, it recalls his
lines:

> But there is neither East nor West, Border,
>   nor Breed, nor Birth,
>   When two strong men stand face to face,
>   though they come from ends of the earth!

Azerbaijan shares borders with Armenia, Georgia, Iran,
and Russia, all of which have fought regional ethnic or religious wars in recent times. Across the gray waters of the
Caspian are the khanates of Turkmen and Kazakhs whose
untested political institutions are struggling to franchise the
gas stations opening along the Silk Road. The fractured
republics that surround the Caspian could well become the
Balkans of the twenty-first century.

Little about the borders of Azerbaijan relates to the Azeri nation. The country has a population of 8 million, of whom a large minority are Russian and Armenian. Most Azeris are Muslims, and a diaspora of 20 million Azeris makes them the largest minority in Iran. Although the government of Azerbaijan banned a political party devoted to Islamic fundamentalism, it coexists with minarets on its skyline much as it once lived with the stern faces of Lenin and Stalin calling their faithful to prayer.

Between meetings I walked through a park overlooking both the city and the shores of the Caspian Sea. Snow and a biting wind swirled off the sea, making it feel like Cleveland in January.

Along the shore were dockyards, ships swinging at anchor, and the ferries that ply the waters of the world's largest inland sea. In the distance, brushed with white caps, were the skeletal towers of drilling rigs, linked in a few places by an offshore highway like that which connects the Florida Keys.

Elsewhere in the same park were the headstones of soldiers who died fighting the 1988–92 war with Armenia. Both countries staked claims to Nagorno-Karabagh, an ethnic beehive inside Azerbaijan. In contrast to the offshore dreams of plenty, the markers were engraved with the portraits of each fallen soldier, as haunting as Edgar Allan Poe's "Masque of the Red Death," which casts a pall over the glitter of a sumptuous house party.

The fighting filled Baku with refugees and prompted Russia to send one billion dollars in weaponry to the Armenians, whose troops still hold the enclave. Pressured by well-organized Armenian lobbyists, the U.S. Congress cut aid to Azerbaijan, for a while adding the country to the list of politically incorrect nations.

More recently, President Bill Clinton has embraced President Heydar Aliyev as part of a sales pitch for American oil companies, and then Energy Secretary Hazel O'Leary picked up some frequent flyer miles around a Baku trade show. Once Congress discovered that Azerbaijan was heir to an oil fortune, it reopened its doors as if to the Rockefellers.

But the shadow over Caspian oil is that for it to reach Western markets, it must flow either south to Iran, north through Chechnya, or west through the Caucasus, routes that prompt many investors to reach for a second sweater. In *Greenmantle*, a novel of the Great Game, John Buchan writes: "The Persian Moslems are threatening trouble. There is a dry wind blowing through the East, and the parched grasses wait the spark." That sentiment perhaps explains why the Azeri martyrs chiseled into the black and gray granite face the same waters that cover the wealth of many nations.

Business etiquette in Azerbaijan is still conducted along Soviet lines. Everyone referred to our group as a "delegation," as if we were there to negotiate a treaty on Joint Economic Understanding, and all the meetings were held in conference rooms that undoubtedly held planning sessions for the five-year plan.

Although most kapitalists doing business in this part of the world dream of selling prefabricated iron curtains, when the meetings start they usually lapse into discourses that could well be lifted from the collected speeches of Leonid Brezhnev.

As models for its economic development, Azerbaijan has chosen Turkey, with whom it shares both linguistic roots and preferences for secular modernism, and the duty-free emirates such as Kuwait or Bahrain. It wants its oil billions to fuel a secular society and, once the petroleum runs dry, to live as remittance men on the invested fortune.

Nevertheless, Azeri assets are contingent, what accountants

call below the line or, in this case, the sea. Existing oil production simply feeds the country's power demands and inefficient refineries, and only a trickle has reached foreign markets.

The crumbling infrastructure inherited from Lenin's colonialists, like the visions of the British midlands that haunt the suburbs of Calcutta, produces little of value for export markets. Without a supply of raw materials from the union of socialist republics, the Soviet assembly line no more creates wealth in today's world than did the Bombay Cricket Club after the departure of the Raj.

For Azerbaijan to raise cash against its petroleum legacy—much as it once subsisted on allotments from the Supreme Soviet—it must rely on the invested billions of large multinational corporations, whose fickle capital markets are one of the dialectics of materialism.

Among the liabilities of the Newly Independent States are their currencies, which in most cases are as air worthy as the repainted Aeroflot jets that constitute their national airlines.

One of the few successes of the Soviet system was the common currency of the ruble, which was legal tender across nine time zones. But the Soviet ruble was company-store script that neither was convertible beyond the corporation towns nor stored any wealth of the society.

The savings of the Soviets tended to be denominated in the perks of party officials. The new money pegged only to political expedience, without an anchor to either a basket of world currency or monetary discipline, also makes it impossible to save anything of value under a mattress.

While the Azeri manat is not a wheelbarrow currency, it cannot be exchanged at the Zurich airport, and the only restraints on its supply are the checks and balances of a one-party government with marginal opposition.

In the former Soviet republics, deals more complicated than short cab rides require dollars, although most governments have issued decrees against the circulation of the greenback, as if the Bill of Rights came with its acceptance.

In the office of the head of the central bank, warmed by the tea and stale chocolates that go with every meeting, I advanced the theory of letting the dollar circulate legally, as it can, for example, in Bermuda or Panama.

With a stroke, Azerbaijan would reduce its inflation to that of the United States, join the dollar trade zone, and allow its citizens to count their savings in something other than Marlboros.

If Germany and France can give up their national currencies, I asked, why not Azerbaijan? I cited the example of Bolivian silver coins circulating freely in revolutionary America, but the blank looks around the table suggested I was carrying the cross of gold discarded by William Jennings Bryan.

Azerbaijan's full faith and credit rests with President Aliyev, whose portrait in shops and meeting rooms conveniently fits into the frames that once held the likenesses of Lenin.

Like many new democrats of the old Soviet bloc, he took his political education on the central committee in Baku, at the KGB, and as a member of the Politburo in Moscow. His election combined elements of the Risorgimento and a ward meeting on Chicago's South Side. His son is the effective power at the state oil company. But no one I met spoke ill either of President Aliyev or his government, for whom foreign investment has replaced the dictatorship of the proletariat as their revolutionary theory.

One of the more curious aspects of Baku is to discover that many of the other prospectors dancing in the saloons are American politicians. Former national security advisors Brent

Scowcroft and Zbigniew Brzezinski, recent cabinet officers James Baker, Lloyd Bentsen, and Richard Cheney, and ex-White House aide John Sununu are among those panning for contracts. Some, like Bentsen, are direct investors, risking their own capital; others here raise the heralds of large corporations, like crusaders before the gates of Jerusalem.

Most cloak their divining rods in the guise of benevolence, and speak of the public good that will flow west with Azeri oil. But few of these men, as either Washington insiders or prospectors, have ever championed the cause of cheap oil.

As government officials, most of them implemented policies that were struck when President Jimmy Carter made his cardigan sweater the symbol of American energy dependence. On the grounds that the world was running out of oil, the U.S. has supported the cartels that fixed the price of world oil as though it were tobacco in North Carolina or sugar in Louisiana. Only with artificially high prices would Saudi princes or ARCO geologists bother to search for new oil.

Many of those now chanting "Open, Sesame" to the caves around Baku are also among those who drew lines in the sand during the Gulf War—the battle, as it turned out, that made the world safe for expensive oil.

The call to arms was to keep Saddam Hussein's hands off the oil spigots in Kuwait and perhaps Saudi Arabia. Otherwise Western economies would be held hostage either to tyranny or to price fixing. But the war ended not with Iraqi crude oil as a spoil of war, flooding into Western markets, but with Hussein's wells shut in, as if his true war crime had been to threaten OPEC's cozy supply quotas.

On his trip home from the territories, Chaplin staked his second claim, that for true love, while I settled for a flight that departed at 4:50 A.M., breakfast, and a back issue of *The New Yorker* that described the contributions of grateful emirs to the political libraries of James Baker and George Bush.

After the socialist realism of Baku, a magazine so devoted to fashion, political and otherwise, made me realize how fine are the distinctions in American foreign policy between good oil—that of the North Slope or Mexico—and the oil of evil—that controlled by mullahs or agents of terrorism. Imagine the furor if Iran, not Oman, had given money to the James A. Baker Institute of Public Policy.

Men like Baker, Scowcroft, and Brzezinski have made diplomatic careers—almost like wine tasters at the court of Louis XIV—for their ability to distinguish those oils fermented by the faithful and those that are grown in the vineyards of heresy.

Since the so-called energy crisis of the 1970s, crude oils have been ranked not according to price, but by the measure of moral refinement they bring to the American consumer, much like cabernet sauvignon.

But as long as the American dream runs on high-test, found at the pumps of countries like Azerbaijan, the U.S. will need to try its hand at the Great Game, which, as Kim discovered, is usually played out on remote mountain passes, perhaps like those that twist through Nagorno-Karabagh. At least late in their careers, America's best and brightest have taken to his majesty's service.

Although the flags of American oil companies fly over paperweights in various ministries around Baku, the sense even from a short trip is that U.S. diffidence toward Azerbaijan has meant preferences for Russian, French, and English companies. The colonial ties with Moscow have meant generous concessions in the Caspian for Lukoil, the Russian conglomerate, and the U.S. lost another bid when Turkmenistan chose to export its gas through Iran. Will not the next Cold War be between Islam and the West over control of Central Asia's hydrocarbons?

Kipling understood that not all countries have a taste for geopolitics, as he wrote in "Dane-Geld":

> It is always a temptation of a rich and lazy nation,
> To puff and look important and to say:—
> "Though we should defeat you,
> We have not the time to meet you,
> We will therefore pay you cash to go away."

Azerbaijan will be a good measure of American prospects. As Chaplin discovered, it is not always easy to find both the gold and the girl.

Moving to Europe

(1992)

A year ago in late spring, after riding my bicycle through the woods of central Maine, I boarded a commuter flight in Bangor, changed in Boston, and, unceremoniously, moved to Europe.

Whenever in my daydreams I imagined living overseas, I assumed the journey would begin on the ocean: waving good-bye at the pier, enjoying a comfortable deck chair, sipping bouillon at eleven, shooting skeet at five, dressing for dinner. Instead I was squeezed into a coach seat, offered chicken or fish, and then, instead of a midnight buffet, fed another of those mindless comedies that run exclusively in the air.

To be sure, it was a routine flight, programmed by a latter-day Dr. Caligari, whose mission is to fly somnambulists to Europe. But it could have been exciting. The Boeing 747 lifted off the runway as the sun set behind the Boston skyline. We climbed to cruising altitude over the Georges Bank, began the crossing just south of Cape Race, made landfall over Shannon, and descended into Europe over the hedgerows of Normandy. Charles Lindbergh charted the same course sixty-four years earlier, on his own discovery of Europe, and, although there were similarities and differences between his flight and mine, at least he was spared a film with Goldie Hawn.

I was on my way to Geneva, which Henry James took delight in deriding as Calvinist or "the dark old city at the other end of the lake." Except for my junior year spent abroad, in London and Vienna, I had never lived in Europe. Since college, I had visited often, on two-week dashes that took me to meetings in London or Paris, or on vacation to Greece. But on those occasions Europe was a theme park where I would buy admission tickets to conferences or the Parthenon. I never had to register a car, haggle for insurance, or enroll a child in school. I was free to pretend that Europe was a moveable feast, not a mandatory seven-course banquet, complete with finger bowls, where unfathomable regulations govern the procedures of the soup course.

Moving several months ahead of my family, which followed with a wagon train of cat carriers, maple syrup, and such essential items as a two-year supply of Pampers, I arrived in Switzerland with a suitcase, an armload of travel guides, and a bicycle, which on weekends I rode through the vineyards and small villages that hug the hillsides around Geneva.

Spring along the back roads of Switzerland is a symphony of neatly trimmed paddocks, medieval walls, weeping willows, freezing rain, and, when the sun shines, the mixed metaphors of cherry blossoms by the roadside and snow-covered Alps in the distance. I would stop for picnics of bread and cheese, drink espresso at sleepy cafes, and consider myself lucky for getting the chance to live abroad.

There still is much to love about Europe, even though stealing from tourists is one of the national sports in Italy, and Euro Disney is the same size as Paris. On my list of pleasures are: newspapers such as the *Guardian* (London), *Le Monde*, or the *Herald Tribune* (for Doonesbury and baseball scores); railroads, which are ratty, smoky, and reeking of wurst in second class but still connect Geneva to Rome, Nice, and

Barcelona with sleeping cars; Paris on a summer evening, when it stays light until 10:00 P.M. and, after dinner, you can walk to the Île St. Louis for ice cream; bookshops in Oxford and Cambridge where, when you order a book by phone, the clerks ask if you want the American edition published by Scribner's or the British from Jonathan Cape; ferries, like those that ply the Greek islands, on which for thirty dollars you get two deck chairs, a bottle of Demestica, and a trip to Cape Sounion.

In Geneva we settled seven miles from the darkness, in a village that at times seems plagiarized from *A Year in Provence*, Peter Mayle's diary of his adventures with French chefs and local tradesmen, all of whom seem to be played by John Cleese.

Out the backdoor are the vineyards of the local *vin ordinaire*, which is sold from small cellars in neighboring villages. The only shop in town is a tiny *patisserie* that sells superb fresh bread, an array of chocolates, and milk in containers so small that two are needed to satisfy one cat.

Although we do not have the procession of quirky tradesmen that roll up to Peter Mayle's house, we do have a chimney sweep who arrives without request, cites a number of obscure fire code regulations, dispatches his assistant to the roof with long brushes, and then departs with a flurry of handshakes, a Swiss cross between the Belgian ambassador and Batman.

We also have to deal with the *Secrétariat des Inspecteurs*, headed by one Madame Bayard, who would otherwise be known as the truant officer. Mme Bayard must be notified, in writing, twenty-five days before an unscheduled absence from school. When, at the last minute, our four-year-old daughter missed some kindergarten to attend her great-grandfather's one hundredth birthday (we listed Willard Scott as a reference), Mme Bayard wrote us a curt note to explain that we had presented the school system with a "fait accompli" and that she had no way to refuse our request. I can only assume that Otto von Bismarck learned a lot from his school board.

For work I began traveling around Europe as I once did the United States. Instead of flying USAir to Buffalo or Savannah, however, I now found myself making day trips to Frankfurt, Zurich, and Milan, and longer outings to Moscow. Alas, even Paris on a business trip can be reduced to a cramped flight, a cab ride, television in the hotel, a meeting at which people use phrases like "the ball's in their court (*'la balle est dans leur court'*)," and a flight home. Nevertheless, it was on these trips that I began to see Europe, less as the restored Orient Express, and more as a masked ball that, at midnight, will turn into another Great War.

Business-class Europe, where executives are forever excusing themselves to call home on AT&T, has five-star hotels, haute couture, wine lists longer than novels, foie gras, doormen that look like they could date Mary Poppins, five-thousand-dollar watches, and black German cars the size of Trident submarines. Adjacent to that Europe, no more than an hour's flying or a day's drive, is another Europe where neo-Nazis are dousing immigrants with lighter fluid, Serbs and Croats are exchanging massacres, British troops are patrolling Belfast in riot gear, and the average Russian is earning five dollars a month. The contrast recalls Barbara Tuchman's portrait of Europe in the years preceding 1914. Her title, *The Proud Tower*, comes from Edgar Allan Poe:

> While from a proud tower in the town
> Death looks gigantically down.

In 1974, when I last lived overseas, all anyone could imagine was that the continent would evolve peacefully into the United States of Europe. I was studying with the Institute of European Studies, which had an affiliation with Bucknell and the London School of Economics. Our group of about twenty lived in a YMCA—lent excitement by the disappearance of the manager with one of the chambermaids. The classes, which met in various spots around London, were a steady diet of European integration.

The American students in London, however, were not at all like our European counterparts. What we cared about was doing the assigned reading, getting papers in on time, seeing Paris over the weekend and getting good grades—pursuits the locals found pedestrian.

I remember one British student who never did the reading, showed only vague interest in his papers, but who loved nothing more than interrupting a lecture to denounce imperialism, colonialism, and the films of Clint Eastwood. It was always a delightful triumph of rhetoric over facts, but if today he's a Member of Parliament from Gayle or Manchester, he's telling his constituents that the idea of Europe is just another call for *lebensraum*, Russification, American imperialism, or the restoration of the Hapsburgs, not to mention an assignment for Lt. Harry Callahan.

In those years American students took political criticism poorly—Vietnam and Richard Nixon were recent memories. "What about the Marshall Plan" was the stock answer to perceived European impertinence about American encroachment, the implication being that France and Germany would have been Finlandized without billions in U.S. aid. But all the progress toward a common market assured us that the future in Europe was in franchising, not fascism.

Twenty years later, the hope is that Europe's future lies as a federation. There's talk of a central bank, one currency, guardless borders, and three-hour train rides from London to Paris by the end of the decade. But these accommodations are the dreams of bureaucrats, much the way European monarchs used to conclude an alliance by marrying a distant cousin.

Beneath this Pax Bureaucratica, the Swiss are searching frantically to stay independent; the Scots and the Basques are dreaming of secession; the Slovaks want nothing to do with the Czechs; the Poles are terrified of a German economic blitzkrieg; the European Community is busy recognizing the sovereignty of Bosnia, Slovenia, and Croatia; Scandinavia is going broke; and Russians are living in newly independent republics as a reviled colonial caste.

Although it has been overlooked in the din of Western, self-congratulatory praise, the collapse of the Soviet Union revealed that more than half of Europe wants nothing to do with what it regards as a League of Nations.

Ironically, the Soviet Union had many elements that the European Community would now like to emulate: a common currency, one judicial system, national republics coexisting in a union of states, and one military. The only problem was that it took all of Stalin's brutality to hold the coalition together.

That the idea of Europe is fragile became clear when I traveled to the villages of my grandfathers. One was a Serb, born two hundred miles south of Belgrade, near the border with Bulgaria. The other was an Ulster Scot, born in America in the 1870s, but shortly after his parents emigrated from a town near Belfast. Both villages are unchanged in the last hundred years, but in each case the surrounding country has become a symbol of why Europe may not work.

I went to Yugoslavia with a distant cousin, who grew up in Belgrade and speaks English fluently. We traveled on the eve of the civil war, beginning in Dubrovnik and continuing by bus, train, and rented car through Croatia, Montenegro, and Serbia. We stayed with relatives and visited friends. When we had a car, I would drive, and he would navigate, translate as needed, and talk about the year of discontent.

He believed war was inevitable. The Yugoslav economy was in ruin. Neither a product of the East or West, it was an unworkable hybrid of state planning, nationalized companies, and free enterprise—so long as the remnants of Tito's machine held all the shares. A worthless currency robbed workers of their capital, and who wanted to ship agricultural products to central markets in exchange for a promise in a five-year plan? What my cousin described wasn't a religious or nationalist dispute, but the failure of tariff union.

We stayed in and near towns that have been damaged in the fighting. Most Serbs and Croats would rather drink plum brandy under a shady tree and toast a new American friend than cut the throats of neighbors they have known for a lifetime. But on the issue of minority rights, not just Serbs but most of Europe is ready to fight.

In the case of Yugoslavia, my cousin had no quarrel, in theory, with an independent Croatia. But he remembered when it was last independent, as a rump state of Nazi Germany, when thousands of Serbs were slaughtered by the fascists. What now would be the fate of Serbs who fell on the Croatian side of the partition? Who would guarantee their rights—a desk officer in Brussels?—especially when the new Croatian government made it clear they would be second-class citizens. And there's the same fear of Slovaks in Czechoslovakia, Russians in the Ukraine, or Ulster Scots in Northern Ireland.

To get to Belfast, I crossed the Irish Sea by ferry, took a suburban train to York Road station, and was riding downtown on a bus when the driver announced cheerfully that there was a bomb scare and he couldn't go any farther. The rest of the passengers took the news routinely, collected their belongings and continued the trip on foot—ducking under the cordon that indicated a possible explosive. Feeling I had no choice, I joined the march toward doom until I decided that, after all, this was Belfast and that the bus was the best place to wait out the scare. When the driver heard my story, he apologized for the city's "inconveniences" and drove me in the bus to a taxi stand.

I enjoyed my stay in Belfast only because it reminded me of my home in Brooklyn. I went to Andersontown, The Falls, and Shankill, where some of the worst violence has occurred, and, for better or worse, it struck me as similar to Crown Heights, Flatbush, and parts of Bensonhurst. In both Belfast and Brooklyn the jobs, but not the workers, have moved to Taiwan, and there's the sense, in the abandoned red-brick buildings, that the industrial revolution can no longer afford the rent. In the argument over diminishing returns, Belfast is left looking like home to a never-ending riot, and some sections end, as did the trenches in World War I, with razor wire, gun emplacements, and a no-man's-land.

My grandfather's village is twenty kilometers north of The Troubles, but it could easily be a thousand miles away. I had a drink in the local pub, which went silent when I entered, made a few friends, and then spent the afternoon visiting people whose last names were the same as my grandparents'. They never went to Belfast, and it never came to their small farming village of Holstein cows and a stone chapel.

From village to village—even in Serbia or Northern Ireland, not to mention Switzerland—Europe is idyllic. It's only when the villages start to overlap that you begin having trouble.

The people I met in Northern Ireland could have been characters in the novels of Thomas Hardy. And indeed one of the pleasures of traveling in Europe is that it amounts to a Cook's tour of great literature. Who needs a travel guide when you can read Honoré de Balzac in Paris, F. Scott Fitzgerald in Cannes, Henry James in Vevey, Charlotte Brontë in Yorkshire, and Gustave Flaubert in nearby France? (Madame Bovary could never have been Swiss, as she would have had to write too many notes to the *Secrétariat des Inspecteurs*.)

The proximity of Casterbridge or the charterhouse in Parma has made it a lot easier to catch up on my college reading. Like most who passed through Lewisburg, I didn't quite finish all the assignments. What I really did was collect reading lists. Last year, when I finished *Death in Venice* in the Hotel des Bains on the Lido (" . . . the air was heavy and turbid and smelt of decay"), I finally completed the required reading for Michael Payne's freshman English seminar.

This year I'm using a Ralph Rees syllabus on American writers in Europe: Henry James, Edith Wharton, F. Scott Fitzgerald, and Ernest Hemingway. If I have to write a paper, it will conclude that American writers came to Europe to write about America, with the exception of Hemingway, who came to write about himself.

Nevertheless, American writers in Europe do have a genius for character. Today, it's still possible to run across one of James's drawing-room dandies, Wharton's dowagers, or Fitzgerald's troubled heiresses. When George Bush comes to Europe, I think of him as Daisy Miller on the Grand Tour. Secretary of State Baker is Lambert Strether, from *The Ambassadors*, forever on a mission to break up an unsound engagement. Nicole Diver (*Tender is the Night*) is the Duchess of York (Fergie) without a media escort.

One reason I'm always picking up James, Fitzgerald, or even the self-satisfied Hemingway is that it's comforting to hear American voices. To live in Europe as an American, even if you speak the language and can read a wine list, is to be an immigrant and thus an outsider. Most expatriates go through each day with a touch of homesickness, as if it were a low-grade infection.

Not long ago the Rath Museum in Geneva put on an exhibition of Edward Hopper, the American painter from the 1920s and '30s who is best known for his forlorn *Early Sunday Morning*. At the exhibit I found myself thinking less about Hopper's art—is it impressionist, surrealist, Ash Can School?—and looking more at the pictures as though they were lifted from photo albums. I wanted to be reminded of the coast of Maine, a clapboard house on Cape Cod, Wall Street, or a lonely stretch of track in the prairie.

Mal du pays is French for homesickness, and it's compounded by an inability to track the dialogue back home. I read the *Herald Tribune*, bootlegged copies of the Sunday *Times*, and watch Cable News Network in hotels (you can't see the forest for the self-promotional haze), but feel I have lost touch with what *Time* magazine calls the American Scene.

For me the United States has become an interminable rock video. Smoke wafts across the set, lights flash, and, in chaotic order, the camera flicks between George Bush riding in his helicopter, Mike Tyson wallowing in jail, Madonna undressing, Jodie Foster thanking her agent, David Duke chatting with Larry King, or the Rev. Al Sharpton showing up for work as a family adviser. Cut to the rest of America, which is the audience at the Phil Donahue Show, deciding who is due for the next Scarlet Letter.

As an American, I always am asked for instant analysis on the election or the economy, but I don't know why Mario Cuomo decided not to run, whether Paul Tsongas is really Mr. Rogers, how many Dodge Darts George Bush wanted to sell in Japan, or if Hillary Clinton listens near the door when Bill gets a phone call and says, "I'll take this one in the den."

The United States comes across as a nation of soundbites: "The envelope, please," "She only rubbed my back," "Didn't inhale," or "Hasta la vista, baby." Seen from a distance, it appears incapable of thought, reason, courage, or sensibility. Little wonder Europeans look West for pleasure, not leadership.

Even if Europe is not in a mood to emulate the United States, it has to decide where its influences will lie: in the United States of Europe or in a return engagement at Sarajevo.

The clues may be found in Berlin, which I visited for the first time just after the wall came down. I had no business, arrived during a snowstorm, and only by good fortune did I connect with a friend of a friend.

We drove in her small car to Checkpoint Charlie, the Brandenburg Gate, Museum Island (When I asked my friend what was there, she replied, "Oh, just some old buildings."), and to the Rathaus where John F. Kennedy announced, "Ich bin ein Berliner." (The crowd roared because he said, in effect, "I am a Danish," rather than "I am Danish." *Berliners* are cream-filled pastries.)

Berlin is flat, vast, filled with parks, and would be exhausting to see on foot. I'm sure it's delightful in summer to sit on the lawns or in beer gardens. The Reichstag, now a museum, is near the site of the wall, which can be found only in small plastic bags at souvenir stands. The rest has vanished, leaving a scar of vacant lots to divide the city.

West Berliners have no time for East Berliners, who are thought to want their jobs, apartments, and perhaps their identities. But those from the east are a people with neither a history nor a memory. They draw only on the present. Where are their roots? In the Communist bloc? In Marx or Lenin? As citizens of the Third Reich? As Germans of Weimar? As Prussians? Geographically they are now united with the West, but historically they are adrift or, to use a phrase of Aleksandr Solzhenitsyn, one of the "nations in exile."

East Berliners are an extreme example of dislocation, but the same is being asked of the rest of Europe. In Eastern Europe, citizens are learning that their future lies in forgetting the past, while in the West the French, Germans, British, etc., are being asked to sacrifice their nationalism for the common good.

It's a high-wire act. If the British decide they can live without the Bank of England, does that mean that the

Germans can forget Auschwitz? What gets kept and what gets thrown away? Solzhenitsyn wrote in *The Gulag Archipelago*: "It is unthinkable in the twentieth century to fail to distinguish between what constitutes an abominable atrocity that must be prosecuted and what constitutes that 'past' which 'ought not to be stirred up.'"

In Berlin, even on a day's drive in the snow, you see so much that needs remembering, and so much that must be forgotten.

Letter from Serbia

(1992)

When we got back to our room in the hotel, my husband said,
"All this is very sad. Men and women have died and lived for the
ideal of Yugoslavia, the South Slav state; and here are these very
charming people chafing with discontent at the realization of it.
And so far as I can see, however bad Belgrade may be, they give
it no chance to prove its merits. These people are born and trained
rebels. They cry out when they see a government as if it were a
poisonous snake, and seize a stick to kill it with, and in that they
are not being fanciful. All the governments they have known till
now have been, so far as they are concerned, poisonous snakes. But
all the same that attitude would be a pity, if they happened to
meet a government for once that was not a poisonous snake."

—Rebecca West, *Black Lamb and Grey Falcon* (1942)

In its schedule, Air France lists a weekly flight from Nice to
Dubrovnik. But in the autumn of 1990, when I was escorted
onto the Tarmac that sweeps the shore of the Riviera, I found
the markings of Jugoslovenski Aerotransport on the side of a
dilapidated DC-9—the airline equivalent of putting plum
brandy into old wine bottles. I was seated on the aisle in the
first row, next to an off-duty pilot, and throughout the flight
had a clear view of the cockpit. No sooner had we taken off

than my seatmate bolted to the cabin, bummed a cigarette from the captain, and settled down on the armrest to spend the flight regaling the crew with his stories.

Although we were flying over the rough Italian spine and then down the azure coastline of the Yugoslav Adriatic, the conviviality of the pilots gave the flight the feel of a Mexican bus ride. As we landed in Dubrovnik, on a runway carved into barren hillsides, the deadheading captain kept pointing out the cockpit window, as if explaining where his sister lived or the beer was coldest. But there was nothing sinister about the bar-rail scene on the flight deck. In fact, I found it strangely comforting to know that men, not a computer and a disembodied voice, were flying the machine.

I was on my way to Yugoslavia to visit the Serbian village where my grandfather was born and to travel in the country during the year of its discontent. Although my grandfather died in 1973, when I was a freshman in college, it would be easy to write that I never knew him. In 1960, when I was five and he was eighty, he suffered a stroke that confined him to hospitals for the last thirteen years of his life. During that time I visited him often, but we never had a conversation about his life, what he had seen, the books that he had written, or the people that he knew. To a boy growing up in a Long Island suburb, and more involved with baseball and bicycles than a life that had begun in Serbia and was now ending in a New York state hospital, my grandfather belonged more to the house of the dead than to one of the living.

Despite the distance of our ages, I have always felt close to my grandfather. Whether deliberately or not, I followed his footsteps in magazines and business, at Columbia University, and abroad in Vienna and Geneva. In college I made a stab at learning Serbo-Croatian, and after graduation I visited Belgrade. And in 1990, when Yugoslavia started coming apart along its ethnic seams, I decided to travel there again. He always wanted Yugoslavia to flourish like Switzerland or the

United States, countries that prospered despite national divisions, but I thought that he would have liked me to be a witness to the disintegration.

I began my trip in Dubrovnik, because in my grandfather's writing it stands for everything that is admirable in the Yugoslav mind. I also wanted several days by the sea, so that I could recover from jet lag and read Rebecca West's 1942 travelogue about Yugoslavia, *Black Lamb and Grey Falcon*, which covers a thousand years of Yugoslav history in about the same number of pages. I had started it on numerous occasions, but had never gotten beyond page 124. On this trip I wanted her to be one of the narrators, and hoped a few days in a deck chair would get me going.

At first glance, from the airport road that does a catwalk along the coastal escarpment, Dubrovnik looks like an Italian village that has been towed across the Adriatic on a barge. Red-tile roofs, Renaissance bell towers, and medieval city walls appear anchored in the turquoise sea alongside the bulkhead of an ordinary Yugoslav town. Rebecca West found it "as precious as Venice," and said that it "should be visited for the first time when the twilight is about to fall, when it is already dusk under the tall trees that make an avenue to the city walls." And, in fact, after I had settled into the Hotel Argentina, which sits on a bluff overlooking the town, it was in the late afternoon that I wandered the streets of polished cobblestones, feeling as if I were in a gondola.

"A little republic," my grandfather wrote about Dubrovnik, "whose population did not surpass a few dozen thousands of inhabitants, produced from the end of the 15th century a relatively prodigious number of writers and savants, and a great majority of them of superior merit." I am sure everything about it appealed to him: its Renaissance charms, its literary tradition, its livelihood in trade, its political neutrality, and its symbolism as the prow of Yugoslavia pointed toward Western seas. The square mile of narrow lanes, trading houses, and writers' garrets was all that he wanted the rest of the country to emulate, and its senseless shelling in the civil war that was to follow would have confirmed his darkest fears about Yugoslavia's fate.

Rebecca West also loved the idea of Dubrovnik—a city-state of worthy artists and clever middlemen—but she found the twentieth-century version artificial. At one point she says to her husband, who serves as the book's literary straight man: "I can't bear Dubrovnik." She was searching for the Yugoslavia that lay on the fault line between Christianity and Islam, which has produced minarets in Sarajevo and Byzantine frescoes in Kossovo—not to mention villages such as the one I was on my way to visit. But what West found in Dubrovnik was a city more at home with Western tourists than with the shepherds that live up the hillsides in Montenegro, and she couldn't wait to leave.

I, on the other hand, did not mind lingering at all, despite the concentration of T-shirt stands. I swam in the chilly autumn waters of the Adriatic, took a coastal ferry to the delightful seaside colony of Cavtat, and walked the ramparts that surround the old town, which from overhead is a labyrinth painted by Giotto. I also spent a lot of time with the desk clerk, plotting how I would take the train to Belgrade. Why not fly, he kept asking? Just to catch the train meant a five-hour bus ride to Bar, near the Albanian border—and, he warned me, the rail coaches were filthy. But I persisted, remembering as a child the letters and magazine clippings that had come to my parents from Yugoslavia, telling of the line's progress through the mountains of Montenegro. When it was finished, it would connect Belgrade to the sea, and Yugoslavia to the modern world.

To get my wish meant a 4:45 A.M. wake-up call and riding a succession of rural buses over craggy mountain passes to Titograd, the capital of Montenegro, where I had hoped to intercept the train. Titograd, like so many cities in the fading Communist world, is a vast, drab housing project that leaves the impression that the landlord has fled with the rent money. Set in a valley that is surrounded by Alpine splendor are cinder-block high rises, dismal storefronts, and those cubist monuments that show a small group of workers, their fists aloft, celebrating, in this case, the paternal leadership of Marshal Tito, when, in reality, they should pay tribute to anyone who had to endure as one of his tenants.

The train arrived shortly before 11:00 A.M., and for the next several hours it picked its way across the mountain gorges of Montenegro, which Rebecca West describes as "an astonishing country, even to those who know the bleakness of Switzerland and Scotland and the Rockies." As predicted by the desk clerk, I was jammed against a dirty window. Nevertheless, the compartment had the feel of the third ring at an opera, and the stage sets were snow-capped peaks and plunging valleys. I passed the day looking out the window, reading, searching the train vainly for food, and, as we left the mountains for the red-roofed villages and small paddocks of Serbia, thinking about my grandfather's life.

He was born Milivoy Stojan Stanoyevich at Koprivnica in February 1881, the second of four brothers. As a boy he tended sheep and went to school, first in the village and later in Zejacar, a town ten miles to the south on the Timok River, a tributary of the Danube. For reasons I was determined to learn, he escaped peasant life and enrolled at the university in Belgrade. Three years later he was back in Zejacar, teaching in the high school.

He might have lived happily as a rural educator had he not written a pamphlet entitled "Youth and Socialism," which enraged the Serbian monarchy. A villager who knew my grandfather once described the episode to me: "He wrote some articles against the king and he had to go away." The book was offensive so far as it advocated democracy and universal education, but he was sentenced to three years either in jail or exile. After much deliberation with his father, he left Serbia to study in Vienna and Geneva, and then he crossed to America, never to return. He was twenty-three years old.

In the late 1950s he added captions to a photo album that chronicled his life, and as the train, in Balkan fashion, crept between withered stations and stopped in remote fields without explanation, I flipped through the photocopy of the album that I had brought on my trip.

In 1911 he described himself as a "humble scholar and neophyte-explorer." Studying for a Ph.D., first at Berkeley and later at Columbia, he was trying "to get inside knowledge of Americanism, and American way of life." In 1917, he married my grandmother, who grew up on Fifth Avenue in New York and from whom I get the name Stevenson. Like Rebecca West, she was an educated, professional woman with strong literary tastes who fell in love with the romance of the Serbs—probably more than she did with my grandfather. But when their marriage was happy, they collaborated together on several books, including a translation of Yugoslav poetry that sings the praises of Dubrovnik.

In the twenties my grandfather published his thesis about Tolstoy, worked as an editor for the *New York Times*, and taught Slavonic languages at Columbia. But the autobiography-in-pictures is silent on the 1930s, and to hear my father tell the story, my grandfather was a casualty of the Depression. He kept reading and writing, but left teaching to start a number of dubious business ventures, such as Universal Syndicate, whose envelopes floated through my childhood. Before his stroke, he became, in my father's phrase, "a world almanac lawyer," challenging local planning boards in New Jersey or trying to set himself up as a trust.

My sisters and I called him Otac, the Serbian word for *father*, and my only memories of him in good health are from holidays. He had a broad forehead and shoulders, closely cropped white hair, perfect diction but an immigrant's accent, and, to hear my mother speak of him, an ease in social situations that could produce either a dissertation on Herbert Spencer or sustained laughter. I have images of him in a professor's three-piece suit, although here my memory may be borrowing from the photographs. He loved giving us windup, novelty-store toys, such as music boxes or marching bears. In what I consider to be a touching expression of an immigrant's awkward affection for the culture, he once gave me a football, but inexplicably painted it red.

As the train snaked the last miles out of the parched Serbian landscape and into the dreary Belgrade outskirts, I knew that other immigrants had written better books, founded more successful businesses, or perhaps led happier lives. But what mattered was not the degree of my grandfather's successes or his material achievements but the sense that I carry, even two generations later, that the choices he made in his life are part of the same tableau in which my own life is being etched. Earl Shorris, a friend and a writer, once told me that he believed all immigration to be a form of revolution. In that sense, on this leg of the journey, I was searching for the points of rebellion.

Leaving the train at Central Station in Belgrade was like stepping into an airport-rack novel that features Balkan intrigue. The station was dim and smelled of burning coal. The platform was jammed with luggage held together with string and men wearing dark, ill-fitting raincoats, which suggested a convention of spies. Instead of meeting a contact, I was collected by a distant cousin, Stasha Stanojevich, technically the grandson of my grandfather's brother but someone I know as well as a brother. He grew up in Belgrade, works as a filmmaker in Paris, and often comes to visit my family in New York. In his early fifties, he has the kind of beard usually found on Russian poets and a ubiquitous twinkle in his smile and eyes. He greeted me warmly and said, without prompting, "This is the same station that your grandfather saw when he left. It's one hundred and six years old."

Even at rush hour, Belgrade has the feel of wartime Europe. The station was crowded and poorly lit, and the tram ran along forlorn streets where both the pedestrians and the shops give the impression that someone else has all the ration tickets. We were heading toward the apartment in central Belgrade where Stasha grew up and where his brother, Slobodan, now lives with his family. Even though I knew everyone well from meetings over the years, I could tell that my arrival prompted some uneasiness.

I was happy to spend the week sleeping on the sofa, but somehow the notion took hold that I would be much happier at a nearby four-star hotel, which would have not only isolated me from the city but probably bankrupted us all. Once it was agreed that a visiting American could sleep adequately on a sofa, we ate dinner in the kitchen. Children had been summoned for the occasion, and there was an exchange of family news. But mostly we talked about Yugoslavia's demise, as if it were a relative who had fallen on hard times.

As with all political dissolutions, the questions revolved around minority rights. Why, they asked, should Albanians in Kosovo be allowed to secede from Serbia while Serbs in Croatia, also a minority, were denied basic freedoms? They described the largely pro-Communist government in Belgrade as the remnants of a broken political machine, but took issue with the notion, advanced in the West, that the Croats and Slovenes stood for democracy and economic freedom while Serbs simply longed for face-lifted communism. Certainly in Belgrade the party organism was alive and well and did not mind sending tanks to protect its privileges. But, they asked, how did that compare with the heirs of Nazi collaborators who were near power in Croatia or the half million

Serbs who were executed there when it was last independent? Over and over they argued with history, describing Yugoslavia—as Aleksandr Solzhenitsyn wrote about Russia— as a country isolated from its origins. How could there be consensus about the future if neither Serbs nor Croats had access to the past? It brought to mind Franz Kafka's pre-science about the fate of central and eastern Europe when he wrote in *The Trial*: " 'A melancholy conclusion,' said K. 'It turns lying into a universal principle.' "

Even though I will never master the rudiments of Yugoslav politics, I felt at home, nevertheless, not just on the sofa but in the many discussions that week about the Bulgarian question or why Romania has a death wish. Because my grandfather died without an estate, a large part of my inheritance was his political fatalism, especially about the Balkans. It was strangely familiar to give it free reign over coffee with Stasha or in the evening while watching television. The news was full of reports about Serbs circling their wagons in Croatia or Albanians plotting to gain control of Kosovo, and the sense of all conversations was that Yugoslavia at the center would not hold. At one point I asked Slobodan if the family was planning to spend the summer on the Adriatic coast, where they owned a house. "No," he said, in terms that implied the house had been lost in a storm. "We cannot. The house will be in Croatia." Or, as Stasha remarked one day when we were having Turkish coffee, "You know, it is a shooting country."

Koprivnica, which lies southeast of Belgrade near the border with Bulgaria, is a five-hour drive on twisting, two-lane roads that, in early autumn, traverse not simply rural Serbia but seemingly the contours of an impressionist painting. As Stasha and I drove south, mist filled the river valleys, and stacks of cornhusks, as if left by Claude Monet, awaited collection in the fields.

Although I had visited the village in 1976, Stasha had not

been there since he was a child in the late 1940s. For language reasons, he was in charge of planning, and although he is a master tactician (in New York once he navigated the Franklin Avenue shuttle in the distant realms of Brooklyn) our itinerary to Koprivnica produced the most delightful schedule of confusion. On the first day, he arranged two luncheons, and during our trip he was always borrowing a telephone to tinker with the plans. What he was up against was Serbian hospitality, for which no timetable is a match. If we were going to visit one relative, we were going to see them all, and that meant making time for unscheduled meals, Turkish coffee, and the inevitable plum brandy, even if it was ten in the morning.

My grandfather was born in the twilight of the nineteenth century. Two of his brothers never left Koprivnica, except for the First World War, and it was their descendants, who live in the village or in surrounding towns, who awaited us now—their tables set, their crystal carefully arranged.

Lunch that first afternoon was in a high-rise apartment building in Zejacar that, like those in Titograd, suggested the visible hand of a slumlord. Broken glass littered the entrance, and the elevator did not work. But on the fourth floor was a small, well-kept apartment that was a wonderful example of the differences between state monopolies and private dreams. Above the sofa hung the obligatory tea towel of Marshal Tito. But more prominent in the room was the flickering pulse of Music Television, which gyrated throughout the meal.

To say we had lunch is to understate the occasion. It was one of those meals where you eat soup, meat, bread, and vegetables only to discover that the main course, a suckling pig, is on its way to the table. Because the master planner had neglected to brief me thoroughly, throughout the meal I was never quite sure with whom I was clinking wine glasses or pledging eternal friendship. But over coffee, a shoe box was produced with pictures taken of my parents in the 1950s. Maybe they had been sent with Christmas cards or passed through the generations. But in a tenement in Zejacar, seeing a photograph of my parents' wedding and a baby picture of my sister gave the luncheon the festiveness of a baptism.

Each of the four brothers that included my grandfather—Milan, Milivoy, Vidoi, and Milosh had lives whose narratives are the outlines of short stories. Milan, who was the oldest and Stasha's grandfather, left Koprivnica to fight with the Serbian army against Austria. The war included a bitter retreat over the mountains of Montenegro, on the line that the train now follows. It is one of the defeats in Serbian history, like those in the Irish past, that has helped to forge a national identity.

Milan, however, was captured by the Austrians and spent three years in prison in Czechoslovakia. When he was released in 1918, he returned to Koprivnica and built a sawmill on a stream not far from his father's house. He also banished his wife and took in a Czech woman, possibly someone he met in the camps. According to Stasha, Milan was a sullen man. He let Stasha's father, at the age of eight, leave home to live with an uncle in Belgrade. After thirty years of living together, the Czech woman died, and Milan invited his first wife—Stasha's grandmother—to return to the mill. And, for reasons that could only be explained in the short story, she accepted.

At dusk we found the road to the mill, but reached there only by walking the last mile along a grooved cart track. An astonished family of Romanian peasants greeted us suspiciously but warmed to the story of Stasha's grandfather and showed us what survives of the mill, which is now used as a barn. We posed for pictures with the Romanians and walked back in darkness to the car. But I could tell that Stasha was angry. "You know," he said finally, "it's awful to have let the mill run down like that. Why don't they take care of it?" It was an offhand remark, and we dropped the subject quickly, but it offered a glimpse of the discontent in the Balkans as a succession of arguments about property rights.

The third son, Vidoi, inherited the family farm where my grandfather was born. Perhaps it was larger then, but today it is two houses—one of crumbling stone; the other built with rough-hewn brick—where Bosilka, the widow of Vidoi's son, still lives. Near the houses are several paddocks for pigs and chickens. Along the dirt road is an apple orchard and other houses of the village, which from a distance is a cluster of red-tile roofs nestled into otherwise lovely hillsides.

I had met Bosilka in 1976, so she greeted me not as a long-lost relative but as if I had lived my life on the farm and was now back after a semester at college. Her heavy wool stockings, print skirt, kerchief, and thick black-rimmed glasses gave the impression that she had stepped from the pages of a Chekhov novel. She showed us to our room and then cooked dinner in the outdoor kitchen that is unchanged from when my grandfather lived in the house.

After dinner, which was the familiar banquet from the farmyard and garden, and after other relatives had left, Stasha and I sat talking to Bosilka, who spoke of my grandfather as if it were only a few years ago, and not 1903, that he had left the village. She told the story of his exile, and how it was painful for his father, who was determined that at least one of his sons would be educated. To pay for his son's flight and continuing education he sold a wooded fifty-acre lot that had been intended to cushion his old age. Bosilka's telling of the story evoked Willa Cather's description of Mr. Shimerda: "He took a book out of his pocket, opened it, and showed me a page with two alphabets, one English and the other Bohemian. He placed this book in my grandmother's hands, looked at her entreatingly, and said, with an earnestness which I shall never forget, 'Te-e-ach, te-e-ach my Án-tonia!' "

Although my grandfather never returned to Koprivnica, he never left the village either. Bosilka described how he sent money for the building of the church and how letters and boxes of books arrived steadily over the years. One of his goals was to attract his other brothers to learning, but only with Milosh, who was the youngest, did he succeed.

Milosh followed Milivoy to Belgrade and later to Geneva, but decided against going to the United States and settled instead near Belgrade. He won a reputation as an educator and married a Serbian woman, Bosilka said, whom he had first known as a pen pal when she was growing up in Milwaukee. During the Second World War, when the Nazis were searching for Milosh, he came to Koprivnica to hide on the farm. He dressed as a peasant and spent his days in the fields. Seeing him, a neighbor asked: "Why are you looking for the sheep?" With a smile Bosilka said that he answered: "It's the sheep who are looking for me."

The heroes in Bosilka's stories were the schoolteachers of Zejacar, whose ranks my grandfather joined after university in Belgrade. Despite the long Turkish occupation of Serbia, they kept alive not only Serbian history and literature, but spoke of worlds beyond this poor corner of the Balkans. They were no doubt the inspiration that nurtured my grandfather on the road that led from Koprivnica to Palo Alto and Morningside Heights. In turn, no matter where he traveled or worked, the role in which he was most comfortable was that of a Zejacar teacher-at-large, whether he was promoting the idea of a democratic Yugoslavia or sending money so that one of his nephews could study in France.

During my trip and after, I spent considerable time collecting my grandfather's writings, which belong to the monograph school of literature. Some articles, such as "Czechoslovakia and Its People," read like chapters from a work by Hendrik van Loon. *Early Yugoslav Literature* is described in a *New York Times* book review as "erudite without being pedantic." *Russian Foreign Policy in the Near East* is full of speculation about how Moscow will secure its warm-water port. *Slavonic*

Nations of Yesterday and Today makes the case for Pan-Slavism instead of fratricidal disputes or, more specifically, that Serbs and Croats should have "the feeling that they might all belong to a single Slavonic organism."

Even if the books are confined to a specific time and place, what I admire about the writing is that my grandfather could express himself so clearly and forcibly in English, which he obviously did not learn until his twenties. By then he knew Russian, German, French, and Czech. But he chose to write in English; and, although their works are not comparable, in reading my grandfather's writings, I am reminded of Joseph Conrad, another Slav of many languages who also wrote in English.

To my knowledge, my grandfather never wrote fiction, and *Tolstoy's Theory of Social Reform* does not have the narrative force of *Lord Jim*. But, as with Conrad, much of my grandfather's writing can be read as letters home. He understood the experience of exile and the literature of dislocation—both for himself and for Serbia—and although he shares some of Conrad's brooding detachment about a man's origins and his inevitable circumstances, he relieves the pessimism by applying the values of village life and the optimism of a new American to such melancholic themes as Yugoslavia's failure to embrace democracy.

What is also clear from his books is that he read widely, and in many languages. In the preface to one book he wrote: "To the Slav, therefore, the knowledge of languages is an immense stimulus to wide reading, and the necessity of reading is an equally potent motive for the acquisition of languages."

Given his love for the printed word, I would delight now to hear his opinion of *Black Lamb and Grey Falcon*. At its worst, it is the world's longest Fodor's guide and leaves no chapel unvisited or gravestone unturned. But where the writing is sharpest, Rebecca West succeeds in her goal of preserving, in a sealed chamber of printed words, a civilization that she fears will be swept away, not just in the modern world but at the hands of the Nazis then occupying the country.

I am sure my grandfather would have quibbled with Rebecca West's understanding of Serbian history. How could a Serb completely accept an Englishwoman's interpretation? But I believe he would have appreciated her passionate denunciations of imperialism, be it Turkish, Hapsburg, or German. Both my grandfather and Rebecca West saw Yugoslavia as Alexis de Tocqueville saw America: as a society that to succeed at the national level needed to incorporate the values of the villages. "In America," Tocqueville wrote, "it may be said that the township was organized before the county, the county before the state, the state before the union." The same is true in Yugoslavia, but, as both my grandfather and Rebecca West understood, the country too often has been in the hands of outsiders—be they pashas from Turkey or *Gauleiter* from Karl Marx—who had no time for the villages.

In Koprivnica the following day, Stasha and I were free to roam about, even though with our cameras and Western clothes we looked like graffiti on a Russian landscape painting. It was harvest time. The school was closed, and the main street was clogged with ox carts and heavily laden wagons. Men balanced themselves on the stacks of cornhusks while women, identical in appearance to Bosilka, drove the teams. We took pictures of the farmhouse where our grandfathers were born, and then tried to get in touch with a professor, and also a friend, who has done extensive research on both my grandfather and the liberal educational system that thrived in this corner of Serbia.

I'm afraid we disappointed Milan Milosevich by not planning to spend several days at his home in Nish, a hundred miles south. I had visited his family in 1976, and in the early eighties he had come to see our family in America as part of his research. But we had run out of visiting time and were reconciled to miss him when Stasha learned, through one of his phone calls, that Milan was on his way to Koprivnica to attend an aunt's funeral.

We tried to meet Milan at the railroad station, a forlorn building beside a line of single track, but missed him and decided to wait outside the house where the family was holding the wake. A picture of the woman, her name and dates, had been posted around town, and now the villagers were arriving to pay their respects. The scene was a passage from *War and Peace*. The men wore coarse black suits, oddly knotted neckties, and shoes retrieved from the deep recesses of their closets. The women clasped bouquets of flowers hastily snatched from their gardens. About a hundred people gathered at the house, and they huddled on long benches in the garden, evoking a line from King Lear, "The weight of this sad time we must obey," that my grandfather quotes in his book that pays tribute to Tolstoy.

As the mourners began their procession to the church, which inside has an inscription of thanks to my grandfather, we also left for the cemetery. Where we were going was outside the village, to a secluded hillside. Without Bosilka we would not have found the graveyard, which was originally hidden from the Turkish garrison to insure that at least the land of the dead would be free from occupation. And without Bosilka we would not have found my grandfather's grave site.

As at the mill, we had to abandon the car and walk for a mile along a cart trail. All the while I kept looking for familiar landmarks, something to remind me that I had walked this road before. Only when I saw the headstones in the overgrown weeds did I know that I was in the same place I had visited in the summer of 1976, when I buried my grandfather.

He actually died in February 1973. During the last thirteen years of his life, he had nothing for which to live, save perhaps to show whoever was watching that giving up was not in his nature. He was a crumpled figure who, on Sundays, was rolled into a waiting room by an orderly in a loose-fitting olive uniform. What sustained him was not life-support systems but the sense that death, like some occupier of Serbia or a poorly worded sentence, was worth fighting. I can now remember that his eyes had an unusual combination of gentleness and don't-get-in-my-way determination, or, as Erich Remarque wrote of another survivor on another battlefield clinging to life, "He possessed something that made his eyes move and that was called soul."

After he died, his remains were cremated. The family had a service in an Orthodox church, but we had no thoughts on what to do with the ashes. Three years passed with them stored in a closet.

In the summer after I graduated from college, when I was eager to travel in Eastern Europe, it was decided that I would bury his ashes in Koprivnica. When I arrived in the village that first time, I explained to various relatives that I was carrying my grandfather's ashes and wanted to bury them in the cemetery. There were looks of horror on the faces of my hosts, and dictionaries were consulted to find the correct translation for questions about my fear of "evil spirits." But Bosilka's husband, Stojan (now dead) arranged for the burial, and one hot July morning we walked the dirt road to the graveyard with two oxen, shovels, candles, and plum brandy—presumably to counter one set of spirits with another.

Stojan cleared the thickets from the family plot, and I dug a hole near where my grandfather's parents were buried. After we covered the ashes, Stojan lit candles, as Bosilka did this time, and, at a loss for a proper burial service, I repeated the Lord's Prayer, which in a remote corner of Serbia seemed stretched to its territorial limits.

When my father visited the village in 1980, he arranged for a headstone to be cut, and we found it today. It gave my grandfather's name and dates of life, stated that he had been born in Koprivnica and died in New York, and then listed the names of his three grandchildren, including my own. On this remote Serbian hillside I had not expected to find my name, in Cyrillic letters, etched into stone. But it is a link to the village, and my grandfather, that, to use one of Lincoln's constructions about hallowed grounds, I find "altogether fitting." As Stasha, Bosilka, and I walked back to the car along the dirt path, I felt the same as when I visit Gettysburg and try to equate the tranquillity of the farmland and the inspiration of the monuments with the courage that is required for a new birth of freedom.

Gray Footsteps in Northern Ireland

(1990)

I had planned to go to Australia, not Northern Ireland, so when my schedule changed and I knew I could spend a few days traveling from Edinburgh to Dublin, I was unprepared to track down my Gray ancestors. I had the names of my grandfather's parents—Edward Gray and Elizabeth Beggs— and knew that they had emigrated to the United States around the time of the great famine. I thought that my grandfather, David Gray, had been born in New Jersey in 1872. I knew his parents had been born in County Antrim, which spreads northeast from Belfast, but beyond that, my information was hazy.

My meetings in Scotland lasted most of a week. They took place at The Gleneagles, a baronial hotel in the Scottish highlands north of Edinburgh. The shame was to spend several days there in a suit and clutching a briefcase, instead of tramping through the hills in tweed or plus-fours. One night after dinner I did manage to slip away for a walk, and from the formal garden the hotel, clouded in a faint mist, had the look of a *Titanic* painting, an odd-shaped hull in the darkness defined only by flickering lights in what appeared to be port-holes.

When I left Gleneagles, first for Edinburgh and then to Belfast through Glasgow, although I didn't know it at the time, I was tracing the steps of early Grays, who in the late seventeenth century had fled the English by moving from the Scottish border to Northern Ireland. Theirs must have been a slow journey with heavily laden ox carts, but my trip was easy. I caught a commuter train to Glasgow, which took a little more than an hour, and then changed for a country train that ran south along the western coast of Scotland to Stranraer, which is said *Stran-rah*, as only the Scottish would understand.

Glasgow is another city where the imperial sun has set. Although the downtown center gives the impression of formality and prosperity, the suburbs are a mixture of tract houses and tired factories, which have the drab look of industrial production without any of the profits.

Past Troon, which is overrun with golf courses, and Ayr, a nondescript seaside town, the landscape is once again rolling farmland, where whitewashed cottages can be seen perched on hilltops or surrounded by grazing cattle. I circled Barrhead on my map, a lonely skytop railroad station, as a place someday that would be worth a visit.

Stranraer, where you catch the ferry to Northern Ireland, has all the markings of a nervous frontier. Dogs sniffed about the luggage. Several bulky detectives scrutinized my passport, and everything about the boarding seemed designed to unearth explosives in my bags. But it was hard to dwell on the darker aspects of the crossing, as the day was one of warm, brilliant sunshine. From the top deck of the ferry, all that was visible were the treeless, windswept hillsides of coastal Scotland. And the run out the long, narrow channel had the feel of a riverboat passage through a barren frontier.

The crossing to Larne takes three hours. I suspect that

most of the time the North Channel, which is an extension of the Irish Sea, is a nasty stretch of water. The ferry gift shop has several books of celebrated sea disasters—the worst occurring in winter. But today we experienced only a small swell and a fresh southerly breeze, neither of which made any impression on the passengers, who sat expressionless in large smoke-filled lounges, eating chips from paper bags and staring blankly at the television screens posted on the carpeted walls.

The ferry docks at Larne, a small port that handles container ships and oil tankers. The early Grays who made the passage to Ulster settled here or just inland. There was probably no need to go elsewhere, as from Larne one could fish or develop a small farm. A train meets the ferry, but only a handful of passengers made the connection. For the first time, sitting in a dingy day coach, I became apprehensive about entering Belfast, an uneasiness compounded by my lack of a hotel reservation or even a guide book. The best I could manage were some leaflets from a tourist desk at the Larne station.

The train to Belfast, about a forty-minute ride, sweeps along the coast, past Carrickfergus into a suburban station that is as drab as anything in the Brooklyn underground. The neighborhood surrounding the terminal was forlorn, suggesting that I was arriving in mid-winter and not in July. I followed the few passengers from the train to a waiting bus, which was marked "Central Station." From there I hoped to track down a hotel.

Checkpoints seal the main shopping streets of Belfast, and a police inspector boards each bus to search for bombs or unattended luggage. By now it was almost 7:30 P.M., and the skies had clouded, giving Belfast the desolate look of a factory in liquidation. The stores had their outside lights on, and the few shoppers scurried along the wide sidewalks as if watchmen making early evening rounds.

As the bus turned to head up the station road, the driver stopped short in front of a cordon drawn across the intersection.

"Must be a bomb scare on the bridge," he cheerfully informed the passengers.

The news fazed no one. All the locals collected their belongings and headed toward the station, ignoring the roadblock as if it were a billboard for an unpopular product. I joined the party, assuming I had no options. But once past the cordon, I decided that it made more sense to walk back into town, rather than ahead into a bomb. To my relief, the driver noticed my hesitation, told me to get back into the bus, and drove me to another part of the city, where I could find a taxi.

"Welcome to Belfast," was how he wished me into the summer evening.

The cab driver drove me south of center city, to the university district, where there are guest houses and small hotels—but not many. He took me to the Helga Lodges, which seemed the stage set for *Death of a Salesman*. My room had a narrow, spring-loaded bed, a cardboard dresser, a cold-water sink, and a light bulb on a string. Still, I was relieved to be there and got wonderful directions from the desk clerk, an American.

I spent the evening taking an uneasy walk through the Botanic Garden and the desolate streets that surround the university. Each block looked like a news photo of a bomb site. But I think my fears were unjustified. Several times I poked my head into crowded, elegant restaurants, and I ended the evening at a theater that showed foreign films.

My plan for the following day was to start at the university bookstore, to see if there were any books on how to trace ancestry, and then to head to the Public Records Office, which I knew from my leaflets contained genealogical records. The bookstore, alas, had nothing, and I ended up walking the last mile to the Records Office, which is in an affluent neighborhood south of the city, but still well fenced and carefully guarded.

I filled out an elaborate form as a "visiting scholar" and watched a video on how to use the library, but then a librarian set me loose in the archive—two rooms of reference books and closed stacks in the basement. Any original material I wanted to see, they explained, a researcher would retrieve.

Before leaving Scotland, I had made a quick call home to my mother to see if she could provide any additional information on the Grays. She knew that her father's family was from County Antrim. From a cousin she had the name of a village, which I wrote down as "Ballyboley." *Bally* is the word in Northern Ireland that means *town*, and just about every third village is Ballysomething. There is also the large town of Antrim in County Antrim. But Ballyboley did not show up on any of the maps.

Everything genealogical in Northern Ireland is listed by parish records. If you want to find a marriage notice or birth announcement, it can be culled from the parish minutes, which have been Xeroxed. But I found nineteenth-century handwriting impenetrable.

With the help of a researcher, I found that there wasn't a town called Ballyboley, but there was a parish of Ballybolly, which was either in Larne, where I had landed on the boat, or in the barony of Upper Antrim. Next I located some maps published in the 1850s and painstakingly tried to plot Ballybolly. Eventually I marked its coordinates fifteen miles north of Belfast, near the town of Ballynure. It seemed logical to conclude that Ballyboley was really Ballybolly.

Other books in the library list all the emigrants from Northern Ireland who left during the Potato Famine. I went through five volumes, looking in the index for Edward Gray or Elizabeth Beggs, and found that in 1850 an Edward Gray, age nineteen, had sailed to American on the steamship *Stella*.

Is this my Edward Gray? I doubt it, because it would seem too great a gap between 1850 and 1872, when David Gray was born. It seems more likely that Edward Gray would have emigrated to the United States in the 1860s, and those records I could not verify.

What leads me to believe that Ballybolly was the village of Edward Gray is other material I found in the library that described, in general, the background of those with the names Gray and Beggs. (Open the Belfast telephone directory, and there are pages of both surnames.) Seemingly the first Gray in England was Hugo de Gray, who emigrated from Normandy in 1248. Most of the Grays lived near Berwick along the English border in Scotland and emigrated to Northern Ireland to escape persecution from James II. They generally settled around Larne, as did the Beggs family—*Beggs* is an Ulster name, a variation on *bigge*. Most of the Beggses settled in Upper Antrim. So in the mid-nineteenth century both the Grays and the Beggses were scattered among the hills that begin north of Belfast and stretch to the coast around Larne. Geographically, anyway, it seems a most natural union that a Gray would marry a Beggs.

Late in the morning I tired of the library. I had the rough coordinates of the village, but didn't want to devote a week, as would probably be necessary, to hunt for the marriage license of Edward Gray and Elizabeth Beggs, which would have been futile if they had been married in the United States. So I decided to rent a car and search for Ballybolly.

To get back into the city, I hailed a taxi and had the driver give me a short course on The Troubles. Most of the violence in Belfast takes place west of the city, in neighborhoods that take their names from major roads. Hence Andersontown, the Falls, and Shankill are sections of West Belfast, as well as four-lane roads. Riding through the Catholic and Protestant enclaves, it is impossible not to be reminded of a fading

American city, like Detroit or Buffalo, that the modern industrial world has passed by. Belfast is yet another city that has
seen its jobs, but not its workers, shifted to Korea and Taiwan.
Those remaining, in addition to their theological differences,
are fighting for diminishing returns.

The ghettos are clusters of modern, suburb-style houses
made of flimsy brick and concrete and etched with thin
wrought-iron gates and small patches of lawn. But everything
else about the Falls, for example, suggests a never-ending riot.
Houses on the line between Catholics and Protestants have
either been razed or shot up. Those remaining stand like
World War I battery emplacements, concrete filling the windows and barbed wire running along the eaves.

Along the main roads, which are also lined with cemeteries where you expect to see parks, are the hermetic barracks of
the British troops, who wait in hovels of corrugated tin, razor
wire, and cement casings to respond to any disturbances. Only
Huns could emerge from such structures, whose architectural
origins seem divided between a fortified baronial castle and a
machine-gun nest. Needless to say, they make wonderful targets for bullets and bombs, when nothing of greater interest is
around.

You don't see British troops everywhere. Mostly they ride
around in armored personnel carriers, whose windshields
have a retractable grill that can be flipped into place whenever
the oncoming traffic merges with rocks or something worse.
But when you do encounter British troops, they are in full
battle dress and walk in the crouch of troops expecting a firefight. These forces aren't cops on the beat, standing in groups
talking about their moonlighting jobs, but combat soldiers
trying to figure whether they are walking toward or away
from the front lines.

Will The Troubles ever end? Obviously, my one day in
Belfast and the reading I've done since returning home hardly
qualify me to answer. In a positive sense, there is much less

violence today than there was ten years ago, when bombings and shootings were a daily occurrence. The cab driver described a sense of exhaustion having overcome each side. But like the Middle East, Belfast remains on the brink, a conflict without a resolution. Britain will never grant Northern Ireland independence nor cede it to the Republic of Ireland, which, for its part, hardly wants unification with Ulster and its myriad troubles. Instead, Belfast, Derry, and some other angry neighborhoods of the North will continue to be part of Britain, which for its part will try to forget them. Just as the United States can tolerate miles of angry slums, so Britain can endure pockets of unhappy neighborhoods where every few years the residents get together for a gang war whose origins pass, on both sides, for religious education.

Obviously there's a connection between the violence today and the presence of Ulster Scots living in the countryside fifteen miles from the city. But it's a tie that is almost immediately forgotten outside the city. Even from the worst streets in the Falls, you can see the pastures and tree covered hills that surround the city. And when you're driving north and leave the expressway that connects Belfast and Derry, northern Ireland feels more like the farmland of western Maryland than the fringes of a medieval battlefield.

Although I had a rental car and was driving north, I still didn't know what I was looking for, as Ballybolly isn't on any maps. Near where I assumed it to be, I pulled off the highway into the village of Ballynure, a one-street town about fifteen miles north of Belfast. My thought was to ask at the church for information or directions, but it was closed. Fortunately I found most of the congregation across the street at the pub.

I ordered lunch from the bar—this while everyone at the pub grew silent and stared. But as conversation began to refill the smoky room, I asked the group standing near me if they had ever heard of Ballybolly. I explained why I was looking.

Their accent was nearly impossible to decipher. It seemed to combine the most impenetrable elements of the Scottish highlands with the Irish countryside. But my new friends warmed immediately to the search, said I was probably looking for an old graveyard near town, and set about drawing directions on a cocktail napkin, which I used shortly to drive into the hillsides of Upper Antrim.

I was looking for "a farmhouse, after a large curve, down this road, not far from that sign. And if I went past a milk farm, I'd gone too far." I found the farmhouse, incredibly, and what stunned me about the men who were working near the barn was how their expressions and their features—high foreheads, long narrow faces, and boyish grins, even on older men—made me think that I was coming face to face with my grandfather, David Gray. It was eerie and then comforting, as they pointed to that part of the field that had the cemetery.

I didn't find the name Gray or Beggs on any of the fallen tombstones that were scattered in the overgrown paddock. I could imagine a hundred years ago this being the courtyard of a simple church, like those described in the novels of Thomas Hardy. But if this was Ballybolly, the town is only a memory. I did strike up a conversation with a farmer who was mending fences in a nearby field. Yes, he said, he had heard of Ballybolly but thought it was several miles from here. He outlined directions.

Whether the cemetery was that of Ballybolly or where I next drove, several miles northeast, hardly matters, because what I learned, when I stopped to talk to another family in their front yard, was that the area I was exploring was known as Ballybolly Forest. There was a school but no village. The man I was talking to was named McKenster, who seemed about forty-five and was loading his family of two children into his car. He said he wished he could take me around a little, but insisted, instead, that I call on his parents, who lived a mile away. They might know either a Beggs or a Gray.

I did track down Mr. McKenster, senior, who was wearing full tweed, including a cap, and sitting in his living room, having lunch, and watching the British Open on television. No, he didn't know any Grays in this area. But, yes, there were Beggses, and he started listing their names, wondering who I was looking for. Then he said, quite accurately: "The person you need to speak with is my father," who probably was born about the time that my grandfather was born, 1872.

I didn't stay long with the McKensters, as I still wanted to wander through the hill country between Ballybolly and Larne. But when I stepped out of the McKenster farmhouse, I had an unobstructed view of the sweeping valley that descends from the hilltop forest of Ballybolly. The sunshine was brilliant, and hedgerows marked many of the fields that were dotted with cattle and small whitewashed farmhouses. The roads were country lanes, and there seemed no connection between this farmhouse and the angry streets of Belfast.

It was easy to imagine life here, even that which took place more than a hundred years ago. To the east was Larne, the sea, and thoughts of England, which has probably always evoked home. South, about a day's journey, was Belfast, which was beginning to lure the young off the farms. In between, where time probably had a habit of standing still, was the farmland that weaves through patches of Ballybolly Forest. No doubt in the 1860s, when Edward Gray and Elizabeth Beggs married and sailed for America, the famine was a painful memory. But it's also possible that Ballybolly escaped some of the awful suffering, as there were fish from the coast and perhaps a few sheep among the hills.

As I stood looking over the valley, I still had lingering doubts that maybe Ballybolly wasn't Ballyboley and that I had gotten it all wrong. Nor did I know when Edward Gray had emigrated or where he had married. But even if the village is elsewhere or if there's a clearer version of the story, in my mind I had found a distant home.

Firewalking in Fiji

(1989)

The term "savage" is, I conceive, often misapplied, and indeed when I consider the vices, cruelties, and enormities of every kind that spring up in the tainted atmosphere of a feverish civiliza- tion, I am inclined to think that so far as the relative wickedness of the parties is concerned, four or five Marquesan Islanders sent to the United States as missionaries might be quite as useful as an equal number of Americans dispatched to the islands in a similar matter.

—Herman Melville, *Typee* (1846)

Three times weekly, an Air Pacific 747, with markings the color of a rainbow, lumbers off the runway at Kingsford Smith Airport in Sydney and sets a northeast course for the four-hour flight to the Fiji islands. Once clear of the New South Wales headlands, the trip to Fiji is a lazy run, entirely over azure seas that only here and there flicker with whitecaps.

A necklace of coral surrounds Viti Levu, Fiji's main island. From the air the reef first appears as a thin white line, separat-ing the darker ocean from the turquoise waters so evocative of the tropics. The shore is also edged with coral, as many un-suspecting tourists have discovered, and behind the beaches, sugar cane undulates in the afternoon breezes. Ridges of high mountain jungle cover the spine of Viti Levu, so international flights land at Nadi, a flatland on the western coast more than a hundred miles from the capital, Suva.

I had a number of reasons for wanting to visit Fiji, beyond the obvious wish to touch down in Paradise. For the last several years I have read numerous accounts that the Pacific Ocean is no longer "America's lake," that the Soviet navy is filling a vacuum created by U.S. indifference to the region. In the vastness of the Pacific, Fiji offers a strategic deep-water port at Suva. At the start of the Second World War, had the Japanese won at Coral Sea and later taken the islands, our supply lines to Australia and New Zealand would have been cut, making the war in the Pacific that much more difficult.

Fiji had other political points of interest. In the eight years of the Reagan presidency, it was the only democracy toppled by a coup. Numerous countries—Argentina, Brazil, and El Salvador, for example—replaced military rule with free elections. Amidst this exemplary record, only Fiji lost its democracy. Admittedly, it lacks the population or size of Brazil, and the interim government is led by the former prime minister, Ratu (Chief) Sir Kamisese Mara. Nevertheless, it was jarring for a military putsch to succeed in the South Pacific, where coups have never been a way of life.

Most of all, I wanted to meet the deposed prime minister, Dr. Timoci Bavadra, whose Labor government had been overthrown in May 1987. I had seen Dr. Bavadra give many interviews on Australian and New Zealand television. His eloquence was appealing, and he raised a simple, telling point: Why had none of the major democracies aided his government when it was overthrown by the military?

At the time Dr. Bavadra was ousted, Fiji was a member of the British Commonwealth, but neither Britain nor its South Pacific allies nor the United States opposed the coup, except with futile diplomatic language so familiar on evening newscasts. In my mind, I wanted two questions answered: Why didn't anyone care about the fall of the Bavadra government?

Second, what did this silence mean for our relations in the South Pacific?

When I landed at Nadi, I had neither a hotel reservation nor knowledge of how I might make contact with Dr. Bavadra. From press accounts, I knew he lived in a small village, Viseisei, which I located on a map as north of the airport. I assumed that I would rent a car, find a hotel, and then drive to the village and ask around for Dr. Bavadra. I hoped he would be accessible. How many Americans wanted to see him at all? Following the coup, he had traveled to the United States to make a case for support. Little was forthcoming. Instead he was given perfunctory hearings at the State Department and before a congressional committee.

As I was hunting at the airport for Avis or Hertz, and in one of those indecisive moods that can overcome jet-lagged travelers, I found myself in conversation with a hotel tout. "Hey, mister, hotel?" is the basic spiel. Perhaps because of the heat, which was about to give way to a late afternoon thunderstorm, I was agreeable and followed a young Fijian of Indian descent to a hotel van.

It was a ten-minute ride to the Travellers Beach Resort. We chatted about what I might do while I was on the island. The hotel could arrange fishing, mountain tours, or, if I wished, some pig hunting—none of which interested me. It seemed implausible that the driver might know how I could find Dr. Bavadra, but when I said that what I really wanted to do was to meet the deposed prime minister, my new friend got very excited.

"My uncle, who owns the hotel," he said, "knows him well. He can arrange everything. They are good friends. It's no problem."

Not often on my trips does Fate intervene so efficiently.

I was the only guest at the Travellers, which was a hotel

overlooking Nadi Bay. I chose a beachside room that was already occupied by a large family of mosquitoes. A fishing trawler and a rusty steamer were anchored close to shore. Otherwise the bay was empty, save for a few seaplanes, which used the calm waters as a runway.

The uncle's name was G. K. Guddy Karan, known as George, and I met him in the hotel's screened dining room. He joined me toward the end of dinner. I had eaten a meal that made me think I was in Bombay or Delhi: curried chicken, rice, samosa, and chutney. George appeared to be in his mid to late forties. He wore a native shirt. His hair, eyes, and skin were dark, making me think his Indian ancestors were Bengalis.

He was willing to speak at length about the coup that toppled the Bavadra government. He was not a politician, he said. His involvement with the government was a result of his friendship with Dr. Bavadra, who liked to visit the resort. Nevertheless, when the coup happened, George was detained for three days.

Our conversation lasted several hours. It began in the restaurant and ended in his living room, where we watched an underground video cassette that provided a history of the coup. Often during the evening George would rummage through stacks of paper and return to the conversation with a magazine clipping, usually something published in the United States or England.

He was convinced that the Australians and the Americans had a hand in overthrowing the Bavadra government. The evidence for such a case might be circumstantial, he admitted, but its volume made the verdict incontestable. His tone of voice was that of a middle-aged man who for the first time had confronted what he decided was evil, and it made him angry. When he was a boy, the United States had freed many of the islands from Japanese occupation. Now it was abetting military coups and tyranny. His story became a cautionary tale that crystallized the unease in the South Pacific about U.S. relations.

The chronology, in abbreviated form, is this:

On April 12, 1987, the voters of Fiji—its population is 750,000—elected a coalition government, led by the Labor party of Dr. Bavadra, a Fijian who previously ran the Public Service union. Into the opposition went the Alliance party of Ratu Mara, which had been in power since independence from Britain in 1970. Ratu Mara had proved a good friend to the West. He had denied the Soviets an embassy at Suva, spoke against granting the Russians fishing rights among the Pacific islands, and tempered the views of his Pacific colleagues who wanted to declare the South Pacific a nuclear-free zone.

Dr. Bavadra's Labor party was a coalition of trade unions and Fijian Indians, who now were a plurality on the island. Once in office, Dr. Bavadra sided with other Pacific islands in supporting the lead of New Zealand, which opposed U.S. nuclear warships in its ports. His foreign minister, Krishna Datt, pursued a nonaligned foreign policy and announced that under certain circumstances he would agree to technical and commercial agreements with the Soviet Union.

Nevertheless, in the words of the *Economist*, Bavadra was "no radical." He continued to deny the Soviets an embassy. His goal was to raise the standard of living on Fiji, which may be Paradise to tourists but is still a Third World Paradise. He launched an investigation into the financial practices of the previous government.

On May 14, Lt. Col. Sitiveni Rabuka, a staff officer responsible for training, led a bloodless coup against the Bavadra government. The prime minister and his cabinet were placed under house arrest for a week. In the meantime Rabuka secured the cooperation of Ratu Mara to serve in an interim government.

Why had Rabuka acted? Most press reports spoke of the tensions between native Fijians, who are Melanesian, and Fiji's Indian population. Indians first came to Fiji in the late nineteenth century as coolies to work in the sugar fields. Only a third ever went back, and an open immigration policy after World War I brought thousands of Indians to the South Pacific. Rabuka feared that Fijians would wind up a minority in their own land, as happened to the Maoris in New Zealand or the aboriginals in Australia. As he was later quoted in *No Other Way*, his as-told-to autobiography: "I told the governor-general that I had to remove the government and re-write the repugnant constitution to give Fijian people control of their own country."

More cynical accounts of the coup note that Rabuka may have acted more for personal than for political reasons. Thirty-eight years old, he had started his military career with a flourish, was a rugby player of world stature and a Commonwealth Games decathlete. But in recent years his rise to power had been checked. He had been passed over for promotion to brigadier and appeared stymied by a senior commander only a year older than he was. If anyone had fit the intelligence handbook description of a military officer who might be amenable to leading a coup, it would have been Rabuka. Even his thesis at staff college had been on the role of the military after seizing power in a developing country.

Fiji's political turmoil continued through summer 1987. The islands' governor-general, Ratu Sir Penaia Ganilau, asserted that he was the legitimate head of state, and he attempted to organize a coalition government that would reconcile the differences between native Fijians and those of Indian descent. In late September, he put forward a caretaker government that would represent all ethnic groups on the islands. But Rabuka would agree to nothing less than Melanesian supremacy, and he led a second coup on September 25 to have his opinion heard.

After the second coup, it appeared that Rabuka might compromise, if only to keep Fiji a member of the Commonwealth. But he still faced the opposition of the governor-general, who sought to resolve the crisis within the framework of the existing constitution. After some discussion, Rabuka abruptly suspended the constitution, sacked Ratu Sir Penaia, and named himself head of state. As of October 10, 1987, he proclaimed, Fiji would become a republic and withdraw from the Commonwealth, odd as that may sound.

The last chapter of the story, which continues, began on December 5, 1987, when Rabuka convinced Ratu Sir Penaia to serve as Fiji's first president. The former governor-general, in turn, appointed Ratu Mara to act as prime minister. In less than a year, Fiji again had the government that had ruled prior to Dr. Bavadra's election. Its principal mandate was to draft a new constitution that would guarantee the rule of native Fijians. In the new government, Rabuka kept internal security as his portfolio, just in case. And along the way, he found himself at last promoted, not just to full colonel, but to brigadier and then major general.

According to George, the press got the story wrong. Race relations were not the major issue on the island—not sufficient to bring down the government, anyway. Certainly it was disturbing to Hindus and Moslems that Rabuka had declared Fiji a Christian nation. As he writes in his autobiography: "It will be a big challenge for us to convert them to Christianity. . . . We either go that way, or they will convert us, and we all become heathens." But rage was not the issue that deposed Dr. Bavadra.

Fijian Indians would never control the country, George believed, because the 1970 constitution had mandated a balance of power between the races. Further, covenants assured that Fiji's land would always be controlled by native Fijians, who owned 83 percent of the islands, even though many of Fiji's prominent businessmen are Indian.

He believed that the reason for the coup was the decision by Dr. Bavadra to follow the lead of the New Zealand government in wanting to declare Fiji's ports off-limits to nuclear warships. Such a course was intolerable to the U.S. and Australian military services, which conveniently found themselves in agreement with local interests also in opposition to the Bavadra government. Rabuka was a stalking horse for the chiefs and the Americans.

Here is a summary of the allegations that were made on the video and in articles I was encouraged to track down:

• In 1984, something called the Asian American Free Labor Institute opened in Suva to campaign against the proposed nuclear ban. The institute spent more than $1 million, which was funded by the Agency for International Development and the National Endowment for Democracy, which in Fiji is assumed to be a handmaiden of the Central Intelligence Agency.

• After his defeat in the April 12 elections, Ratu Mara traveled to Honolulu to meet with the U.S. Pacific Command. There he was seen in the company of various Asian American Institute officials, including William Paupe, a U.S. embassy official in Suva. Paupe is one of those larger-than-life government figures whose work for AID began in Vietnam in 1967 and continued in South Korea from 1977 to 1981. According to the film, he was sent to Fiji to coordinate efforts against South Pacific trade unions that favored a nuclear ban.

• On April 30, two weeks before the coup, U.N. Ambassador Gen. Vernon Walters showed up on Fiji to urge Foreign Minister Datt to drop his plans of nonalignment for Fiji. Walters also met with Fiji's third-ranking officer, Lt. Col. Sitiveni Rabuka.

• Five days prior to the coup, Rabuka was spotted at Nadi International Airport, chatting with five Americans. According to a Bavadra cabinet member, one of these men was among the masked gang that stormed Parliament and seized power on May 14.

• At the time the coup took place, retired American Maj. Gen. John Singlaub, of Iran-contra fame, was in Fiji attending a conference on democracy sponsored by the Pacific Democrat Union.

• During the coup, Rabuka and his mysterious lieutenant—known only as Captain X and hooded, like the rest, throughout the operation—spoke to their men only in English, not Fijian, leading to speculation that mercenaries were among the rebels. Other reports mentioned in the film describe some black American troops landing on Fiji several days before the coup.

• Two months after the first coup, Ratu Mara was again in Honolulu, meeting with the U.S. Pacific Command—this time to request arms for Fiji.

Needless to say, the array of allegations was difficult to assimilate. I didn't think of them as facts so much as articles of faith, similar to what one hears from any such aggrieved party. In the days leading to the coup, it appeared as if the islands had as many operatives as honeymooners. Nevertheless, the charges were serious. If only a few were true, who could blame the Indians for coming to their conclusions? They had, after all, lost their say in government after winning a freely contested election. No one had ever charged that Dr. Bavadra had won other than fairly.

When the conversation broke up, it was arranged that we would visit Dr. Bavadra the next day. But it would be imposing to arrive without a gift, and what would be most appropriate would be *kava*, a drink from *yagona* roots, which George wanted to go to Suva to find. As it was a two-and-a-half-hour drive to the capital, it was decided that we would leave at six-thirty the following morning.

The Queen's Road winds along the southern Coral Coast

to Suva, the kind of Pacific port etched many times in the writing of Joseph Conrad. The Grand Pacific Hotel, a splendid colonial retreat, overlooks the harbor where the modern version of tramp steamers swing at anchor, awaiting a turn dockside. Across the street from the Grand Pacific are the government buildings, including Parliament—which has as its front yard an expansive parade and cricket ground, making the connection between this group of coral islands and the British Empire.

We spent the morning searching several markets for the *yagona* that would please Dr. Bavadra. George finally found roots to his liking at a market several miles north of Suva. Afterwards we ate lunch in a small Chinese restaurant with an Indian civil servant. The man said that the government had made life difficult for Indians; many were being forced out of the civil service. Like so many others, he spoke openly of his plans for emigration. When his papers cleared, he was leaving for New Zealand. When he had enough money, he would send for his family.

We headed back through the late afternoon showers. To the left was the Beqa Passage, a palm-fringed strait like many in the Caribbean. On the right was tropical vegetation and, in the background, sharp mountainous peaks. Frequently we came up behind trucks carrying workers home from the fields. Crammed into the back and sitting on piles of straw or dirt would be groups of native Indians and Fijians. It wasn't a sight I had expected on what had been described as a racially divided island. The men waved each time we passed and seemed to be joking with each other, in that Miller-time manner, about the day just past.

At dusk we drove north of the airport to Viseisei, Dr. Bavadra's village. We parked in front of a Methodist church, covered in white clapboard, similar to what one might find in New England. I had expected Indians to be Hindu or Moslem. What I didn't expect to discover was that Fiji is a religious polyglot. It has Sikh temples, mosques, Hindu shrines, Protestant churches—even the Church of the Latter-Day Saints. Apparently every group of seamen who visited the islands left behind one of their churches, a condition that may bode poorly for a nation officially declared Christian.

The sun had nearly set when we found Dr. Bavadra, who was supervising the construction of a new house. Primitive cranes had sited long oak trunks in two lines, which gave the foundation the air of a Greek ruin. George explained that Dr. Bavadra needed a grander house to recognize his position as the leader of the Indian community. The parlor floor would be elevated from the ground. He used the Fijian word for chief, *ratu*, to describe Dr. Bavadra's position, even though it was the chief system that, as prime minister, he had opposed.

All the men in the village were milling about the construction site, as if part of an Amish barn raising. Most were trying to coax the last timbers into position, and Dr. Bavadra was watching impassively as we approached.

Not more than fifty-five years old, he wore a white polo shirt, slacks, and thongs. His sunglasses were tucked into his vest pocket, in the manner of a golf pro. Although he was a medical doctor before entering government service, his handshake implied that heavy stints of manual labor were part of his background. He had a broad, round face and clear, determined eyes. His mood was one of subdued resignation. But why would he welcome wholeheartedly a strange American determined to meet him?

I had expected a bolder, more strident man. Some press accounts had described him as a bellicose liberal, determined to push Fiji to the left. Words like comrade had drifted into his speech during the short time he was prime minister. But his manner was more deferential than I expected, and as we stood watching the men from the village move about the foundation, he spoke about the coup without a trace of rancor.

Dr. Bavadra believed his government had been over-thrown by the chiefs, who feared his investigation into the past government's financial dealings. When I asked what he had wanted to do in office, he said flatly: "We wanted to tell the truth."

He described the Fijian economy as if he were reading from a case study on Third World underdevelopment. An Australian multinational, CSR, controlled the sugar fields, he said. Another, Burns Philp, ran the stores and imported most of the consumer goods. Tourism didn't put much money into the local economy because the hotels and airlines were owned by outsiders. The average wage was $3.50 a day, hardly enough to support the large families that were typical on Fiji.

As for outside involvement in the coup, he didn't believe that the U.S. alone had toppled his government, but U.S. concerns had mixed well with local interests. He recited some of the litany that George had outlined the night before. The U.S. had wanted to keep Suva as a port for its nuclear war-ships. An Australian operative on the island, Rod Kelly, who had been featured in last night's video, had once been photo-graphed with Australia's prime minister, Bob Hawke. Articles published in Britain and the U.S. outlined the American com-plicity. Lt. Col. Rabuka had not thought up the coup on his own; he was a front man.

Dr. Bavadra would not even consider the notion that racial differences on Fiji had led to the coup. He gestured toward the men working on his house. They were from his village. Half were Fijians; the rest were Indians. "We have no problems," he said. "That's something made up in the foreign press."

What interested me most was to hear his account of how the rest of the world reacted to the coup. As soon as he was released from house arrest, the Indian community on Fiji raised money to send Bavadra and his wife first to England

and then to the United States. In London, he hoped to meet with the Queen. But his request was denied, because it was pointed out that he was not the head of state—that was the governor-general, Ratu Sir Penaia. So the Bavadras took what sounds like high tea with the secretary of the Commonwealth, who, while sympathetic, delivered one of those "tough luck, old chap" messages.

In the United States, Bavadra made even less headway. He wanted Congress to investigate the charges that the U.S. had played a role in overturning his government. He wanted to meet Secretary of State Shultz, but he was out of town. He met with an aide, who temporized. Ironically, Bavadra got the most sympathy from the Black Caucus in Congress—ironic because it was blacks on Fiji who in the cause of ethnic purity had overthrown his largely Indian government.

Finally, Dr. Bavadra described a hopeful meeting he had at the end of his trip with a well-known lawyer, a man who used to be in government, who promised to investigate the charges. Did I know this man, Ramsey Clark? Did I think anything would come of his investigation?

While on Fiji, I made no effort to speak with Major-General Rabuka. I had no introduction, nor did I think he would be as accessible as Dr. Bavadra. Nevertheless, I was able to get a copy of *No Other Way*, which he dictated to an Australian and a Fijian journalist after the coups, no doubt to soften his image as a strongman.

To be sure, it is full of asides such as: "I believed I was acting in the best interest of Fiji as a nation" or "I thought to Myself 'God is telling me to do this.'" But the book has the fresh quality of a long conversation with Rabuka, who speaks with few doubts about the righteousness of his effort to save Fiji for Fijians.

Rabuka has the look of a mail-order dictator. He often

wears a military uniform and a beret, and appears more comfortable in a barracks than at Parliament, where pictures taken of him express a forlorn impatience with the tedious aspects of democratic government. A stock photograph shows him in jungle fatigues, reviewing the troops. Others show him commissioning a patrol boat or greeting schoolchildren—playing the role of a father to modern Fiji.

His strongman persona, however, contrasts with what are obviously streaks of geniality. He has a firm, somewhat rounded black face, a full mustache, and a toothy, almost Kennedyesque smile, the kind usually worn by victorious athletes. He exudes a boyish enthusiasm, especially for the camaraderie of sport. In many photographs, if you didn't know he had seized power and suspended the constitution, you would get the impression he was running for local office. Indeed, Rabuka's speech is not the clipped growl of a Stroessner or Somoza so much as it is an echo of the homilies and allusions to the Lord usually heard on the stump or perhaps in postgame interviews.

Rabuka says he intervened to prevent a civil war on Fiji. He was the mediator between the left-wing fanatics of the Bavadra government and the *Taukeis*, the nationalist movement of the right that threatened violence to remove the Labor party from power. *Taukeis* had support from native Fijians who were angry that Indians had better jobs and material comforts. He writes: "I had [to take] over the Government, not for power or personal gain, but to save my people from bloodshed."

Rabuka sees in Dr. Bavadra someone with little use for the Great Council of Chiefs, Fiji's traditional ruling bloc. Instead he believes influence in the coalition government comes from India, which in turn is allied with the Soviet Union, or from Libya, where Labor party officials traveled while in opposition. No wonder, he concludes, Dr. Bavadra wanted to declare Fiji a non-nuclear zone and pursue a foreign policy detached from traditional alliances with New Zealand, Australia, and the United States.

Another concern to Rabuka is the 1874 Deed of Cession, the agreement under which the chiefs gave Fiji to the British Empire. Native Fijians ceded the islands to the Queen. Hence, in 1970, when Fiji was granted independence, the land belonged once again to those who had originally ceded it: the chiefs and native Fijians, not postwar Indian immigrants.

Lastly, he says he intervened to make Fiji a Christian state: "If this land is run by Christians, or Fijians who are Christians, everything will be in place."

The earnest, plodding qualities of the book point against an international conspiracy bringing down the Bavadra government. Rabuka needed little prompting to overthrow Dr. Bavadra. He perceived little respect for the army, and that was sufficient reason to act. The night before the coup he sat up until nearly 5:00 A.M., outlining his reasons for a military takeover. Since immortalized as Fiji's declaration of independence, OPORD 1/87 nonetheless reads more like notes for a military briefing than Thomas Jefferson's "On the Rights of Man":

> • Our mission is to overthrow the govt. and install a new regime that will ensure that the RFMF [Royal Fiji Military Forces] and national interests are protected.

> • Coalition is based on Labour Party [Trade Unions] and NFP [Indian Party] supported by WUF [Western United Front]—dissident group. . . . Communist influence spread by Labour, Peace Movement, Church movt.

> • India is a great friend of Russia. . . . Our allegiance to the Crown is threatened.

• Party members do not trust RFMF. . . . Nonalignment
will mean pulling out of Sinai—500 (+) unemployed. . . .
RFMF morale will nosedive.

Rabuka scoffs at the notion that he was a stalking horse
for the CIA: "I do not know anything about them, and I think
they know very little about me." On the issue of mercenaries
participating in the coup he says: "Everybody involved in my
coup of 14th of May were people I personally picked and
trained . . . no foreigners came into the country to help." Nor
can he understand the opposition from Australia and New
Zealand to the coups: "We wanted to strengthen the links
with [them] especially, yet they were the first ones to go." He
asks how he could be the marionette of Australian intelligence
if Australian Prime Minister Bob Hawke was so opposed to
the outcome of his coups.

Rabuka insists that his goal is not unlimited personal
power, but simply Fijian control of the government, which
would respect the rights of Indians and other outsiders: "The
only thing we wanted is to give Fijians 40 seats [in the new
one-house Parliament], Indians can have their 22, the
General Electors [Europeans and other races] can have their
8. . . . Fiji is to be a Christian country. The constitution to be
reviewed after every ten years. Those were the only things I
wanted."

Nevertheless what he got was a nation that for the moment
can be run only by a general, and what he introduced was the
precedent of military intervention in the South Pacific. For
the United States, his presence invites the suspicion, whether
it is deserved or not, that it is prepared to play the Great
Game even here, on coral islands better known for their fair
weather than their threats to American security.

Having ignored the South Pacific for so long, why would
the U.S. now decide that Fiji mattered? For some time the

U.S. has believed that the Soviets are behind much of the movement in the South Pacific that would declare the region a non-nuclear zone. Perhaps in New Zealand it was local politics that caused the rift in the joint-security agreement, but elsewhere Washington senses invisible red hands behind the agitation to ban nuclear warships.

Under those circumstances, it is easy to see how the U.S. Pacific Command might have reacted to the election of an opposition, non-nuclear party on Fiji. What responsible commander would want to lose calling privileges or landing rights on the largest islands between Hawaii and New Zealand? If the local political establishment also wanted Bavadra out, so much the better. How difficult would it be for the U.S. to turn a blind eye if it learned of plans for a coup on a remote Pacific island?

Certainly the evidence suggests that, odd as it may sound, events in Suva mattered to Washington. Generals like Vernon Walters or John Singlaub don't turn up anywhere on a whim. Or as U.S. Navy Admiral Ronald Hayes, commander in chief, Pacific Command, said to Simon Winchester of the *Guardian* prior to the coup: "Of all the problems that I see arising in the South Pacific in the coming months, the formation of the Fiji Labor party seems the most pressing. It could lead to all kinds of instability."

During the time that I was hearing about U.S. complicity in the coup or listening to complaints that it was no longer a friend in the Pacific, but a colonial master, another American came ashore on Fiji. This one brought along his own Boeing 727 aircraft and 151-foot yacht, in whose wake floated enough celebrity gossip and photo opportunities to satisfy even the grouchiest Hollywood press agent.

Malcolm Forbes, the owner and publisher of *Forbes* magazine, made Fiji a port-of-call on his fourteen-nation goodwill tour of the Pacific. He arrived on the yacht *Highlander* about the same time as his Boeing jet, *Capitalist Tool*, set down at Nadi, bringing along additional passengers for that segment of the journey.

When he arrived, the local press spent several days examining the possibility that Elizabeth Taylor might be on board. Finally that rumor proved unfounded. She would be joining the *Highlander* later. Other than Forbes himself, the only celebrities of note were the editor of *Architectural Digest* and Liz Smith, the gossip columnist, who presumably was the voyage's Darwin. But along the way the passenger list would include Roger Smith, chairman of General Motors, Sadahei Kusumoto, president of Minolta, and the exiled King and Queen of Bulgaria—not to mention Liz Taylor.

The government of Fiji turned out to greet Forbes as though his were a state visit. The papers showed President Ratu Sir Penaia and Prime Minister Ratu Mara leading the magazine publisher to elaborate welcoming ceremonies. Less prominent, but still on hand, was a smiling Brigadier Rabuka. They treated their guest to a luncheon and later a display of traditional firewalking—a ritual of penance and cleansing, not another hardship for Indians under the Rabuka government.

Forbes returned the hospitality with an elaborate party held on the off-shore island of Laucala, which he owns. He said the tour was to strengthen the friendship between the United States and the Far East.

"Countries rimming the Pacific," he told his guests, "are increasingly where it's at these days for the businesses of America and for every multinational corporation. What happens in or to any one of us affects all of us."

The president took the opportunity to assure the rest of the world that tourists no longer had anything to fear on Fiji.

"We don't want to look back on what has happened in Fiji," he said. "This is the time to look forward. To look back, we have to apportion blame."

Forbes added: "We hope to get the word to the rest of the

world, particularly our neighbors in the Pacific Basin . . . that the sun shines on Fiji."

At one point in the ceremonies, Mr. Forbes arranged for the *Capitalist Tool* to fly low over the beach on Laucala. The picture published the following day shows the money-green and gold airplane, its flaps extended and its wheels down, just above the tree tops. In one corner of the picture is a palm. Nearby are the thatched roofs of Fijian huts.

Below this photograph is another showing schoolchildren in native dress, performing what Fijians call *meke*, which is an epic set to song and dance. At the top of the page is the head-line: "Festivity Forbes Style Hits Fiji." It's hard to look at the collage and not think that, once again, the natives are being instructed in the ways of civilization.

The Playing Fields
of Terrorism

(1987)

The journey to the frontier between Jordan and Israel began on the runway at the Athens airport, brushed as it is by gentle sea breezes of the Saronic Gulf and a terrorist past. Passengers for Amman, before boarding, were asked to point to their luggage, which was scattered beside the boarding stairs. Only then was it loaded into the fuselage. A matter of caution, perhaps, but it was a fitting introduction to the fatalism of the Middle East: the exercise didn't insure that there wasn't a bomb on board—only that, if there were, its courier would go aloft with the suitcase.

Royal Jordanian flight number 132 avoided a direct route to Amman, which would have meant flying over Israel, and flew a long arc over the dry riverbeds of southern Turkey and Syria. Approached in the half-light of dusk, the Jordanian desert reflected a gray, lunar complexion. Seemingly the plane could have set down anywhere in this wasteland and rolled the last fifty miles to the terminal, which appeared first as a winking electronic oasis and later as a Potemkin village.

Like so much else in Jordan, the $85 million Queen Alya International Airport was paid for with Saudi petro dollars.

Completed in 1983, before traffic warranted a field the size of that serving Houston, it was intended to mark Jordan's accession to the front rank of Middle East nations. Late that afternoon, however, the linoleum corridors from the arrival gate echoed the loneliness of footsteps in a mall where the shops are closed. The unused baggage carousels gave the impression that only ghost flights had landed. And the grand concourse—Jordan's gateway arch—had more portraits of King Hussein than arriving passengers.

My trip coincided with a number of events that, when recalled as one, fix the image of the Middle East as the Balkans of the late twentieth century. While I was there and after: Israel launched an air raid against the Palestinian Liberation Organization in Tunisia, in retaliation for Israeli yachtsmen killed on Cyprus; Palestinian gunmen hijacked a cruise ship, threw an American invalid overboard, and then escaped the fate of pirates by disappearing into the Italian judiciary; an Egyptian policeman opened fire with a machine gun on Israelis sunbathing at Taba, the disputed beach on the Gulf of 'Aqaba, and more than a month passed before official condolences were received in Jerusalem; Vice President George Bush conducted a political barnstorm through Jordan, Israel, and Egypt, as though each were a primary state on Super Tuesday; American hostages, seized in Beirut, were released in Syria after President Reagan authorized an Israeli agent to deliver weapons to Iran, fighting a seven-year war with Iraq, the ally of our allies in the region; and, after being the object of thrown rocks, the Israeli military on the West Bank shot more than a dozen Palestinian demonstrators, killing two.

Rather than interpret actions that, in history, may read like the intrigue that preceded Sarajevo, I decided to visit the land that, in my mind, lies at the heart of the Middle East conflict: the West Bank and Jordan Valley. On the East Bank of the Jordan River, in Jordan, are many of the Palestinian refugees from the Arab wars against Israel. Occupied by Israel since 1967, the West Bank is a kaleidoscope of Palestinian villages and, lately, Jewish settlements. In either land it is possible from many of the hilltops to took down on the spires of Jerusalem, a city whose divisions are a tapestry of the conflict.

To my surprise, as an American I was welcome at Palestinian refugee camps and Israeli settlements, and was free to cross the Jordan at the Allenby Bridge. In New York, before leaving, I had collected several names of Jordanians and Israelis, but otherwise went with an open itinerary. I left, however, with the despair that is the region's most freely traded commodity. As if in a time warp, I felt I had visited Europe during a feudal period, when countries were forming and wars were fought over religious questions or village squares. My impression of the Middle East was that it was in the early stages of a hundred years war. Nor was there any urgency to finding solutions to the problems. It reminded me of the Austro-Hungarian Balkan policy at the turn of the century, the preference to "muddle through"—even if a small act of violence, an assassination, perhaps, eventually has larger consequences.

The international symbol of squalor—corrugated tin roofing—interrupts the Irbid road north of Amman. Behind cement walls, wire, and halyards of fluttering laundry, as if part of some landlocked fleet, rows of cinder-block houses give shape to a restricted town. The main gate is a dusty intersection where trucks, buses, Mercedes taxis, and pushcarts jostle with the pedestrians drawn to such commotion.

This is Baqa'a—a Palestinian refugee camp. Even though Jordan is sparsely populated, and some of the rocky hills give way to expansive farmland, the camp is crowded into an area not much larger than the playing fields of an American high school. A satellite of the United Nations refugee constellation, it began in 1967 as a tent camp, with a few central spigots for water; later came the block housing, electricity, and the open sewer that snakes through the side streets and alleys.

I found the camp's director, Mr. Alfattah Wheidi, in a tin shack, seated behind a plain wooden desk. A dark-haired man in his late forties, he was wearing sunglasses, a light cotton suit, and an expression as impassive as the drab olive paint on the walls. As testimony to the far-reaching adaptability of bureaucracy, his desk had an in-box, a black rotary telephone, and several neat stacks of paper. While talking with the camp administrators, he motioned for me to sit in a wooden chair against the long wall in his office.

Adjacent was a large blackboard that kept the camp's daily ledger. That particular morning 65,370 people were living at Baqa'a, which broke down to 9,091 families living in 7,650 dwellings or about eight to each family and house. Three of every four houses had a toilet. The roster listed 7 doctors and 186 teachers on duty, and reported 240 cases treated the day before at the clinic. Seventy-one sanitation workers picked up the garbage, and there were 76 water points with 242 taps. One thousand six hundred fifty refugees were eating in one of the camp's three feeding centers, as they were called. Each month 3,200 rations of dry milk were issued to children under the age of three. No epidemics were present.

After his meeting broke up, Mr. Wheidi talked of the symbolism expressed by camp life. The Arab refugees from the 1948 war with Israel first settled in the West Bank, but were pushed east again in 1967. Jordan had offered citizenship to the refugees and the opportunity to assimilate into the culture, and while some did, most clung to the camps—their only link with towns and villages in Israel. The refugees were free to come and go as they pleased, and many commuted to Amman. But most of these families maintained a camp residence, because it was temporary, because one day they would be going home. Dreary as it might be, Baqa'a was Paradise Lost.

Escorted by a squadron of flies and several small, darting boys, one of whom wore a Houston Astros T-shirt, we walked to a school, a soup kitchen, and a clinic. The open sewer festered under the high sun. A bazaar that choked the main streets filled the air with dust. And at the clinic the head doctor said that while, in general, the health of the refugees was good, such social problems as teenage pregnancy were devastating. Nevertheless, it would be misleading to etch Baqa'a in terms that evoke Calcutta or the slums of Rio.

At Baqa'a Preparatory School No. 2, the schoolgirls lined up for morning exercises, frolicked at recess, and filed reluctantly, like all students, into their classrooms. The school resembled a field warehouse, and the girls had their heads covered with flowing, Arabic headdresses. The principal, Mrs. Ayshed Diab, spoke excellent English, something she was trying to pass along to various sixth-grade classes. Graceful and determined, she displayed the qualities of patience, leadership, and good humor that I remember from the best of my own teachers. She knew each girl by name, and when we talked—first in her office and later in class—she would interrupt the conversation to revise a lesson plan with another teacher or to restore order in the school yard.

Like Henry Adams, she spoke of life as a political education. It disturbed her that the classes, on average, had fifty pupils. Moreover, her students had neither pencils nor paper, which disappeared from the supply trucks after the 1982 war in Lebanon. She suspected supplies were short because of cuts in American aid, but all she knew for sure was that her students had to learn by repetition. Homework, sadly, was an abstract concept. Only a few of the thousands that passed through her charge would ever go on to a university. Many of the girls would leave school to have babies. It was a future she was trying to change.

She spoke about the United States with an ambivalence that I heard often in the Middle East. She admired its open society—both she and Mr. Wheidi asked to be sent magazines and books—but she saw its politics only as an extension of Israel's. It was a lesson she intended to pass on to her students.

"I want them to know," she said, "how Israel stole their land. I want them to know that one day they will return." On this point she was inflexible, as only a principal can be.

On the walk back to the office, Mr. Wheidi and I stopped at the house where, a week before, Margaret Thatcher had paid a visit during her own tour at Baqa'a. It had given this family with nine children, living in several concrete rooms, fleeting celebrity status. Later we passed a vacant lot where goals for soccer were set up at either end. Some of the smaller boys were chasing a ball while the older ones milled about on the sidelines—of what another British prime minister might have described as the playing fields of terrorism.

The house of Laila Sharaf, until recently Jordan's minister of information, straddles a ridge that overlooks Baqa'a. From her back lawn the camp spreads out as a desert labyrinth— with the streets showing up as tunnels through the maze and the perimeter as an ancient rampart.

A striking woman in her forties, with coiffed black hair and an elegant bearing, she spoke about the Palestinians from the perspective of an Arab who has lived in the United States. During the 1970s her husband had represented Jordan at the United Nations—a diplomatic life recorded by the pictures around the house. After his death cut short a promising political career, she served in the Jordanian government until she resigned over a difference in policy—by all accounts, an act of considerable courage.

When living in the United States, she had found it impossible even to discuss the question of the Palestinians. Not only did she encounter prejudice against Arabs, but Palestinians were seen only in the veil of terrorism. At public meetings whenever she spoke on the issue, she was reminded of the Holocaust. "Why," she asked, "should the Palestinians alone bear the guilt for this tragedy?"

She questioned the ability of the United States to serve the region as an honest broker. In the Kissinger shuttle missions and at Camp David, the U.S. had cast itself as a disinterested party, yet she believed the peace that it offered implied sympathy for the Israeli position.

"What's mine is mine, and what's yours is negotiable," is how she summarized the various Israeli peace initiatives. She cited the example of Jerusalem, which Israel annexed after the 1967 war. The Arab claim to the city "was not even up for negotiation." Further, on the West Bank and the Gaza Strip, Israel was strengthening its occupation through the settlements and not searching for compromise solutions, such as those offered by the various U.N. resolutions.

"What's left for us to concede?" she asked.

She resented the American fascination with the phrase that Israel had "made the deserts bloom." To her it dismissed the achievements of the Palestinians or their claim to Palestine. It implied that the land was barren prior to the Balfour Declaration in 1917 and the immigration of the Jews.

She explained why she believed Americans had such a difficult time understanding the demands of the Palestinians. Americans were happy living anywhere, she remembered. Yes, hometowns were important, but usually for mythic beginnings. People in the United States don't dream of spending their lives where they were born. But, she said, Palestinians were rooted to small parcels of land, most of which were now inaccessible in either Israel or the West Bank. The ancient towns, like Jaffa or Nazareth, were just as important to Arabs as to Jews, and the various national and religious claims to Jerusalem were duplicated throughout Palestine. Much of the anger stemmed from the inability to go home.

She neither avoided the subject of terrorism nor condoned it. It was endemic to the region, she believed. She recalled the tactics of Menachem Begin's Irgun Zwei Leumi and other groups, but said the only hope for peace was through a Geneva convention, attended by all the powers, including the Soviet Union. It had the ability to wreck any settlement so it ought to be party to any agreement. But she thought it doubtful that the United States or Israel would ever agree to such a concord, at which the Palestinians would have to speak for themselves.

On leaving, I asked if Palestinians and Israelis ever got together informally, away from the headlines, and talked quietly about the land they divided. No, she said quickly, that never happened. She remembered the time she and her husband were invited to watch the launch at Cape Kennedy of Apollo 9. As they stood waiting for the lift-off, she pointed out to her husband that the Indian and Pakistani ambassadors, also invited to the occasion, were clearly enjoying each other's company. When Mrs. Sharaf said to her husband that she could not imagine such a scene between Arab and Jew, he answered: "Not everyone's as crazy as we are."

I met Fawzi Daoud, a member of Jordan's parliament, in the lobby of the Amra Forum Hotel, located off what in Amman is called the Seventh Circle. He wore a sports jacket, gray slacks, and had his necktie loosened in end-of-the-day fashion. Like most Palestinians, his hair and complexion were dark, and his trimmed beard recalled sketches of the Arab noblemen. Rather than take a table in the bar, we simply talked on the sofa where I had been waiting.

When I complimented his English, he said that he had lived in the United States from 1964 to 1972, first attending Xavier University in Ohio and later earning a doctorate in psychology from the University of California. After he returned to Jordan, he developed his practice. In 1984 he was elected to parliament, representing a district on the East Bank. Most of his constituents were Palestinian.

From what he said, it was clear that he admired much about the United States. Nonetheless, our conversation repeatedly came around to how Americans perceived Palestinians. It dismayed him that the only Palestinians Americans recognized were those who seized airplanes.

"Never are we portrayed as a people or a nation, but always as some outlaw gang, " he said. "Just as it would be un-fair to sum up Israel as a country that occasionally launched strafing missions against Palestinian camps, so too is it unfair only to equate Palestinians with acts of terror."

He feared that the Israeli settlement of the West Bank marked a turning point for the Palestinians and for the chances of peace in the region. There were now more than a hundred settlements and 60,000 "colonists," to use his description. He saw the 900,000 West Bank Arabs being squeezed into smaller quarters, as Israelis took more of the land. It was a re-run of what happened earlier in Palestine. That the United States had offered only token opposition, he said, implied approval of the venture.

"Just as Israel is an American dream, similar to those that pushed West, settled the frontier, so, too, are the colonies," he said. Idealistically, he could see a negotiated peace over the West Bank, agreed to by Israel, Jordan, and the Palestinians, in which control was returned to Jordan. But he could never imagine any of the settlers peacefully submitting to such a plan. Nor would the Israeli military ever mount a large-scale action against its own people.

"What then," he asked, "is the point of no return?"

The crossing from Amman to Jerusalem began at first light, when a small bus, the kind rental car agencies use at airports, made the rounds of the hotels. On board was an assortment of Europeans, Asians, and Americans. To make this trip at all it was necessary to obtain a permit from the Ministry of Interior, which involved three days of dropping off and picking up my passport, standing in line at barred windows, and even buying a tax stamp from a robed clerk, whose office was a card table on the island of a busy intersection.

The guidebook described the crossing as "time-consuming and unpleasant" and went on at length about the Orwellian ritual necessary to go fifty miles between the ancient, sister cities: "The bridge closes at 1 p.m. daily and is completely closed on Saturdays, the Jewish Sabbath. It's necessary to begin your journey early (via taxi) to reach the Jordanian security point, where you must board a bus, the only vehicle authorized to make the crossing. You cannot cross over in a taxi or your own car. The last bus leaves the security point (on both sides) at 11 a.m."

At sunrise, the bus descended one of the wadis, or dried river beds, that slope into the Jordan Valley. The road had none of the fortifications or tensions of, for example, the passage through the demilitarized zone at Panmunjom. The customs house, dedicated to King Hussein, was more a turnpike rest stop than security checkpoint. Inside, seated behind a wooden desk, a Jordanian officer struggled to make sense of passports not written in languages he understood.

It took more than an hour to clear the Hussein barracks, but less than a minute to cross the Jordan at the Allenby Bridge. The river is no wider than a mountain stream, and the bridge, despite its aura, is a drab overpass of expressway proportions. Prior to the crossing, an Israeli soldier boarded the bus, drew the shades, and warned against picture taking, since, as it turned out, the far side was heavily fortified. Technically, because Israel only occupies Jordan's territory in the West Bank, the river isn't an international boundary. Nevertheless geopolitics have invested it with the rituals of Berlin.

Another Israeli soldier met the bus at the modern immigration building. An Uzi machine gun hung casually from his shoulder. With a flick of his head, he ordered two Arabs, dressed in blue smocks, to unload the baggage. Across the parking lot an older bus, jammed with Palestinians, pulled up to a second frontier point. In this building—I was told repeatedly in Amman—Arabs were routinely asked, as part of the inspections, to strip and pile their clothes in a basket.

From the checkpoint the road to Jerusalem raced across dry farmland north of the Dead Sea and, outside Jericho, passed a ghost village, which turned out to have been a refugee camp until 1967. Traffic slowed on the rocky foothills that lead into the city. Altogether from the Allenby Bridge it was an hour's drive—as it would be for tanks in an invasion.

Even though it is difficult to think of the Middle East as a tourist attraction, something called Diplomatic Services advertises "Israel Beyond Tourism" and operates briefing trips of the occupied territories. My group of ten included an Israeli family, an English couple, and an American scriptwriter from Hollywood who spent much of the day explaining to his various seatmates how soap operas are written.

The briefing before we left was an outline of local history. Israel refers to the two administrative districts of the West Bank by their biblical names, Judea and Samaria. On a map their borders—once the U.N. Green Line between Jordan and Israel—are a silhouette, perhaps that of Abraham Lincoln. To the north Samaria is the hair and face, while

Judea in the south takes the shape of the shoulders. Appropriately, at the throat or jugular vein is Jerusalem. From the northern border to the south is a day's drive along a tortuous two-lane road. East to west, however, is a matter of an hour or so. And at its widest point, the West Bank is nine miles from the Mediterranean Sea.

The story of the West Bank reads like that of Poland or Czechoslovakia, or any land which, because of its strategic placement, has as its history a chronicle of occupations. Turkish rule lasted until 1917 when General Allenby took Jerusalem. The British ruled Palestine, including the West Bank, until they departed following the Second World War. A 1947 U.N. Partition Plan designated the West Bank for a Palestinian state, but the Arabs rejected such a compromise. Jordan then annexed it in 1950 and remained in control until the 1967 war. Not until the mid-seventies did the Israeli government authorize settlements, and then only for defensive reasons. But the government of Menachem Begin pushed settlements to incorporate what it believed were Israel's historic lands.

Our first stop was a hilltop churchyard that overlooked the spires of the old city. The prophet Samuel was said to be buried here, although our interests were less biblical and more tactical. We reviewed the skyline as though sighting artillery. Until 1967, Jordanian troops were entrenched around three-quarters of the city in siege lines. In addition, Arab neighborhoods encircled those of Israelis, a position that continued even after the city was annexed. To redress this imbalance, the Israeli government constructed a ring of settlements in the hills around Jerusalem. From the churchyard these houses resembled the condominiums that dot the Washington Beltway, although their placement re-enacted a crusader investment. The white prefabricated townhouses and their picket roofs glistened in the morning sun as the latest city wall. Someday, we were told, the West Bank might be returned to Jordan, but never again would Jerusalem be an Arab city.

The occupation of Judea and Samaria presented Israel with a colonial mission: that of governing 900,000 Palestinians. At the office of civil administration in the West Bank—in appearance, a military base—we heard from an American-born Israeli officer how local government operates. The civil service comprises 300 Israelis and 1,200 Arabs, who enforce a hodgepodge of Jordanian, international, and military law. In rare cases the Israelis prosecute Arabs under the same hated statutes that the British used against Jews under the Mandate.

The briefing compared the Israeli colonial record with that of Jordan's. By any measure—except perhaps that of hearts and minds—conditions have improved on the West Bank since 1967: fifty percent of the villages now have running water, as opposed to twenty percent; infant mortality is down; ten thousand students attend five universities which have been founded under the Israeli occupation; more than seven thousand families have moved from refugee camps into new public housing; and the local administration has introduced a number of social services, including day care, job training, and programs for the elderly and sick.

Nevertheless, the West Bank remains the tar baby of Israeli politics. Were it established as a Palestinian state, either independently or in federation with Jordan, questions about security might topple any Israeli government, even if the territory were demilitarized and Israel were to establish a defense around all boundaries. Only a few Israelis would solve the problem by expelling the Palestinians from the occupied territories. Judea and Samaria could be annexed, as with Jerusalem and the Golan Heights, but that might raise the prospect that one day the majority of Israelis would be Arab. Nor has it been easy to deal with Jordan on the question. King Hussein, a Bedouin, rules a country with a Palestinian majority, which could use a state or federation on the West Bank to overthrow the Hashemite Kingdom. Finally, Israel must contend with the settlers, who while small in number have a powerful hold on the electorate. No one is eager to live under Arab sovereignty. As a consequence, the stalemate on the West Bank is now in its twenty-first year.

The typical settlement is a condominium in the hills, fenced by barbed wire—a lonely outpost in enemy lands. Images of Vietnam's strategic hamlets come to mind, only these are equipped with air-conditioning and two-car garages. Some are religious communities where members participate in all aspects of village life, as if at a kibbutz.

The first settlements in the Jordan Valley formed a trip wire to signal a Jordanian attack. They provided the Israeli government with reservists at the frontier. Later came the religious settlers, for whom the West Bank represented a return to biblical lands. But the larger design of the settlements was to create a demographic club sandwich that would intersperse Jewish communities between those of Arabs. On a map, simply by connecting the dots of the settlements, it is easy to see the entrenchment lines that run north-south through the West Bank. Maginot had only one line in France—here Israel has three or four.

Ariel, where we stopped for lunch, is a linchpin in this defense. Twenty-one miles from both the Jordan River and Mediterranean Sea, it sits abreast the Patriarch's Road, a major thoroughfare. Several years ago it was another windswept barren hillside with more rocks than trees at the top. Today the population is 2,000, which is planned to increase to 160,000 in the next century. Those who don't find work in one of the local factories or in an adjacent industrial park will commute to Tel Aviv. In the grand design the settlers will become suburbanites.

Leaving Ariel to the northwest, we drove to the point where from the hills of the West Bank it is possible to look across the entire width of Israel to the sea. During the 1967 war, Israeli fighter pilots nicknamed this spot "Mickey Mouse," because of two ear-shaped towers that protruded from the landscape. Even in hazy sunshine the high-rise apartments in Tel Aviv were clearly visible, as were cooling towers from a nuclear power station and Boeing 747 jets making lazy turns on their final approach to Ben Gurion airport. Whoever controls the West Bank controls this high ground, with its natural defenses as stubborn as those at Gallipoli.

Near the Allon Road east of Nablus is an early settlement, Ofra, which in the 1970s was established on the grounds of an abandoned army camp. Ending the day here, we came to listen to Shifra Blass, a spokeswoman for the Council of Jewish Settlement in Judea, Samaria, and Gaza.

When the first families arrived, Ofra was a tent camp. To hear a description today, it was the Middle East equivalent of Injun country—with Arabs serving the role of Indians. Each night settlers huddled together behind the wire. The men carried guns. The only jobs were in clearing the land.

Eventually the crops took hold in the rocky soil, and the tents were replaced with row houses, which could have been ordered from the Levittown catalogue. A hundred families with 350 children moved in, and, in addition to a metal factory, the settlement put up a silk-screening plant and various craft shops.

As though on a sales tour, we saw Ofra by bus. Shifra Blass acted as guide, and her descriptions of the settlement made it sound like one of the utopian communities in nineteenth-century America, perhaps Putney or Oneida. Residents were carefully screened. Anyone wishing to live at Ofra had to pass a trial year and then receive community approval. Only Orthodox Jews were admitted, and everyone shared in the chores, be they farming or child care. All agreed that Israel had a biblical, moral, and political right to settle the West Bank.

Mrs. Blass exuded an air of manifest destiny. Her plain, rough-cotton dress and fortitude, despite the latter stages of pregnancy, were consistent with Ofra's prairie setting. In an earlier time she might have been found leading wagons through the Cumberland Gap. In fact, when she spoke later in the community center, she said she had grown up in Philadelphia and emigrated in the early 1970s.

The Israel that she found along the Mediterranean coast, however, did not mesh with her Zionist ideals.

"Tel Aviv wasn't mentioned in my Bible," she said, adding that to her Israel was the biblical town of Hebron or Nablus or Jericho. "What does Zionism have to do with living in a high-rise overlooking the water?" she asked. It further offended her, when she lived in Tel Aviv, that these biblical lands were off-limits to Israelis. Of this policy she said: "What hypocrisy to speak of Israel, of Zionism, of a return to the lands of the Bible and then not to let people settle in the holiest towns."

Having won the right to live in the West Bank, the settlers were working to purchase as much of the land as was for sale and to defeat any peace initiative that would put them under Arab rule. Mrs. Blass said that land was being purchased fairly, despite the Palestinian claim that the Israelis were pressuring Arabs to sell. As for living under Palestinian or Jordanian rule, she could not imagine it. It brought to her mind Jerusalem under the Jordanians. They had let the city, especially the Jewish quarter, deteriorate. She said it had been "an ugly city, dirty." Israelis had been forbidden to enter their holiest shrines, which were allowed to fall into disrepair. What comfort did that offer for a future under the Jordanians?

Nor could she imagine any Israeli government forcibly removing the settlers as part of any peace plan. When Israel returned the Sinai to Egypt after Camp David, the military needed weapons to remove some of the settlers there. But it was an ugly scene, not to be repeated, especially on the scale of the settlements of the West Bank.

As she concluded: "What the settlers are doing today is no different from what the first Zionists did when they reached Palestine."

We rode home through Ramallah, an Arab town fifteen miles north of Jerusalem. It was almost dark when, on the edge of the town, an Israeli officer stopped the bus. Up ahead, he explained, rocks were being thrown at cars. It was up to us whether to proceed. After deliberations with the tour guide, the driver went ahead, grinding his way through the low gears until the van settled into overdrive.

When we reached the town center, Ramallah had the eerie look of Northern Ireland or Soweto. Troops in full battle gear lined both sides of the main street. Machine guns were drawn. Lurching side to side from the speed, the van followed several trucks past this formation. No rocks were felt against the windshield, however. In fact, few Arabs could be seen on the street. Outside Ramallah, we blended into the rush hour traffic and arrived safely in Jerusalem, although I couldn't help wondering whether someday a rock thrown in anger would become, yet again, a shot heard 'round the world.

The Road to Petra

(1985)

Early on a Thursday evening, Queen Alya International Airport—thirty-five minutes from downtown Amman—had more portraits of King Hussein than arriving passengers. My wife and I cleared immigration, collected our bags, and stood almost alone in the modern airport's concourse, like plastic figures in an architect's model.

We were in Jordan to see Petra—the Mount Rushmore of cities, which the Nabataeans and later the Romans literally carved from the hills of the desert. "A rose-red city half as old as Time" is how Dean Burgon describes it in his often-recited poem, "Petra," which begins "It seems no work of Man's creative hand. . . ." But for more than a thousand years, Petra was lost to the Western world. Only the wanderings of a Swiss explorer in the nineteenth century rediscovered this lost city of fable.

More accessible today, Petra is three hours south of Amman, just west of the Desert Highway, Jordan's main highway. We knew from the guidebooks that tour buses make a daily run to Petra, but instead we wanted to drive there by going south along the King's Highway, once a caravan route to the Red Sea.

Standing in the airport's empty arrival hall, we felt ourselves at a crossroads. Should we set out on our own or retreat to the sanctuary of a tour bus? Friends who had lived in Jordan had warned us about the dervish qualities of its traffic. But we didn't want to be tied to the schedule of a group or to the oppressive banter of tour-bus narratives.

We decided to rent a car, but that meant we would face the dilemma of arriving on the eve of the Jordanian Sabbath—the first of many forks in the road. Should we rent a car now at the airport, or could we get one in the morning and thus be spared a night drive into Amman?

There was an agent on duty at the Avis counter, but he answered my question by saying that the office was closed. A clerk at a tourist information desk said it would be "no problem" to rent a car the following morning in the city. But when we checked into our hotel, the desk man shook his head no. Tomorrow was Friday. Didn't we know it was the Sabbath? We should have rented a car at the airport.

Despite his gloom, the desk clerk said that he would try to help. After several phone calls, he found an agency that would be open on Friday. It was agreed that at eight in the morning we would present ourselves to the manager, who would be waiting with a car.

Nobody in Jordan was friendlier than Mr. Imieri, the proprietor of Kada Rent A Car. Unfortunately, he had only two cars on his lot. Both were Dodge Colts, each closer to stud than starting gates, so it wasn't much of a choice. Eager to please, Mr. Imieri readied one by scooping trash from the back seat and shoving it under the car.

"You take this one," he said proudly. "It's the best."

I paid in cash. He fetched maps from his own car and tried to hurry us along with a cheerful, "Okay, you go," but I protested that the gas tank was empty.

Mr. Imieri couldn't understand my objections at all.

"You take it empty," he explained, "and you bring it back empty," adding that this was standard procedure in the local rental market. But after a standoff, and my primer on American rental practices, he grudgingly followed us to a service station and paid for a tank of gas. Then once again we were waved away with his favorite: "Okay, you go."

We went, but in circles. Amman is built on seven hills—like Rome, the guide books say—and on top of each is a traffic circle. None, however, had signs directing traffic to Petra or even to the King's Highway. We stopped at a Holiday Inn for directions, but "no problem" was how that futile discussion began and ended. Eventually a policeman headed us in the right direction.

The King's Highway runs north and south between Amman and 'Aqaba on the Red Sea. A leaflet I picked up at the airport said that the highway "has been the pathway of traders and caravans, of armies and conquerors, of Romans, Byzantines, Crusaders, and the armies of Islam." It would take eight hours to get to Petra, as opposed to three hours on the Desert Highway.

No road I've been on so evokes the passages of the Old Testament, which is read as local history in towns like Hisban or Ma'daba. Bedouins encamp on either side of the highway. They can be seen clustered under tents, like latter-day Moabites or Amorites, the biblical tribes who once wandered these lands. The hot sun has bleached the towns a monochromatic clay color. The road is punctuated with Crusader fortresses, spaced a day's ride apart, or about forty miles.

We stopped mid-morning at Mount Nebo, one of several places where Moses is said to be buried. The courtyard of a small Byzantine church overlooked the valley of the Jordan River. Faint in haze was the Dead Sea. On clear nights, we were told by an old man watching the church, the lights of Jerusalem flicker across the valley.

As I now recollect the drive, I probably knew right from

the start that the clutch on the Colt wasn't right. It needed pumping close to the floor to engage the gears. But more than anything we wanted to see Petra, so I judged the loose clutch another quirk of the Kada Rent A Car system, like the empty tanks, and convinced myself that it would hold a day or two longer.

The King's Highway traverses a number of steep valleys, known in the Middle East as wadis. Dried riverbeds, they are best imagined as small versions of the Grand Canyon. Wadi Mujid, south of Dhiban, drops thirty-eight hundred feet and is over two miles wide. The twisting climb from the bottom sounded the death knell for the clutch. Only by grinding the gears into second was I able to coax the car into Kerak, a hill-top town dominated by a Crusader fortress.

The car came to rest on the edge of the bazaar, not far from a government rest house. The manager, who spoke a little English, listened sympathetically to my narrative of the clutch, but shrugged that today was Friday, a holy day. It was also lunchtime for his guests. But I managed to convince a waiter to come with me to the old quarter to search for a mechanic.

The waiter assembled a full mechanical crew simply by hollering. As if summoned by the muezzin, five men followed us to the car. They weren't really mechanics, had no tools, spoke no English, but who was I to argue? In an instant, one man was jacking up the car, another was leaning into the engine, and a third sat in the driver's seat, revving the engine. A self-appointed head mechanic slid under the chassis on a discarded piece of cardboard.

By turning a bolt under the engine, the mechanics tightened the clutch and then, mostly in reverse, went for a gleeful, horn-punctuated test drive around the medieval block. A ceremonial picture was taken. The tip I offered everyone took slightly longer, as no one would accept money for himself.

Each had to accept some for one of the other mechanics. So we had the pantomime of everyone stuffing money into someone else's shirt.

After lunch in the guest house and a walk through the Crusader fortress, which held out until Saladin took it in 1189, we made a triumphant exit from Kerak. From inside a darkened café, the mechanics cheered at the sight of the car, and we returned to the King's Highway for the remaining eighty-five miles to Petra.

In about fifteen minutes it became clear that we were being followed. A motorcyclist, dressed in studded black leather, rode either on our tail or just ahead of us—this on a road with no traffic. Nothing indicated that this was a friendly escort, and it was unnerving to have him along as we approached the desolate Wadi Hasa, the grandest we were to cross.

From where we were, there was no other road to Petra. Nor did we need a return visit to Kerak. Near a widening in the road, I pressed the brakes and watched the biker shoot past. Up ahead he stopped to watch us, but didn't return in our direction. We talked over the risks of going forward, decided that it would be Petra or bust, and descended into Wadi Hasa.

In the valley of the canyon, where the road parallels a riverbed that runs to the Dead Sea, two men, waving their arms, stepped in front of our car. They wore blue uniforms that gave the impression of a thrift-shop fitting. Perhaps they were local police, or maybe military, but they lacked the crisp professionalism of the officers who had given us directions in Amman. It also seemed a big joke to both of them that we had stopped at all.

The older of the two was about nineteen. His half-friendly, half-sinister smile revealed a mouthful of golden fillings. Leaning into the car, he rubbed his right forefingers on the palm of his left hand. I interpreted this as the international symbol of bribery. Maybe all he wanted was identification, but we were on a lonely road in the middle of nowhere, and he offered none in return. Nor did he have a gun, a squad car, or a roadside command post.

Not wanting to give this man either money or my passport, I feigned a search of my pockets while gently lowering the clutch, of all things, to the floor. For once the Colt moved briskly from the gate, and as we bucked forward in first and then second gear, I watched the two highwaymen in the rearview mirror give a half-hearted chase and then flail their arms in anger.

Up ahead we had to climb four thousand feet to leave the wadi. Would there be a police roadblock waiting at the top? What about the motorcyclist? Was he involved? And to make our day, I again detected incipient failure in the clutch. Clearly Kerak had never fallen to Midas.

Out of the wadi, the car ran smoothly across the high plain leading to Tafila, after which it was clear that no one was following. The landscape, now almost comforting, had qualities of the New Mexico desert. But outside Dana, a town thirty-five miles from Petra and not far from King Solomon's mines, the clutch failed.

Using a maneuver that I perfected in college on a 1966 Volkswagen, I put the Colt in third gear and roll-started it down a long incline. Until Petra there would be no gear shifting. Third would be it. That meant scattering hitchhikers and roaring through village crossroads. Near Shobak, where there is another Crusader fortress, we nearly stalled when trapped behind a truck. More than a few hills produced a death rattle in the engine.

Fortunately, the road skirted a deep wadi and ran mostly through a stony desert. We swept through Wadi Musa, the town adjacent to Petra, and, after a few loops in a parking lot to build engine speed for the last hill, coasted to a stop in front of the four-star Petra Forum Hotel, whose swimming pool appeared more a mirage than an oasis.

Petra was worth the ride. Were it on today's tourist trails, as it once served the caravans, it would be as celebrated as are the ruins of ancient Greece. We first saw it at sunset, when the light on the surrounding hills spins as if in a kaleidoscope. The next morning we set out on foot before dawn to watch the sunrise perform the same magic show on the city lost to the world for most of the last millennium.

The entrance to Petra (the Siq) is a half mile from the hotel, and the only way in is by pony or on foot. The Siq is a narrow defile, three kilometers long, that slices through canyon rock two hundred feet high. It leads to Khasneh, or treasury, a Roman temple engraved in the rock face. This architecture—that of classical buildings carved from canyon walls—is why Petra deserves consideration as a wonder of the world.

Nabataeans founded Petra around 800 B.C. Put crudely, they collected protection money from the caravans that plied the routes from Arabia to the Mediterranean and Red seas. The Romans captured the city in 106 A.D. and added such touches as Corinthian columns and friezes to the existing splendor.

Petra remained an imperial crown jewel for several centuries until Rome faded and the trade routes shifted. The city was slowly abandoned and forgotten. Sandstorms covered the valley where most of the city developed. It became a lost city of fable until 1812, when the Swiss explorer, John Burckhardt, wrote in his journal: "It appears very probable that the ruins in Wadi Musa are those of ancient Petra."

After several hours among the ruins and a climb to the High Place of Sacrifice, where an offering of the Colt would have complimented the sweeping view of antiquity, we decided to hike back to the hotel to deal with the car. When we had checked in, the hotel manager had called Kada Rent A Car to explain the situation. He relayed our message that if the car couldn't be fixed soon, we would have to leave it at the hotel.

By 2:00 in the afternoon, when we got back to the hotel, there was word at the desk that mechanics were on their way. We swam and ate lunch, but by 3:30 no one had arrived. It meant we had to give up our plans of driving to 'Aqaba, the Red Sea port that T. E. Lawrence captured from the Turks in 1916. Now we simply wanted to get back to Amman. The only public bus serving Petra had departed, so I arranged for us to hitch a ride with a tour group that was leaving shortly for the capital.

As we prepared to board the bus, two men dressed in mechanics' overalls pulled up in a Dodge Colt very much like the one we had rented, or, for that matter, like the one we had left behind in Amman. The mechanics neither spoke English nor had many tools, but they set to work, Kerak style, on the disabled Colt. Moments later they were inside the hotel, announcing to the hotel clerk that our car was "100 percent."

For obvious reasons I was unconvinced that the clutch could be repaired in ten minutes. Nor was I prepared to take it on a night drive to Amman. As there were two mechanics, I told them that they could keep the car, which wasn't what they wanted to hear.

The lobby discussion grew heated. Their style of debate was surly and intimidating while mine developed into that of Billy Martin arguing a call at second base. Using the desk clerk as a translator, the mechanics insisted we return the car to Amman. They delivered a full litany: we were under contract to Kada, the car was "100 percent," the only problem was a loose clutch bolt. At one point the chief mechanic claimed that his partner could not drive a gear shift, which is not what you want to hear from clutch repairmen.

Finally a compromise was reached. We would take their car, and they, in ours, would follow us to Amman. We would take the main highway.

After a stop for gas—of course their car was on empty—the mechanics drove in front at high speed, littering the landscape with empty water bottles. At least this wouldn't be a slow ride. But twenty minutes from Petra, high on a barren, rocky hillside, the accelerator cable on our replacement Colt snapped. The car died immediately. Meanwhile, oblivious to my horn, the mechanics rolled on.

We pushed the Colt off the road and awaited their return. A number of Bedouin children appeared on a hillcrest to watch the excitement, which lacked only vaudeville music to capture the mood. Eventually the mechanics returned, but, for reasons I still find incredible, they had neglected to bring with them any spare parts or cable. When they began searching the roadside for wire, it was clear we had a problem.

Needless to say, in this dry, biblical land of the Edomites, no accelerator cable was found. But four or five miles away, twisting slowly out of the valley near Wadi Musa, I spotted the tour bus from the hotel or, as my wife said, "the last train to Shanghai." As if in slow motion, it wound its way up the hillside until we flagged it down.

In the last of our great debates, the mechanics returned to the proposition that only one of them could drive a stick shift. The driver of the waylaid bus translated this contention with a deadpan expression. When I delivered a harangue on the Kada Rent A Car company and scoffed at the idea of a mechanic unable to drive, our mediator had a wonderful response: "I'm not telling you what to do. I'm only telling you what they said."

Any more discussion was pointless. The mechanics had a working car to return to Wadi Musa for the necessary parts. Then there might be the short course on gear shifting, assuming the clutch could be made to work. But we were through with Kada. It had delivered us, barely, to the city Dean Burgon said "seems no work of Man's creative hand," which had also become our view of the Colts. We boarded the bus and never once looked back on the road to Amman.

Old South Africa

(1985)

Johannesburg could be an American city. The Carlton Centre, one of the better hotels, has an observation deck similar to those atop monoliths across the United States. From the hotel rooftop, the streets below spread out like an inner-city fortress. The perimeter is a moat of expressways, the gates being the cloverleafs at each of the four corners. Inside these fast-moving, six-lane city walls is a familiar downtown, evocative of Dallas or Denver. The glass exteriors of the office buildings shimmer in the prairie sun. Across the tracks the department stores, judged by suburban standards, look a little shabby. There is the forlorn sense, even during the day, that this is a place where people work and shop, but don't live.

The city's power, and, by extension, that of white South Africa, comes from the gold on which Johannesburg literally sits. Like Aztec ruins, heaps of golden residue are piled throughout the city that was founded as a campsite during the 1885 rush. Operating mines can still be found in the suburbs, and it is not an exaggeration to say that Johannesburg's pulse can be taken from the quotes bid and asked on the London or New York exchanges. It is this modern skyline rising from the Transvaal plain that gives South Africa a sense of might and invulnerability. It seems to have conquered a number of frontiers. During a conversation on the possibility of change, a leader from one of the opposition groups pointed toward the colossus and said to me: "How's anyone going to overthrow that?"

In recent months, however, the specter of rebellion has hovered over South Africa. Since September, more than two hundred blacks and one white have died in riots, clashes with the police, or random violence. When I decided to go there, the decision was received among friends and acquaintances with reservation, if not hostility. At a dinner in New York before I left, an angry woman said: "I can understand your wanting to go to Africa. But not South Africa. Go to Kenya. Go look at wild animals. Anything but South Africa." But the purpose of the trip was not to go on safari. I wanted to judge for myself a country I knew secondhand from books, headlines, and the silhouettes that are often shown on television.

The trip began with a seemingly endless flight that crossed the Atlantic to Cape Town and then continued northeast, over prairie like the American West, to Johannesburg. After arriving, I was free to go where I pleased. Technically, the black township of Soweto was off-limits to visitors, especially foreigners, whose safety was questioned because of the continuing violence. But that didn't prevent me from talking to blacks or from visiting the township so synonymous with black life in South Africa. The trip ended with a walk at the water's edge at the Cape of Good Hope. I departed with the sense that instead of being a world apart—some underground set aside for evil practices—South Africa's society bears similarities to our own. I left also firm in the belief that its cures lie in greater contact with the West, especially the United States, rather than in isolation. As the former editor of the *Johannesburg Star* said one afternoon: "Cut us off more and we'll become even queerer than we are now."

With introductions ahead of time—from sources as discrete as South African diplomats and black dissidents living in exile—I was able to meet a number of persons whose lives are in politics—be it through the government, writing, or in the churches. Both blacks and whites in the country have the sense of living under an occupation, and the Vichy-like atmosphere has produced a political discourse as vibrant as in any state of siege. In many of these conversations, the common ground was speculation over whether apartheid would end with a whimper or a bang. Would the precedent be *Brown v. Board of Education* or Sherman's march to the sea?

In my time in South Africa, I did not become an expert on U.S. investment policy or African tribal politics, but I was fortunate to meet two men, Beyers Naude and Alan Paton, whose lives have already shaped the course of the country's history. On returning, I came in contact with Desmond Tutu. So much of what South Africa was for me is summed up in these three voices, all in the opposition, telling the experiences of an Afrikaner, a British descendant, and a black.

For anyone arriving at Jan Smuts Airport, South Africa begins as a tale of two cities. Neither Johannesburg nor its black satellite, Soweto, could exist without the other. Nor could the residents, who are bound together in one of the many symbiotic twists of apartheid. The essence of the system that legally separates whites from blacks emerges in this most unlikely pair of sister cities.

What comes as unexpected is that, by day, Johannesburg is a black city. Whites go downtown to file themselves away in the office buildings, but the blacks come to be on the streets: to work as laborers, to shop, to sit motionless in the parks, as if posing for the camera of Walker Evans.

Under the laws of apartheid, which isn't one but many acts of parliament, blacks in the Johannesburg area must live in the township that, even on a clear day, is only faintly visible from the Carlton. But the shopping, like everything else in Soweto, is meager even for food. So beginning before dawn, trains and buses from Soweto start to ferry blacks into the city for their work or shopping. An unforgettable scene, worthy of the pen of Dickens or the eye of Daumier, is that of railway carriages jammed with blacks as they pull into the platforms at Johannesburg station. One imagines the passengers, wedged together in silence, to be fleeing some catastrophe instead of making their everyday commute.

The shopping district is a postcard of an American southern city before integration. Few buildings are taller than two stories, and the blocks are a grid as you would find in Memphis or Birmingham. On the sidewalks a number of blacks still step aside to let a white person pass. In certain situations some of the older black men doff their straw hats. The city operates two bus systems, one each for whites and blacks. The few whites who rely on public transportation ride brand-new Leyland double-decker buses in which the air-conditioning works and it's easy to get a seat. The buses for blacks look twenty years old, are covered with dirt and exhaust, and even at odd hours appear packed, as though they were transporting migrant workers through California.

In the evening Johannesburg has a curfew. By 10:00 P.M., like grounded teenagers, all blacks must be off the streets and presumably back in Soweto. Hence, beginning in the late afternoon, the Stygian trains and buses reverse the directions that they ply in the mornings. What is remarkable—to an American visitor—is how compliant most blacks are with the conditions of apartheid. No police with nightsticks are needed to enforce this lockup. In fact, the evening rush hour would appear normal if everyone leaving from the station's underbelly weren't black. When the last train departs, however, the city of gold becomes a ghost town.

For a white visitor, there are several ways to get to Soweto, and all have qualities of the absurd. "Sowetour" is a government-sponsored bus company that drives tourists around the nicer sections of the township, which envelops 100 square miles and has a population greater than 1.5 million, making it one of the largest cities in Africa. The flyer advertising the tour shows an air-conditioned Mercedes coach. The accompanying photographs make Soweto appear to be yet another African game park. On the leaflet are phrases like "Book Now" and "Don't Miss This Opportunity." Pictures of houses on the tour show a split-level in a neighborhood called "Beverley Hills." Other pictures of a swimming pool and a band shell give the impression that blacks have chosen to live in Soweto the way retirees might move to Hilton Head.

Those whites wanting to go to Soweto on their own need a pass, which is obtained from a municipal building in Johannesburg. Applying for a pass makes it clear why in the course of a lifetime many whites only encounter blacks as servants or in other menial jobs. With double bulletproof doors at the entrance, the building has the appearance of a headquarters for an army of occupation. Desk-bound officers, wearing pale-green uniforms and expressions of contempt, treat any white requesting a pass as either a traitor or a subversive, perhaps on a gun-running mission. My request for a pass was dismissed with the wave of a hand, as the presiding officer said: "We're not issuing any passes until things settle down." From his intonation it was hard for me to tell if he meant that I would have to wait until the next day or perhaps the next century.

I drove to Soweto in a rented car, without a pass, as things had yet to "settle down." The paper that morning had numerous items on the violence that since last September has fed on the grievances of miners and students, and later on the violence itself. In the newspaper that morning, a typical dispatch began: "In White City Jabavu, Soweto, a delivery van was stoned by about 200 youths who also looted the van. When police arrived at the scene, the youths fled. The driver was injured and the van damaged." Another item read: "A woman sitting in a moving bus was shot in the neck from the street outside a Soweto shop at 5:00 P.M. yesterday." Nearly all such violence, including the recent shooting of funeral marchers near Port Elizabeth, takes place in the townships, far removed from the white enclaves.

About ten miles from downtown Johannesburg, surrounded by wire fences, Soweto is no more a threat to white South Africa than one of the camps in the Gulag is to the Kremlin. On the main road, at the eastern end of the township, the South African military maintains a base that, at the first hint of trouble, can rapidly deploy troops. A familiar sight in Soweto is an armored personnel carrier, painted the light browns of desert camouflage, on patrol with a squad of white soldiers.

Unlike the slums around New York, which visually are more menacing than Soweto, this one has a rambling, suburban quality. It spreads out across what used to be farmland on the veld, and the clusters of tract housing resemble a misplaced Levittown. But whatever Soweto may have over the South Bronx, it remains a dreary image of tract housing, dirt roads, garbage-strewn lots, and children playing in the roadside squalor. The family I got to know lived in the garage of a four-room house. By local standards they were by no means poor. The husband worked for an American corporation; his wife was a nurse. They had enough money to build their own house, but there was no land available, nor could they get the required bureaucratic approval, even though the South African government is making an effort to improve housing.

In apartheid's grand design, all blacks in South Africa are guest workers. Soweto is the hostel for these migrants, who, in theory, will use it as a bunk room for several years before going back to places like the Ciskei, Lebowa, or Qwaqwa—tracts of land that the South African government has set aside for blacks. In the pronouncements of apartheid, South Africa is for whites; Africans have their own countries. All the races shall be accorded a separate development to preserve languages and cultural diversity—a concept that matches the separate but equal notions of the American South. But as so often happens in partitions, white South Africa got the gold, the diamonds, Cape Town, and the beaches of Durban, while blacks were consigned to townships like Soweto or to grazeland that in the arid Newspeak of apartheid becomes an ancestral homeland.

What struck me first about Beyers Naude, an Afrikaner and a leading critic of the Pretoria government, was his precision. Over the phone, as we were arranging a time to meet, he said, "I have an appointment at nine and another at eleven, so we'll have to meet at ten." Cheerful openness was not what I expected from someone who had been described to me as being under a form of house arrest. The following morning, almost to the minute, there was a knock on the door of my hotel room and in came the cleric who has since replaced Bishop Tutu as the General Secretary of the South African Council of Churches.

He wore a light-blue leisure suit and Hushpuppy shoes, not exactly revolutionary garb, and we talked for fifty minutes over coffee ordered from room service. His manner of speaking was direct, clear, forceful, and engaging. There was little small talk and, likewise, no monologues. Around seventy, although with surprisingly few gray hairs, he must have told the stories of his life and his encounters with apartheid many times before, but he remained cheerful throughout the conversation, even when the subject was his own sufferings.

The education of Beyers Naude has an ending not dictated by the early curriculum. His father, Joshua Naude, served with distinction on the Afrikaner side in the Boer War. He was a chaplain and close adviser to many of the Boer generals and, afterwards, at the Vereeniging Peace Conference, voted with the minority to continue the war against Britain rather than submit to its terms. In the 1920s, while serving as a minister in the Dutch Reformed Church, he became an early member of the Broederbond, the Afrikaner secret society that grew notorious for serving as an underground for the extreme Nationalists who after 1948 ran the government.

Beyers followed his father into the Dutch Reformed Church. Also, for twenty years, until 1963, he was a member of the Broederbond. The split came when he was unable to find justification for apartheid in the Bible. He resigned from the Broederbond and made public his reasons, an act that infuriated the membership. When he accepted the directorship of the Christian Institute, he was defrocked by the Dutch Reformed Church. Since then, however, he has continued to speak out against the white, minority government, but at great cost. In 1972, for example, after a sermon in Cape Town, the church where he had spoken burned to the ground. In 1977, by a peculiar South African practice, he was banned.

Ancient Greece had ostracism and modern Russia has retained the sentence of exile, but neither is a precise precedent for banning orders. In Naude's case, the minister of justice informed him by a hand-delivered letter that, henceforward, he would comply with the conditions or face charges whose penalty might be death. No trial or hearing preceded the banning; nor was explicit reason ever given for its issuance. Nevertheless, from that point, Naude wasn't allowed to address any public meetings. In fact, he could meet only with one person at a time, meaning his wife would have to leave the room when a friend dropped by to see him. He was restricted to an area around Johannesburg, although he pointed out that had he chosen he could have fled the country. The media were prohibited from quoting him in their dispatches.

In our conversation, he made the distinction between the current situation in South Africa and segregation as it existed in the American South. "There," he said, "you had recourse to the law and the courts. Here parliament runs everything and, as it chooses, can pass an act to stifle any change."

In South Africa's case, parliament has enacted a series of laws that, were they not the cornerstones of apartheid, might be thought to have been plagiarized from George Orwell's *1984*. Naude went through some of the stipulations: the Liquor Act prevents whites and blacks from drinking together; the Publications Act gives the government a free hand at censorship; the Reservation of Separate Amenities is the essence of petty apartheid; the Prohibition of Political Interference Act outlaws multiracial parties; the Group Areas Act keeps blacks from living in white neighborhoods; the Black Urban Areas Consolidation Act regulates the flow of labor into the cities.

Because so many peaceful avenues of change are barricaded, Naude fears that violence will precede any structural changes in South Africa. He abhors the prospect, and said so sincerely more than once, but doesn't see how it can be avoided when normal political dissent—as practiced throughout the Western world—can be classified as traitorous under the broad definitions of the Internal Security Act.

"I don't know when it will come or how," he said on leaving, referring to a general upheaval, "but when it does, first the blacks will suffer. Then it will be the whites."

Like many others, I first wanted to visit South Africa after reading the books of Alan Paton, who is best known for his novel, *Cry, the Beloved Country*. Published in 1948, the book remains a current reference on the country's racial dilemma. But in reading that and other books, I found South Africa difficult to visualize. *Cry, the Beloved Country* begins: "There is a lovely road that runs from Ixopo into the hills. These hills are grass-covered and rolling, and they are lovely beyond any singing of it." But it was still hard to imagine them. I wanted to fix images to the words.

I also wanted to meet Alan Paton. From a book jacket I

learned that he lived in Hillcrest, Natal, which on the rail line is between Kloof and Botha's Hill. Ixopo is not far away. I addressed a letter of introduction to "Alan Paton, Hillcrest, Natal, South Africa," and several weeks later a reply came from his wife, encouraging me to visit.

The Natalian hills above Durban are reminiscent of a plush London suburb: parts of Surrey and Sussex came to mind. But the view from the hilltops isn't hedgerows but the sweep of the Indian Ocean. The Patons' house, down a quiet lane, might also be found in Larchmont or Oyster Bay— except for the gardens. Along the driveway, beside the house, and on the terraced back lawn were trees, shrubs, and flowers that made it clear that this was the tropical tip of Africa.

Although he has published ten books, many of them best-sellers, it is not as a writer that Paton has spent his life. Born in 1903 in Pietermaritzburg, forty-five minutes north of Hillcrest, he became a school teacher after being educated at the University of Natal and a teachers' college. For thirteen years he was the principal of a reformatory for black boys at Diepkloof outside Johannesburg, which is now part of Soweto. In 1953, he founded the Liberal party, the country's first multiracial party that attempted to wrest the parliamentary majority from the Afrikaner Nationalists. Only since the party was outlawed in 1968 has he had uninterrupted time to write.

His eyes are what you notice first. They have a searing quality, in the sense of Scottish righteousness, but also a twinkle of benevolence. His hair is white, and with age his shoulders have rounded. Sometimes he doesn't answer a question immediately, but instead stares off pensively, his hand cupped under his chin. Then he will turn square and face you, very much the school principal addressing a pupil.

We talked in his studio, whose double doors open to the view of the Indian Ocean. It is not surprising that he began his most recent novel, *Ah, But Your Land Is Beautiful*, with a description of a related vista: "At night it can draw gasps of wonder, for you can see spread out below you the lights of the city of Durban. . . ." In the same book, which is partly autobiographical and in many respects my choice among his novels, he asks the question: "Can white hopes and black hopes be realized together, in this southern land to which both white and black have given their devotion?" Over tea, he offered some answers.

He began by saying that for as long as he could remember visitors have come to South Africa, seen the despair of places like Soweto or Crossroads near Cape Town, and predicted that "things can't last" more than a year or two. But in Paton's lifetime, which is also that of South Africa as a nation, apartheid has only grown more entrenched. He noted that the pass laws, which require blacks to carry identification at all times or face arrest and a fine, date to the last century. The land was segregated before 1948, but since then, especially with the development of the homelands, the demarcation has grown sharper.

Unlike many Americans who assume that time will begin to heal most political differences, he will not say that he is hopeful about the country's future. Instead he chooses the awkward construction that he is "not hopeless" that peaceful change will come. But to those who only see gloom in the world, he points out, somewhat elliptically, that "the miracle of my lifetime is what happened in Germany," by which he means the defeat of the Nazis and the coming of peace to the European continent. Clearly he struggles between the desire for change to come and the reality of the strength of the ruling party.

Like Beyers Naude, he is not without scars for his outspokenness. Because of the international fame that accompanied the authorship of *Cry, the Beloved Country*, he said he was probably spared being banned or imprisoned. For many years after he founded the Liberal party, four security policemen followed him everywhere. *Ah, But Your Land Is Beautiful* has this passage: " . . . And then the Security Police. You know my aunts and uncle are very respectable, and they didn't like the police attending my cousin's funeral. When I say they attended it I mean they parked a little way off, and got out of the car and leaned against it, watching. You know how they are taught to look at people with that merciless stare that frightens the wits out of the more timid ones." In conversation, he told a similar story from his own experience with the police.

Before the visit ended, he recounted a trip he made in 1954 on commission for *Collier's* magazine to write about the United States on the threshold of desegregation. That was the year of the *Brown v. Board of Education* decision by the Supreme Court. On the journey, which lasted several months, he saw white privates in the army saluting black officers and other irreversible signs that never again would the United States embrace policies like those Paton deplored in his own country. On a trip to New Orleans in 1981, Paton saw again a man that he had interviewed on that earlier assignment. He remembered the man as an extreme racist, and when they met at a dinner, Paton asked him how he had adjusted to integration."

"Oh, I still have my prejudices," the man said, "but thank God my children don't have them." Looking right at you, Paton recites these lines as an exemplary tale, so as to leave no doubt that he hopes the same dialogue might someday be repeated in South Africa.

It had been my hope to meet Bishop Desmond Tutu while in South Africa. Despite his accomplishments as the General Secretary of the South African Council of Churches, I knew little of his day-to-day work. A mutual friend agreed to arrange an introduction. But just as I left for South Africa, he arrived in New York for a semester's residence at Union Theological Seminary. While there, he learned that he had been awarded the Nobel Prize for Peace. Our meeting was thus lost in the commotion.

I never did get the opportunity to speak directly with Bishop Tutu. The Nobel Prize transformed him into a media darling and placed on his doorstep a standing corps of journalists. At various functions around New York, however, I was able to hear him speak. Each time was a pleasure.

Nobody will ever describe Desmond Tutu as Lincolnesque, even if his effect is to transform South African society as Lincoln did ours. Rather than being tall and brooding, he is short and ebullient, perhaps the most cheerful man ever to take on so somber a task. At 53, his gait remains spry—it reminds me of a sandpiper's—and even on the subject of apartheid there is a springtime melody in his speech. His favorite weapons are humor and an observant eye. He fondly recalls a sign he once saw in a homeland: "Drive carefully. Natives cross here," which he would amend to: "Drive carefully. Natives very cross here."

After hearing him speak on several occasions, I came to the conclusion that he won the Nobel Prize because of his ability to describe apartheid in the plain, sparse language that recalls some vivid chapters of the Bible. His work for peace is to try to convince his countrymen that unless peaceful change comes soon, general violence will.

South African blacks, in his words, are the "little people—the unsung heroes who have their noses rubbed in the dust every day." He has an Orwellian ear for the language of the system that believes in "foreign natives" and that passes laws to invent homelands. On the tests conducted to determine race, he explains: "They put a pin in you, and your expression is supposed to tell them which race you are. One child is classified as white and another 'of color' when both are of the same family. It is like Hitler's Aryan madness." But, then, in what I would describe as his stump sermon, his eyes will twinkle as he tells of an early encounter between whites and blacks: "We had the land and they had the Bible. When they said, 'Let us pray,' we closed our eyes. When we opened them again, they had the land and we had the Bible." He frequently ends by saying that "we will remember later those who helped us now," but his tone is never threatening, except to pretense.

When he says that apartheid is "an evil system, a system as evil as Communism," he makes a point that occurred to me frequently while traveling in South Africa: that is, its similarities to the Soviet Union and its political system. One reason that the Reagan Administration advocates its policy of "constructive engagement" is to bolster a government perceived to be a bulwark against Soviet penetration in southern Africa. Defense of strategic minerals and vulnerable passages off the Cape of Good Hope is another reason why Americans are often ambivalent toward taking a strong position against the South African government. But everything the Reagan Administration deplores in Soviet politics—the denial of the rights to think, travel, and work freely—I encountered over and over again in South Africa. The justifications for the homelands reminded me of the agitprop I heard repeatedly on a trip to the Soviet-occupied Baltic states. The wire around townships like Soweto looks like what you pass through on the way from Vienna to Prague. Tutu's genius has elements of Solzhenitsyn's.

It is easy to hear men like Naude, Paton, and Tutu and believe that there are solutions to the problems in South Africa that exclude violence, or at least might keep it to a minimum. But such hopes leave aside the historical interests and fears of the Afrikaners, whose decision it will be to make war or peace.

Before leaving South Africa, I visited Blood River, which

is as indicative of the country, in one sense, as is Soweto. In the development of Afrikaner nationalism, no event was more pivotal, save perhaps the Great Trek, than the 1838 battle against Zulu tribesmen on the banks of a river that evokes a past like that at Antietam Creek.

I drove the last fifteen miles to the Blood River battle site on dirt roads through a vast landscape whose hills were only a silhouette at dusk. I expected the battlefield to be the South African equivalent of Bull Run or Yorktown, with the attending visitors' centers and concession stands. But only a small sign, difficult to read in the twilight, indicated the way to a small museum and the more striking, life-sized replica of the laager that fought here on the night of December 16.

Led by Andries Pretorius, fewer than one thousand Afrikaners killed three thousand Zulus in about six hours of close-quarter combat. The victory secured the Afrikaners land for farming and settlement that was up-country from British rule. The anniversary of the battle is celebrated as a national holiday—the Day of the Covenant—that is much like our Thanksgiving, although the feted imagery isn't cooperation with local Indians but the rout of a black nation.

In his study of the Afrikaners, *The White Tribe of Africa*, David Harrison writes: "Blood River still matters, of course, because it offers the perfect symbol for the Afrikaner Nationalist view of South Africa today—a gallant, God-fearing country surrounded by the forces of evil. It is the theme of countless politicians' speeches every 16 December: 'South Africa is on the brink of another Blood River. . . .' "

I lingered at Blood River until after dark, when the only light came from the stars. Under such a sky it is easy to make the connection between the Afrikaners and those Americans who settled the West. Around eight o'clock headlights appeared on the dirt road leading to the battlefield's entrance. The car approached mine, and its front window was rolled down. I expected the driver to be a security guard and asked: "Do you speak English?" The answer, in gruff self-assurance, was: "Speak any damn language you please."

In the car, it turned out, was a middle-aged Afrikaner and his wife. They had driven out to camp on the banks of Blood River—in reenactment and homage to those who did the same 147 years ago, before the fateful encounter. Such an evening under the stars amounted to a reaffirmation of the faith. When the man's interior car light came on and lit up his face, I saw in profile a portrait whose determination matched those cast in bronze inside the museum. His streaked, gray hair looped around his ears, as you might find on a New England farmer unconcerned about his appearance, and there was sharpness to his stare that indicated he could withstand a great deal of suffering, should it be necessary. Looking at his callused hands as they gripped the steering wheel, I couldn't help but think that when the fight starts in earnest, men such as this will defend the lines.

One leaves South Africa with a sense of relief. As the Pan American jet lifted into the night sky over Johannesburg, I was finally freed from the tension of a society divided along racial lines. Signs like those in Durban, "This bathing area is reserved for the sole use of the white race group," are a constant reminder of the ideology that would post such a notice. It is also easier, once airborne, not to be reminded of the similarities between South Africa's racial history and that of our own country.

At the first Lincoln-Douglas debate in 1858, Abraham Lincoln said: "I have no purpose to introduce political and social equality between the white and black races." Nevertheless, he continued: "I have never said anything to the contrary, but I hold that notwithstanding all this, there is no reason in the world why the negro is not entitled to all the natural rights enumerated in the Declaration of Independence, the right to life, liberty, and the pursuit of happiness." But it took one of the world's deadliest wars for Lincoln to have his way.

Traveling
the Afghan Archipelago

(1984)

Pakistan's capital, Islamabad, is a patch of tranquillity on the Asian mainland. Twelve miles from Rawalpindi, the fading British way station between Kabul and Delhi, it appears at the end of a four-lane parkway, rather the way Washington, D.C., surfaces on the ride in from Dulles International Airport. Islamabad is a new city in the fashion of Brasilia and Canberra, capitals that have sprung fully formed from an architect's drafting table. Before, it was a town, at best, surrounded by cool mountains and an expansive prairie. Now it is Islam's first suburb, a grid of neatly laid-out bureaucracies and vacant lots reminiscent of an industrial park near Houston. So few people actually live there that one can't help wondering if, when the American embassy was sacked in 1979, the demonstrators were bused in for the performance.

Wanting to find out more about the refugees from the war in Afghanistan, I arrived in Islamabad shortly before midnight on a cool evening late last summer. The train from Lahore goes only as far as Rawalpindi; a taxi brought me the rest of the way. The choice of hotels—between the

Islamabad Hotel and the Holiday Inn—seemed a tidy symbol of modern-day Pakistan's dichotomies. I chose the Islamabad, as it was nearer the ministry of public affairs, and the following day went next door to a small cluster of shops where, over a drugstore, I found the department that handles press credentials for anyone wanting to visit the refugees.

The office was a replica of so many on the subcontinent. Officials in traditional Pakistani cotton suits sat behind tired wooden desks. Paper the consistency of newsprint was stacked everywhere. Only the strategic use of paperweights kept it from scattering in the jet stream created by the ceiling fans. True to form, I was greeted warmly and served lukewarm tea with milk. After an hour of polite conversation—interrupted by numerous phone calls and document signings—it was arranged for me to visit some of the refugee camps in Peshawar, the provincial capital of the Northwest Frontier Province.

First, however, I was scheduled to meet General Said Azhar, the high commissioner for Afghani refugees, whose office in Islamabad is literally on the edge of town. General Azhar, a sturdy man in his late fifties, welcomed me in what had been the living room in a ranch-style house. On the walls, in military fashion, were a number of maps, all seemingly charting Pakistan's proximity to danger. Several showed the region: Iran and Afghanistan to the west; the Soviet Union and China to the north; India to the east. Another showed the archipelago of the nearly 350 refugee camps along the border with Afghanistan, yet another volcanic chain of islands forced to the surface by Soviet cruelty.

The general summarized the refugee situation for me. In 1973, after Sardar Daoud overthrew the monarchy of Mohammad Zahir Shah, a few hundred opponents of the new Afghan regime trickled across the border into Pakistan.

But the flow was insignificant until April 1978, when Muhammad Taraki staged a successful coup. The Daoud family was eliminated, and in the general upheaval more than 100,000 refugees fled Afghanistan. That September Taraki himself was swept away in yet another coup and replaced by his prime minister, Hafizullah Amin. Again the refugees took to the mountainous trails that lead into Pakistan. At the same time violent opposition to the Moscow-supported Amin threatened to topple his frail government. It was at this point, in December 1979, that the Soviet Union intervened, anxious to protect a potential client and buffer state. In the turmoil, Amin died mysteriously, and Babrak Karmal, then Afghanistan's ambassador to Czechoslovakia, was brought in to run a puppet government. The resistance now began in earnest; so did the flight of the Afghans.

Since the Russian invasion, more than three million Afghans have actually registered in Pakistan as refugees. Who knows how many more have crossed the border and ignored the bureaucracy? Many Afghans are nomadic by tradition and persist in their habit of migrating in summer from the mountains to the valleys and back again in winter, despite the fighting. Now, however, Pakistan is a long stop on these wanderings, a safe harbor from the war. In the spring of 1980 the number of refugee immigrants reached a high point of 130,000 a month. At the beginning, General Ahzar's agencies and colleagues provided emergency shelter, food, and clothing. Tents were supplied wherever the Afghans camped, producing the network of tent villages that is now, more or less, a permanent home for these uprooted Afghans. The state within a state stretches from the red deserts of Baluchistan in the south to an area in the mountains near the ancient kingdom of Swat.

In 1983 the cost of maintaining the refugees came to $441 million, or about $12 for each refugee. Pakistan paid just under half of this, no mere gesture for a country as poor as any in the Third World. The United States committed itself to donating $8 million, 170,000 blankets, used clothing, and 240 International Harvester trucks. Other nations gave tea, medical supplies, food, tents, and other relief supplies. But considering that the Afghan dislocation constitutes the greatest population dispersal in the world since 1947, such assistance barely meets the needs of most refugees. When each Afghan registers as a refugee in Pakistan, he is entitled to cash, food, and other assistance totaling 150 rupees a month—not much, with the Pakistan rupee worth about nine American cents. Worse, for all concerned, is that the longer the war continues, the more the status of the refugees appears to be permanent.

Said Azhar has visited all the 350 or so encampments under his jurisdiction. He made arrangements for me to see several near Peshawar the following day and then dropped me off at my hotel on his way home. On the way, we passed the ribbed-iron and marble skeleton of the unfinished parliament. If Islamabad is a model city, this will be the model capitol; and if function follows form, Pakistan will soon resemble Gladstone's England.

The next day began in the rain. I met my driver, Omar, in the hotel lobby at 6:00 A.M., and we set off through a cloudburst for Peshawar, seventy-five miles to the west. The road was mostly two lanes, with an occasional aspiration to expressway status. The trucks and buses on the highway looked like advertisements for Islam. Each was decorated with colorful stencils and chrome embroidery, giving their front ends the silhouette of a mosque. Some of the stenciling showed landscapes. One, I noticed, was the vivid detail of an armored vehicle shooting down a Russian plane. Others had portraits of departed war heroes. It made the journey to the frontier a festive occasion.

At first impression, Peshawar seems to have been built for the purpose of buying and selling guns. Signs advertising "Guns" and "Ammo" are everywhere, making the place look like one's idea of Cheyenne during the era of the six-shooter. But this is indeed a frontier city—be it that of internal Pakistani squabbling or the Cold War.

Peshawar's importance lies in its location. Kabul, the capital of Afghanistan, is through the Khyber Pass to the west, and, until the war started, a narrow-gauge train took passengers as far as the mountain town of Landi Kotal near the border. Peshawar is also the strategic intersection between Islamabad and the sometimes rebellious province of Baluchistan. And from Peshawar one can take the only road north to Chitral, the northwest corner of Pakistan, close not only to Afghanistan but also to the Soviet Union, China, and India. Little wonder that the military government in Islamabad has kept its defense establishment in Peshawar. In any conflict larger than the present one in Afghanistan, it would take on the significance of El Alamein.

While I was there, I heard someone refer to Peshawar as "a page from *Homage to Catalonia*," an allusion to the factionally divided Barcelona that George Orwell described in his memoir of the Spanish Civil War. Peshawar is indeed headquarters for the principal factions of the resistance in Afghanistan, though in the beginning, despite their common cause, these groups barely spoke. Now they have coalesced into two tenuous wartime alliances, "the group of seven" and "the group of three." Still, the struggle among the groups is almost as fanatical as the struggle with the Soviets.

Long before it became the shadow capital of free Afghanistan, Peshawar was notorious for sheltering undergrounds. In the days of the British empire it was a favorite of intelligence agents slipping in and out of Afghanistan, which the empire never managed to subdue in the course of three wars. And though the names of the clandestine rivals have changed, the city still feels one part Kipling and one part Le Carré. The Soviet mission in Peshawar has lately taken to verifying Russian casualties in Afghanistan by buying back the dog tags that have been stripped from killed Russian soldiers and returned to the city as booty.

Nevertheless, the principal commodity traded between Russian intelligence and the divided Afghans is disinformation. It is in the Soviets' interests to keep the resistance divided—fratricidal, if possible. And it's easy to feed the bad blood with rumors and an occasional killing. Nor could there be a better cover for both sides than a city of bazaars and narrow, cobbled streets through which intrigue passes as quietly as small boys with bare feet.

At Dabgri Building, yet another dim municipal office with paper-strewn desks and languid ceiling fans, I met Mr. Affridi, the local press attaché. He was about forty and, although not in uniform, looked like a major on assignment. He introduced Mr. Nawaz, who was to accompany me to the camps, and then talked about the negotiations on Afghanistan in Geneva.

"You know," he said, "there is a proverb that says the Russians never withdraw."

A number of proposals have been put forward in Geneva to end the fighting in Afghanistan. One suggestion even has the exiled king returning to Afghanistan from Rome. But what prevents any kind of settlement being reached is that neither the resistance nor the Soviet Union has any incentive to end the fighting. The Afghans may be fragmented, but they are at least agreed on fighting until the Russians leave—even if that isn't for another hundred years. The way the Russians see it, withdrawal would result in the overthrow of Babrak Karmal's government and perhaps the establishment of a fundamentalist Islamic regime hostile to Moscow. As Mr. Affridi remarked, "The only thing that would change their mind on this would be heavy losses, heavier than those they are now suffering." But casualties on both sides are difficult to estimate. The resistance is reported to have suffered 100,000 casualties. The Soviets may have lost 10,000 to 15,000 men killed, but neither side is especially concerned with body counts; nor, I might add, with taking prisoners.

Before I could actually visit the camps, I needed yet another signature on my papers—this one from the district commissioner for Afghan refugees. The otherwise nonde-script two-story building that housed his office was distin-guished by a milling crowd of Afghan men near the front door and in the lobby. They wore pajama-like cotton suits and full beards and were remarkable for the intensity of their expressions, with eyes that seemed eternally fixed on distant enemy encampments. These were *mujahidin*, or holy warriors, on leave from the fighting, and they appeared uncomfortable away from the front lines, without their guns.

Waiting in the district commissioner's office, I leafed through the *Jihad Days*, an English-language magazine of the resistance produced on faded newsprint. It contained profiles of soldiers killed fighting the Russians. One, Dr. Man Nasrat, was described as having "girded up his loins as soon as the Red coup of communists gained victory." In a desperate last stand, according to the magazine, he killed thirty-five Russians before "the soul of this heroic man and of this bril-liant beacon went loft high to the creator of the world." There was another article entitled "A Liberation Gained Through Muskets and Axes," a fairly accurate summary of both the weaponry of the resistance and its determination.

Nasir Bagh, which means "green garden," is the first piece of flatland down from the hills of the Khyber Pass. The encampment's eastern boundary is an irrigation canal, edged by graceful hanging trees—no doubt the first water found by refugees filing out of the mountains; the rest of the settlement spreads out over an arid, almost lunar landscape whose hard-packed sandy soil is divided by culverts from the storms that sweep the plain. The drab olive-green military tents recall the fate of refugees all over the world, except that this lot seems even more tenuous than most.

It is misleading to call the "refugee tent villages"—their bureaucratic description—camps. No barbed wire or guards surround the Afghans, who are free to come and go as they please. It's easier to think of them as entire villages that have migrated across the border. Tribal discipline and rituals have remained intact.

Mr. Nawaz and I were greeted by an elderly Afghan. He was over six feet tall, with a stringy white beard and the long, precise gait of someone who has spent a lifetime climbing through mountain passes. Now he is a village elder, looking after the women and children while the men are away fighting the Russians.

Walking through the encampment was like touring an adobe village in the American southwest. As a supplement to the original emergency-supply tents, which keep one neither warm in winter nor cool in summer, the Afghans have put up their traditional houses from blocks of dried mud.

Children followed us everywhere. First they would peek from behind a mud wall; then, with urging from our guide, join the tour. Not one begged for food or money, even though it was clear they could use both. All posed solemnly for the camera whenever asked.

Amid the monotony of mundane routine—school for the children, hauling water for the women—life in the refugee villages is reduced to a never-ending series of expectations:

waiting for the Russians to leave; waiting for the men to return from the fighting; waiting for the supplies of food to arrive.

As I left Nasir Bagh along the absurdly stately irrigation road, the villages seemed transplants not just from Afghanistan, but from the Middle Ages. Only the few jeeps of the relief agencies interfered with a landscape that would have been familiar to anyone living five hundred years ago. Since then foreign invaders have come and gone with the regularity of supernatural tides, but the Afghans have always held on, somehow.

That afternoon, I found Louis Dupree, the author of several books about Afghanistan, and his wife eating lunch and packing for departure to the U.S. in their room at Dean's Hotel.

Dupree is a short, vigorous man in his late fifties. During the Second World War he jumped into the Philippines with an American airborne division. He got a doctorate at Harvard and has taught and lived in Afghanistan whenever possible ever since. Just before the last coup and the Russian invasion, he was jailed for a week in Kabul as an "undesirable" and then deported. He is now in Pakistan working on a book about the Afghan refugees. Needless to say, Dupree is no supporter of the Karmal government; nor, for that matter, of U.S. indifference to the Afghan cause.

He described the fighting in Afghanistan as a cross between the Spanish Civil War and the resistance against the Nazis in Yugoslavia. "The one difference here," he said, "is that the Western world hasn't been drawn to the cause of the Afghans as it was to the Republicans in Spain. The tactics the Russians are using are worse than anything used by Franco, only nobody seems to care."

One problem is how to supply guns to a badly divided resistance, whose armies tend to be tribal and rarely larger than 4,000 men. In any event, of the estimated 100,000 *mujahidin*, only about 30,000 have rifles. For the rest, it's the way *Jihad Days* described it: a holy war fought with muskets and axes.

Russian broadcasts would have it believed that the West, especially the United States, is funneling substantial arms to the resistance. But Jere Van Dyk, the author of *In Afghanistan: An American Odyssey*, described the military assistance as "rifles and sleeping bags." Before he was assassinated, President Anwar Sadat said that the United States was purchasing some of Egypt's surplus of Russian arms for shipment to the Afghans. Yet the reluctance of the West is in supplying the *mujahidin* with the weaponry—notably heat-seeking "Red-eye" missiles—that will knock out Soviet helicopters. The problem, Louis Dupree said with exasperation, is one of accountability. "No one wants to be responsible for aiding the Afghans and killing Russians, however indirectly. It's fine to go all out in Latin America. But the Russian army is here. And the Afghans feel bitter. They think, and rightly so, that they are fighting the West's fight against communism and the Soviets. But then they don't see any help."

Those neighboring countries that also live in the Soviet Union's shadow are no less afraid of antagonizing the Russians. Pakistan has been careful not to appear as a participant in the struggle. Aiding the refugees is all very well, but the regime of President Zia ul-Haq fears that the war would spread if Pakistan openly supported the Afghan cause. China is reluctant to help the resistance for the same reason.

"What I would like to see," Dupree told me, "is the U.S. and other Western governments guaranteeing the territorial integrity of Pakistan. Not the regime, but the country. Since the end of World War II, we've been backing regimes, not countries. This would be different. Announce that you will defend Pakistan. That would free up a lot of aid for the re-sistance. Tell them that a Russian footprint in Pakistan is the same as a Russian footprint in Washington, D.C. We should be one of the policemen of the world; not the only policeman. That's when we get into trouble."

So far, however, the extent of the American commitment to the Afghans has been to use their suffering to score moral-istic points against the Soviets. President Carter canceled American participation in the Moscow Olympic games after the Russian invasion, but didn't do much else. This summer both Secretary of State Shultz and Defense Secretary Weinberger—on separate occasions—flew by helicopter to the Khyber Pass to address the *mujahidin*. Secretary Shultz told them: "Fellow fighters of freedom, we are with you." Secretary Weinberger said: "I want you to know that you are not alone." Each then flew off to other appointments, leaving the Afghans still facing the Soviets with their muskets and axes.

There is yet another reaction to the resistance in Afghan-istan, one that sees it as "a self-sustaining revolt," which means: As long as the Afghans, with nineteenth-century guns and a few bombs, can keep bleeding the Soviet army white in mountainous combat, why should the West do anything to disturb things? Louis Dupree stands in the doorway to his room at Dean's and says, rapidly: "I find that notion obscene."

Late that afternoon, before leaving Peshawar, I went to a house on the outskirts, hoping to find Abdul Haq, one of the leaders in the resistance. The guards near the front door of the two-story house said he was in, and the one with a machine gun slung across his chest showed me to a small office toward the back. Inside was a couch, a few chairs, and an empty desk. A few minutes later in came Abdul Haq, a bearded man in his late twenties. He looked remarkably like

Fidel Castro but had none of the Cuban's stridency. Haq spoke English effortlessly and said he had been in Peshawar for two weeks. He was here to visit his wife and family. Soon he would be going back to the fighting where he commanded four thousand men in the Kabul region. In the war's most crucial theater, he led possibly the largest single body of Afghan troops.

He grew up in Nangarhar, a province along the border with Pakistan. His father worked as a civil servant; his mother raised the family of eight children. One of the influences in his upbringing was clearly the code of *Pushtunwali*, the ethos of a major tribe in eastern and southern Afghanistan, which serves as a guide for all Afghans. According to *The Struggle for Afghanistan*, an excellent book about the war by Richard and Nancy Newell: "It is simple but demanding. Group survival is its primary imperative. It demands vengeance against injury or insult to one's kin, chivalry and hospitality toward the helpless and unarmed strangers, bravery in battle, and openness and integrity in individual behavior." In accordance with this, the Haq family has divided the responsibility for the struggle. Several brothers are working abroad—in Saudi Arabia and West Germany—to earn money. Several other siblings live in the camps, taking care of the elderly and the children. The rest, led by Abdul, are fighting the Russians.

As a commander in the Kabul sector, he organizes everything from guerrilla raids to major offensives—or at least what can be mounted with the weaponry available.

"In the beginning," he said, "we were using the tactics that had defeated the British in the last century. Now we are learning, changing. We have no teachers. We learn from experience." The warrior-poet is one of the ideals of Afghan society. Louis Dupree told me that a lot of poetry was coming out of Afghanistan these days—much of it dreary—and that, like it or not, many men were happy to be back in the traditional role of fighting an oppressor. Abdul Haq struck me as neither a warrior nor a poet. He was fighting because his country had been overrun. What choice did he have? He spoke of his experience in combat, but expressed none of the awe of the Soviet army currently in vogue in the West. Russian soldiers, he explained, are "very stupid."

He went on to say: "They have two kinds of soldiers. One, the draftees, who don't want to be in Afghanistan. They're scared of everything. Second, the regular army. They have all the latest equipment. Tanks. Helicopters. Everything. But they can't do anything for themselves. We know the land: every stream, every hill. They know nothing. When we attack, they have to wait for orders as to what to do next. But then we are gone." He described how the Russians would march arrogantly into a battle behind all the latest machinery but would be left vulnerable as soon as they were in hand-to-hand fighting.

"Without their officers, the soldiers are lost," he said. "The Russian army is trained to fight against governments. They are trained for tank battles in the desert. But they are no good against the *mujahidin*. This is our home."

Despite such brave words, the war remains a stand-off. The Russians control the cities and the major supply routes. Nearly half their troops are in or near Kabul, maintaining the Karmal government that is reportedly despised by a majority of the Afghans. In Kabul and Herat and Kandahar, the principal Afghan cities, there are few men between the ages of eighteen and forty-five to be seen on the streets. The Soviets have taken to door-to-door sweeps to bolster "enlistments" for the Afghan army, which averages about thirty thousand men. The Russians might just as well be recruiting for the *mujahidin*, since there is a steady underground flow of troops out of the Afghan army to the resistance. The defectors take with them guns and ammunition, and as a consequence the Russian army is the greatest source of weaponry for the Afghan resistance.

With the support of the rural population—or what's left of it—the resistance can move freely through large portions of the country, especially in the mountains. They receive food and shelter from local residents and try to fight the Soviets in isolated guerrilla actions. Abdul Haq likes to say: "We started on the mountaintops. Then we came down the mountain. Now we are in the valleys and the towns. Next we want Kabul."

The Soviet response has been to concentrate large amounts of firepower against villagers and encampments. Helicopters, unchallenged by ground-to-air missiles, can move Russian troops anywhere for a surprise, concentrated attack, often backed up by artillery and air support. The idea is to discourage the villagers from aiding the *mujahidin*, but the effect has only been to lengthen the historical roster of massacres.

For the Afghans the decisive battle of the war is Kabul, but the action there remains fragmented, if brutal. Abdul Haq said that office workers in the Russian-occupied capital often join the resistance on their nightly raids. But these actions are far from the divisional-size attacks that would dislodge the Russians. And as long as the Soviet government is willing to tolerate high casualties, the war will continue as a vicious stalemate.

If you ask Abdul Haq why the Soviets decided to invade his country, his answer contains none of the qualification that a similar question might prompt at a symposium in the West.

"They took Afghanistan to drive a wedge into the sub-continent. Look at a map," he says, with a trace of irritation. The map, in fact, shows Afghanistan at the crossroads of Asia, midway between India and the Middle East. Control of the country puts the Soviet Union within striking range of the

Iranian oil fields and Baluchistan, which might like to be rid
of both Pakistan and Iran. Afghanistan is also rich in minerals, which the Soviets are already exploiting. Their invasion,
which has tapped deposits of iron, chrome, copper, and possibly uranium, can produce a balance of trade surplus—mineral
profits less military costs—even if things stay exactly the way
they are now.

To Abdul Haq, the war is simply a matter of geopolitics,
but one of surprisingly little interest to the Western allies.
Because of his flawless English, Haq is occasionally pulled
from the front lines and sent to Paris or Washington to state
the Afghan cause. Last year, on a trip to the United States, a
cousin actually took him to Disney World. There can hardly
be a greater metaphor for the gap between the resistance and
the West than the image of a commander from the Kabul
region taking a trip around the Magic Kingdom.

In the West, he notes, there has been some outrage at the
Soviet use of poison gas against the Afghans. But the greater
problem for the villagers, he says, is the cluster bombs that the
Russians scatter about. These small, black fragmented objects
look to the children almost like candy or little toys, and more
than one child has paid with a limb or a life for his curiosity.

As we talked, the room slowly filled up with *mujahidin*
until they were crowding the door. They were there to listen
to and watch their leader. Who knew—maybe this would be
the conversation that would secure substantial Western aid?
Abdul Haq finished by talking about supplies for the refugees.
Air conditioners, destined for the Afghan hospitals, were
winding up in the houses of relief workers, he said. His tone
was that of a man with many burdens and none of the breaks.
We walked outside, and each Afghan came forward to shake
my hand. It took some time. Each looked me directly in the
eye; their firm expressions were those of the old men at the
tent village. Abdul Haq walked me to the car. He said he was
sorry that we could not talk further. Perhaps someday we

would meet again? I wished him well and said good-bye. And every time I read of Afghan casualties in the newspaper, I think of the eyes that watched my car move down the narrow lane and turn onto the highway.

The Night Train
to Prague

(1986)

Without straining the marriage, I convinced my wife that we
ought to make a bicycle trip in Poland. What won the case
was not my arguments about Poland being flat, and thus ideal
for bicycles, or my descriptions of Cracow as the Florence of
Eastern Europe. I only prevailed because of a promise to end
the trip in Prague, the Czech capital, which I knew she longed
to see. I sweetened the deal by promising that we would take
a sleeper from Poland to Prague. It didn't matter that
European trains are slowly going the way of Amtrak; in her
mind they still convey the romance of the Orient Express. As
it turned out, Graham Greene, with a rewrite by Franz Kafka,
could have narrated the tale of our train ride.

Our bicycle riding ended in Cracow. Not even a flat tire
marred the previous eight days, which took us through
Warsaw, parts of the Lake District, and Gdansk, the Baltic
coast city. Cracow lived up to my predictions of Renaissance
charm, and, as we spent several days trying to steer the bikes
clear of cobblestones, our thoughts turned to Prague and how
we would get there.

Before leaving New York, I had unsuccessfully tried to

buy rail tickets from Cracow to Prague. "Get them in Poland," was what I was told by several travel agencies and the Polish tourist office. In Warsaw, the lines were such at the railroad station that I decided to wait until Cracow before getting serious about the tickets. In my mind, I could not imagine that many people would be traveling first class on a Sunday night to Prague.

All travel arrangements in Poland are made through the state tourist agency, Orbis, which had an office off the Main Market Square. To buy a ticket for Sunday, we arrived first thing Friday morning, having heard from everyone, and seen for ourselves, that Poles wait in line with the same devotion that Americans clog freeways.

Even though we were early, we still had several hours of waiting, enough to get a small taste of what the British might call the life of the queue. The cramped ticket office was full of strangers, yet everyone acted as though they knew their neighbors in line. Once a position was established, anyone was free to leave for other errands or, as we started to suspect, other lines. Every so often a head would poke through the door to check on progress. But since the tickets were issued manually, and phone calls had to be made to verify seat assignments, there was little chance of someone losing his place because of efficiency.

Not wanting there to be any misunderstanding, we brought along a phrase book. We even had the woman behind us in line write a sentence in Polish explaining that we wanted two first-class, sleeping-car tickets to Prague and that we were traveling with bicycles. When our turn finally arrived and I stumbled through, "Prosze dwa bilety—pierwsza czy—do Pragi," the clerk answered in garbled English that the train was full. But after a few phone calls, presumably to the station, she said that she could sell us open tickets and that we could get sleeping accommodations on board from the conductor. I was doubtful about such a possibility, but we had little choice. Our visas expired Sunday night, and we had a prepaid hotel room in Prague, starting Monday. As for the bicycles, the agent said that we could check them in Katowice, an hour west of Cracow, where we would have to connect with the express from Warsaw to Prague.

These loose arrangements left me unsettled. On more than one occasion I have run up against Eastern European border protocols and found myself having to produce passport-size photographs to avoid being thrown off a train. My preference was for us to leave early Sunday morning, take local trains to the border, walk the bicycles into Czechoslovakia during daylight, and then pick up other local trains to Prague. It would mean missing the sleeper, but we would avoid having to cross the border after midnight. My wife dismissed my proposition as alarmist, pointed to our first-class tickets, and then planned a last day of sightseeing in Cracow.

As it turned out, we spent the day in a salt mine outside Cracow, assigned, because we didn't speak Polish, to a Bulgarian tour group. After a farewell-to-Poland dinner at a hotel near the station, we boarded a local train for Katowice to connect with the Silesia, the sleeper to Prague. Our car, half baggage and half coach, quickly filled with day-trippers who had spent Sunday in Cracow. Many of the children fell asleep in the arms of their parents. Most of the men smoked unfiltered cigarettes. Because it was raining, the train windows grew thick with fog. It was easy to imagine many of the passengers, back at work the following day, descending one of the many mines around Katowice.

At the Katowice station shortly after 10:00 P.M., I gamely lined up under a sign that indicated that sleeping-car reservations could be obtained. An hour later, when I had a fleeting moment at the window, I heard again that we could only get berths on the train. As for the bicycles, we could check them in the baggage room underneath the main concourse.

Neither of us was surprised to find the baggage room closed. It meant that not only would we have to get ourselves on the train, but we would have to try to bring along two ten-speeds. The alternative was to spend the night in Katowice and try the same exercise Monday night—there being only one express train a day. Or we could try my local train odyssey in the morning. In the end, we decided to try our luck with the conductor. On previous train trips, we had found Polish conductors friendly and accommodating, and more often than not mildly amused at the sight of two Americans, dressed in bicycle gear, resembling wayward Martians.

When the Silesia arrived at 12:42 A.M., we tried boarding one of the sleeping cars, bikes and all, waving our first-class tickets. The porter would have none of it, so we madly checked the bikes into a baggage car and boarded a second-class coach. Less than twenty seconds later, the train departed.

Walking the length of the train, we petitioned the sleeping-class porters about getting a compartment for the night. A few consulted their manifests; the rest waved us away. Not only could we not find a bed, but all the seats were also taken. Eventually, we settled in the corridor of a second-class coach, standing with perhaps fifteen others who seemed to share our predicament.

It didn't matter at all to the Polish conductor that we lacked a reservation. As we weren't in a seat, what did it matter? But I was still apprehensive. We were approaching the Czech border, notorious in Eastern Europe for its difficult crossings. I had concerns also that the Polish officials might notice that our Polish visas had expired at midnight—it was now approaching 2:00 A.M. At worst, they would remove us from the train for questioning. At the least, we might be asked to change thirty dollars for another day in Poland, which is how much currency two foreigners must change each day they are in the country. And there was the problem of the bicycles, which were checked only to the Polish border, Petrovice. How could I be sure that they would make it into Czechoslovakia?

A border crossing in Eastern Europe creates the impression that the Second World War never ended. Guards with machine guns walk the length of the train, checking for refugees who might be hidden under the carriages. Dour uniformed immigration officials, walking in groups, begin the long process of checking the papers of everyone on board. Always there are those whose travel documents are not in order, and they are led away to the station for questions. Sometimes the lack of a correct passport stamp or visa means a return trip home. At night these rituals are played out in eerie silence.

This evening, however, I was relieved that everything went so smoothly. Nothing was said by Polish immigration about our visas having expired. The Czech border guard, an attractive woman in her forties, could not have been more genial. She even consented to write on my visa that we were traveling with two bicycles.

With Czech arrival stamps in our passports, I left the carriage and ran alongside the train to the baggage car. There I found an empty compartment (save for our two bicycles), the agent, and several Czech customs officials, who were about to remove the bikes from the train. Nothing I said made any impression on the group. But I did remember that the word *bicycle* was on our visas, and I proudly showed it to everyone. After the agent and customs officials conferred among themselves—no doubt they were wondering if all Americans were as crazy as this one—they told me that the bicycles would stay on the train to Prague, where I could claim them in the morning.

Back in our car, I began to feel as if we might make it to

Prague. Now all we needed to do was find seats. For a few stops, long enough to fall into the half-sleep that comes with riding coaches at night, we managed to squeeze into a compartment filled with a group of Poles, whom we nicknamed "the Bad Hats," because it was clear that they were up to no good. Just before the border we had seen a woman burst into their compartment with a package that she obviously wanted hidden. Now, well into the night, they were riding with the lights on, as if running a lookout. But for us, these seats were an improvement over standing in the corridor.

After about an hour, we lost our seats to passengers with reservations and ended up standing at the end of the car in the company of a Japanese student. He had attended a student conference in Athens, had made a number of friends from Eastern Europe, and was on his way to visit one of them in Prague. Actually, his friend would be boarding the train sometime during the night. We exchanged travelers' tales for a while. Then everyone tried to sleep, either by leaning against the wall or in a campsite of arranged luggage.

I dozed for about an hour until awakened by the conductor. She wore a drab, olive green uniform. Her hairdo, permed and colored somewhere between blonde and orange, jutted from the sides of a conductor's cap. She didn't have an expression so much as a permanent scowl. She wanted our tickets, which I produced. But instead of punching them, as the Poles had done, she flew into a rage. Although she spoke a little English and some German, the only word I understood was "No."

From the tone of her voice it was clear that we had a major problem. I tried the universal assuager, but she wasn't interested in American dollars. Occasionally she would take a break from her harangue, punch a few other tickets in the car, and then return to us—and the Japanese student—to continue her invective.

Although I didn't know why, I figured out that she wanted

twenty Czech crowns. She communicated this by tracing her forefinger on the wall. Our answer was that it was illegal to carry Czech money into Czechoslovakia. But she replied that we could have changed money at Petrovice, although I had not noticed a brisk currency business when we arrived at 2:10 A.M.

My father's golden rule of bloc-country travel is always to carry in some local currency, no matter what the regulations say. I had tried to find Czech crowns before leaving New York, but did not succeed. My only recourse now was to change money—another illegal act—with someone on the train. Followed by the Japanese student, I set out through the train, hoping to find someone who might change money. My problem was that I had not a clue as to the worth of the dollar against the crown. Was it like the Polish zloty—200 to $1—or the German mark at 2 to $1?

Although nearly everyone on board was asleep, several cars away I found a group of attractive women in their early twenties, explained to them that I was about to be railroaded by the conductor, said I needed twenty crowns, and offered five dollars. When they didn't immediately respond (I'm sure it was surprise, not a bargaining ploy), I offered eight dollars, at which we did the transaction. Sympathetic to my problem, and clearly enthralled at the exchange rate, they began pulling wads of Czech money from their purses. Did I need more money?

I didn't think I did until I tried to give the conductor the twenty crowns. She scoffed at them, shook her head in the familiar "No," and now said we needed to give her eighty crowns. Unlike most nightmares, this one was beginning to get expensive. From my suitcase I fished out a guidebook, leafed through it frantically, and discovered that in 1985 one dollar fetched twelve crowns. No wonder those women had nearly embraced me.

Back I went to them, this time with my guidebook. I explained that the rate, unfortunately, had dropped. Now I was offering five dollars for sixty crowns, although the thought did occur to me that this was an absurd time for the dollar to appreciate. But the women were still happy to do business, and both the Japanese student and I returned to the conductor with eighty crowns.

My fear with the conductor was that she would have us removed from the train if we didn't comply with her demands—even though I was at a loss to comprehend our offense. My wife noted that she was unable to understand Polish and kept referring to the tickets as second-class. We wondered then if she thought the "1," denoting first class, meant number of passengers traveling and hence thought we were trying to get two persons to travel on one ticket. But at 4:00 A.M., not a lot makes sense.

As the Japanese student and I walked back through the long corridors to find the conductor, I could feel the train slowing down. I knew that if the eighty crowns didn't make her happy there was a good chance she would summon the police at the station. This time when I offered her the money, she again scoffed, tucked our tickets into her leather pouch as if to say, "Too late, smart guy," and disappeared.

We awaited our fate with touches of black humor. My wife, who was resolute throughout the ordeal, remembered my fondness for the expression, "Better to go first class than to arrive." We began using the name of the Polish travel agency, Orbis, as a verb that meant to be forcibly evicted from a train while holding valid tickets. My wife said that it was a good thing the Czechs were encouraging Western tourism. "Can you imagine if they weren't?" she sighed.

Around 4:30 in the morning, the train stopped in Ceska Trebová, about four hours east of Prague. The conductor left the train and returned with several policemen, who also wore olive green uniforms, although these were decorated with braids and ribbons. Although I knew we were doomed, at least as passengers on the Silesia, I told my wife and the Japanese student that we should wait here at the end of the car for the police to find us; it would be silly to give ourselves up for the crime of holding first-class tickets. One of the reasons I didn't want to be "orbissed" was that it would mean losing our bicycles, for which I had not been given a receipt at the border.

The police came aboard, went directly to the compartment of the Bad Hats, and arrested them. One of the Hats was hiding in the WC and had to be tracked down. Then the four Hats were led unceremoniously from the train. Who knows why they were removed, although both my wife and I agreed that they deserved it, for something, even if we were about to join them.

After the Hats had departed, the conductor briefed the police on our crimes, but they didn't get back on the train. Instead, the conductor waved her flashlight at the engineer, and the train pulled out of the station. Although we were happy still to be on board, we knew that our problems were unresolved.

At this moment of relief and perplexity, we were joined by the Czech friend of the Japanese student. He had boarded the train at Ceska Trebová and was now acting as translator. He spoke perfect English.

He explained that our offense was that we did not have seat reservations. Thus began a dialogue that might have been lifted verbatim from one of the novels of Franz Kafka. It didn't matter at all that, with first-class tickets, we had passed the night standing in the corridor of a second-class coach, after having been led to believe that we would find accommodation in a sleeper. We needed seat reservations. Normally they cost twenty crowns (about two dollars), the conductor explained, but on board we had to pay forty crowns each (about $3.50). When she said that it was a simple matter, however, to get reservations on the train, we wondered if perhaps Conductor

Hyde had gotten off the train in Ceska Trebová and we were now speaking with Mrs. Jekyll, the friendly Czech railway employee.

I handed her eighty crowns and asked for our tickets. Unfortunately, the translator explained, they had been given to the police in Ceska Trebová. But we were not to worry. We would have "no problem" from here to Prague. But, I asked, what if another conductor came through the train and found us with reservations but no tickets? There was no answer.

Finally, I asked our nemesis where we would be sitting. We had visions of at least two hours' sleep before Prague. But it was not to be.

"Seats," she replied, "there are none on this train."

South Korean Crossroads

(1985)

It was Korean Air Lines flight number 001, not its doomed sister ship, that took me to Seoul. I boarded at Narita Airport, forty-two miles northeast of Tokyo, and the 721-mile hop across the Sea of Japan was routine, save for a cone's-eye view of Mt. Fujiyama shortly after the 747 lifted off the runway. But as I think back now to those two hours in the air, an image of the airliner's crew haunts me. They were all remarkably young. I think of them occasionally, wondering which crew of such boys and girls had the misfortune to draw duty on flight 007.

Had that plane been able to finish its appointed rounds, it would have landed at Kimpo International Airport, which sits in a valley north and west of Seoul. On all sides are the sharp, jagged peaks that distinguish the Korean landscape. The travel guides describe it as the "Land of Morning Calm," but at dusk, which was when I arrived, it looked like a medieval dungeon, with the shaded peaks appearing as gargoyles.

Nevertheless, the reality of Korea as a modern nation living at the edge of war also emerges at Kimpo. Somber gray transports of the American and South Korean air forces are lined up on the tarmac. Kimpo is less than three minutes' flying time from North Korea, where, officially speaking, the war has never ended; in any renewed conflict the airport would be one of the first targets hit.

The ride from the airport to the capital follows roughly the course of the First Marine Division which landed behind the lines at Inchon in September 1950 and quickly moved inland to recapture what remained of Seoul. Today sentries still stand at checkpoints along the route—their expressions as rigid as the M-16 rifles at their sides. The road is choked with traffic. Seoul's reputation for urban sprawl and carbon monoxide is on a par with that of Lagos or Mexico City; but if you approach downtown from the expressway running alongside the banks of the Han River, the city seems less threatening. The hills around which the modern city has grown faintly resemble those of Seattle or San Francisco, and the Han, though the guidebooks forever liken it to the Potomac as it passes the Jefferson Memorial, actually looks more like the Susquehanna flowing through Harrisburg.

In less than thirty years, Seoul's population has grown to eight million. North of the Han, inside the ring of hills that define the city's natural borders, is an expansive dish filled with a mix of glass-and-steel office buildings and houses with red clay roof tiles. The wide boulevards convey imperial grandeur only when they converge near the old National Assembly; elsewhere the eight lanes or so—a challenge to the bravest pedestrian—are merely a means of accommodating traffic so helter-skelter that ownership of a car also usually implies possessing the affluence and wisdom to hire a driver.

The original purpose of my trip to Korea was to write an article on the country's preparation for the 1988 summer Olympics and on how South Korea remains a model for economic development in the Third World. But after I arrived I began to realize that one of the biggest hindrances to understanding Korea is that it is too easily reduced to the status of a metaphor. Instead of seeing the country for what it is—a prosperous nation that has serious political problems and faces a hostile enemy to the north—the United States, led by a succession of Presidents, has always wanted it to be something more, usually for reasons of domestic political consumption. Hence the disappointments with Korea over the years.

During the Cold War, for example, Korea, a divided nation that had suffered from years of Japanese occupation, was required to be the spot where—by necessity—the West had to draw the line against Communism. Later, during the 1960s, its assigned role was as a model of development and showcase of democracy—with all the implied expectations and disappointments. When Jimmy Carter was president, South Korea and its military government were an albatross of ugly Americanism: examples of what went wrong when the U.S. military got too close to a client state. Lately President Reagan has returned Korea to its earlier symbolism, that of an Asian Berlin; his visit last year to Seoul and the demilitarized zone was, in effect, a photographic rendition of "Ich bin ein Korean." Some aspects of all these metaphors are true; but they overstate the case if they become the encompassing view of the country.

If anything, Korea is a prisoner of its own tragic history—something that's often overlooked in the West. For most of the last century, the peninsula, which forms a strategic crossroad in East Asia, has been divided and conquered by one of its neighbors. China, Japan, and the Soviet Union have taken turns marching their armies across the mountainous terrain that is nearly a land bridge between the Chinese mainland and the Japanese islands. Control the peninsula, and you have something that amounts to an Oriental Gibraltar. Hence Korea's history is one of occupations. When, for example, during the closing days of World War II the Russian army seized territory down to the 38th parallel, it was recapturing ground lost to the Japanese in the 1904–5 war. In effect, the tensions today are an extension of those forces that have competed for Korea since the Russian and Japanese fleets joined at the Strait of Tsushima, which is just off the Korean south-eastern coast.

Because violence has been such a frequent visitor to the Korean landscape, the American impression of the South today is that of a nation at war with itself. Headlines in the newspapers or film clips on the evening news—if they show the country at all—usually depict students on a rampage or poets on their way to prison. However true the specific incidents may be, what is not shown is the historical context of a country that has existed for barely a generation and that faces—less than three minutes by air to the north—an enemy waiting for its chance to finish off the war that started in 1950. Under such pressure, South Korea has done well to create an economy that has flourished; and despite a nasty reputation, few people are as open to visitors as the Koreans. True, its government is repressive, but the reference point should not be Jeffersonian democracy, but the sad reality of American politics during our own Civil War.

When he left office, George Washington advised his young nation to avoid foreign entanglements. In its first one hundred years, the U.S. more or less succeeded. But in its brief existence, South Korea has never known the luxury of isolation. Foreign entanglements are all the Koreans have known. Both China and Russia still covet the peninsula for their spheres of influence. And while Japan may now be an ally and protector of the South, few Koreans can forget the brutality of the Japanese occupation. Instead of growing up in a political incubator that might have allowed the ancient civilization of Korea to develop its political institutions slowly, the South came to life as a stepchild of geopolitics. To repeat Abraham Lincoln's metaphor, its house is still divided. Hence any understanding of the country must begin with a journey to the frontier.

Difficult as it may be to believe, the Cold War is something of a tourist attraction, at least for foreigners, and each morning a bus takes a handful of travelers from one of the downtown Seoul hotels to the demilitarized zone that separates north from south.

The ride north forms a collage of recent Korean history. The bus passes the deceptively tranquil façade of the Blue House, South Korea's presidential home, where in 1979 a cabinet minister assassinated President Park. What followed were months of unrest, street demonstrations, and a military restoration led by President Chun Doo Hwan.

Behind the Blue House is a large forest, protected by chain link fences and barbed wire, where South Korean forces can be seen at various intervals entering for routine patrol. It all seems a bit extreme until the bus passes a statue to mark the spot where thirty-one North Korean commandos were captured a decade ago before they had managed to complete a suicide mission to kill the president. Perhaps a similar marker will be erected in Rangoon to commemorate the spot where a North Korean bomb assassinated nearly half the cabinet of the South.

Farther north, as the city gives way to a landscape of rice paddies, the bus passes an innocent-looking checkpoint. But overhead is a concrete slab loaded with explosives, which can be dropped at a moment's notice to deter tanks from reaching the city.

South Korean civilians are permitted to go no farther north than the southern bank of the Hant'an River—the country's Rubicon as it were. Fences line both riverbanks, and the buoys that appear to be marking the channel are actually mines strung out to deter enemy frogmen.

Across the river, the terraced rice paddies give way to scrub pines of the sort found in the American South—and to military installations as well. The traffic on the two-lane road is all one color, the drab olive green of jeeps and canvas troop carriers, with the occasional platoon of American soldiers, their faces red in the summer sun, jogging past in the other direction.

There are forty thousand trip-wire American troops stationed in Korea, and for those assigned to forward positions, duty on the frontier often means being posted to Camp Kitty Hawk, one of the many bases on the southern edge of the DMZ. As the name implies, the camp is a parody of a peaceful American town, carved into the dusty Korean hills. Near where the bus parks for lunch are some tennis courts; behind the officers' club a few GIs can be seen splashing in a swimming pool.

Despite this illusion of calm at Camp Kitty Hawk, where it is even possible to get a cheeseburger for lunch, the crossing into the demilitarized zone conveys as much about South Korea as the roadblocks do about Beirut or Northern Ireland. The DMZ is 151 miles across and a couple of miles wide, and a combination of the U.S. Second Infantry Division and South Korean forces guards a swath cut along the southern line. The strip, which looks as if it were shaved by a razor, is protected by a barbed-wire, chain-link fence and illuminated by spotlights every ten yards. Behind it an antitank wall, made from bleached concrete, looks like something dug up from a Roman fortification.

The "peace village" of Panmunjom is two kilometers from Camp Kitty Hawk, across desolate terrain. For all its newspaper fame, Panmunjom is no more than a collection of Quonset huts and several façades. Not surprisingly, about half of the village is the press center.

The border is a series of meter-high white stakes, like part of an unfinished fence. The line runs through the middle of an eggshell-blue Quonset hut, which is where all the negotiations take place. Except for a few United Nations observation towers, the rest of the village consists of two large façades—elements of the burlesque that occasionally intrudes on deadly matters.

Each side has erected buildings on its half of the border to lure converts from the other country. These buildings are wonderfully representative. Panmunok, the North Korean showcase, is an accurate advertisement for Communism. Though only three feet deep, it is three stories high and apparently modeled along the late Stalinist lines of a Bulgarian ministry. On the other side of the border, however, is Freedom House, the South Korean exhibit. It is part pagoda and part Disney World and surrounded by the only garden and clipped grass to be seen for miles. It would appear to appeal to anyone smitten with thruway rest stops.

Still, the architectural histrionics of the DMZ are in keeping with its more sinister aspects. Rarely does one side ever give an inch: hence the absence of a formal peace treaty after thirty years of truce. Back in Seoul, I was told that when North and South Korean patrols stumble on each other in the DMZ, a firefight often ensues. The last official incident, however, took place in 1976, when North Korean soldiers wielding axes attacked a tree-trimming party led by two American officers. Captain Arthur Bonifas and First Lieutenant Mark Barrett were killed in the mêlée, which lasted four minutes. Some now think it was the inspiration of Kim Il Jong, son of Kim Il Sung, the North's president, as a way to prove his hatred of Americans. Nevertheless, several days later the United States launched Operation Paul Bunyan and reduced the tree in question to a gnarled stump. In Korea, symbolism is the continuation of war by other means.

The tour ends at Observation Post 5, a small bunker with a commanding view for miles into North Korea. In the distance a flag hangs over what the troops refer to as Propaganda Village, which, like Panmunok, was built to show off the prosperity of the North. One of the world's largest flags flies over Propaganda Village, and it might indeed be a pleasant place— if anyone lived there. But this workers' paradise is a ghost town, save for the keeper of the flag.

Before returning to Seoul, the bus makes a little swing past the small, one-lane Bridge of No Return. In 1953, on this stone bridge, the only man-made link between North and South Korea, prisoners of war were allowed to choose where they wanted to live—with no going back once the decision was made. Grass is now growing up between the cracks in the pavement of this forlorn monument.

I found Peter Hyun in, of all places, an office on the second floor of the Hotel Shilla, which is in the deluxe category. Not a very likely place to find a serious writer, perhaps, but there he was, sitting behind a desk that should have been filled by someone booking banquets or conventions.

He was dressed like an investment banker in a summer suit from Brooks Brothers, a Pierre Cardin shirt, and Gucci loafers. He said that he spent half his time in Seoul and the rest in New York City, where he had a rent-controlled apartment. In addition to his books and magazine articles published in the United States, he writes a column for one of the English-language dailies in Seoul. He said that he had once worked as an editor of children's books for Doubleday, the publishing company.

I wanted to meet him to learn more about North Korea and to get a realistic appraisal of the chances for reunification. Hyun was born in what is now the North and lived there until the autumn of 1945, when his family fled the Russian army that was then moving down the peninsula. The Hyuns settled in Seoul. Several years later, Peter Hyun left Korea to study in the United States, where he eventually became a citizen and entered his careers in publishing and journalism.

During the 1970s, while living in New York, he decided to make a trip to North Korea. The State Department refused to guarantee his safety; the North Koreans delayed the journey with the usual red tape. But eventually he got a visa and flew to Pyongyang, the North Korean capital, via Moscow. He was naturally nervous that because he had been born in the North the government of Kim Il Sung might not let him leave once the trip was over.

Peter Hyun returned to New York after a month in North Korea—one of the few Western travelers to make such a trip—and the result was *Darkness at Dawn*, which is less a travel account than a meditation, of the Koestler variety, on the bureaucracy that runs the North. From the moment Hyun lands in North Korea, the itinerary is by George Orwell and the dialogue by Eugene Ionesco. Instead of staying in the capital and mingling with the people, whose language he speaks, he is sequestered miles away at a villa for special guests. When he asks to meet other writers, he is handed collected speeches of Kim Il Sung. He asks repeatedly if he can eat with typical North Koreans, and when his hosts relent, he is taken to an empty restaurant. When he rides the new subway in Pyongyang, it is in the empty car reserved on every train on the off chance that Kim Il Sung will decide to pop down into the system. No matter where he turns, Peter Hyun is struck by the absurd presence of Kim Il Sung in all aspects of North Korean life; an entire country has given itself over to government by iconography.

From Hyun's descriptions, it is clear why peace talks and those on reunification between the North and South have always failed. There was a hope that as a result of the Reagan summit in Beijing the talks on reunification might be restarted. But little progress on that matter is in evidence. Likewise, on his visit to Seoul, Pope John Paul II urged a reconciliation in the divided country, but again the words were not followed with action.

The tragedy is that reunification remains the one dream that both Koreas share. Many families that have lived apart for thirty years long to be back together. Peter Hyun, as an example, traveled to North Korea in part to see if he could find his father's grave, which he did and which is described in the book's most moving chapter. Reunification is an emotional issue, rather than a political one, but it is the obvious political gulf that prevents anything from happening. Neither side has a clue as to how unification might work. During my trip I heard a number of solutions, although none seemed feasible. Some talked of a federal system; indeed, the National Assembly in Seoul even has an empty chamber awaiting North Korean legislators. But that would require a constitutional convention on a par with Philadelphia's in 1787, which is difficult to imagine since both sides barely speak. Others dream of ending the division by force, but that would take everyone back to the stalemate that began with the armistice in 1953. Sadly, the best hope for the future isn't reunification, but evolutionary change in the South—the North is probably beyond the pale of reform—that would allow the country to develop a political tradition to match the opportunity for advancement now afforded under its economic system.

In the minds of many South Koreans, economic progress and democracy are incompatible. Democracy implies a kind of disorder that not only would reduce the gross national product, but also would weaken the country to a point where the North might once again be tempted to rush south. Further, the question of succession in Korean politics remains a constant fear. After President Park was assassinated, student demonstrators had their run through the streets and the continuing order was threatened with collapse. Democracy to many in the South seems almost to imply numerous assassinations—with constant changes in the leadership and the economy always threatened. Easier to let the military run the show instead, with American aid.

A further obstacle to a functioning party system in Korea is the absence of any democratic tradition at all. For all its history Korea has been governed by one kind of strongman or another. The last king was poisoned in the imperial palace in the 1920s. Although in recent times outsiders have challenged for the presidency, the military remains one of the few groups that has any experience in government, producing a vicious circle familiar to anyone who has looked for his first job. Even observers like Peter Hyun are reluctant to support opposition leaders without experience. The opposition is often charged with failing to come up with specific alternative programs, and its answer, as Hyun summarized it, is: "How do you expect us to come up with specific proposals when it is the government that has all the money to hire any expertise it chooses?" No work without experience; but how do you get some unless you have a job?

A partial answer may be prison. Jails have had a combustible effect on politics in the twentieth century—Gandhi comes immediately to mind, and at some point in the future prisons may have an impact on Korea. The idea did not occur to me until I was home from Korea and went to Columbia University to hear Kim Dae Jung give a speech. He first ran for the presidency in 1970 against Park Chun Hee and received 40 percent of the popular vote. Later he was kidnapped off the street in Tokyo, smuggled back to Seoul, and kept in jail or under house arrest from 1974 until 1981. In 1980, he was one of the so-called "three Kims" who would have run for president had they been permitted.

Kim Dae Jung is one of the few political men I have heard speak recently who has had kind words for both President Carter and President Reagan. He credits both for helping to save his life and is grateful to be living in the United States, teaching and writing at Harvard University. Although perhaps less dynamic, Kim Dae Jung invites comparison with Benigno Aquino, with whom he was friends until the exiled Philippine leader decided to return home and was assassinated.

Kim Dae Jung was a senator before he ran for the presidency and subsequently went to jail, but even so, for him prison was a political education. It gave him time to think and read. At Columbia, he recounted how he passed the time reading Toynbee's histories, Reinhold Niebuhr's *Moral Man*, some books by John Kenneth Galbraith, and other writers one might associate with a freshman seminar in political theory. He also wrote. Guards gave him pens, but only a limited amount of paper. So he developed a microscopic style that enabled him to put 18,000 Korean characters on a page—a record, he now muses. Through the experience, during which his only joy at times was a small prison garden, Kim Dae Jung seems to have grown into a mature political leader, capable of thought and action.

Ironically, when I first heard him speak, I began to wonder how the hopes of many in the opposition were pinned on such a speaker. To be fair, he struggles with English, but, still, he read his speech in a monotone voice with little inspiration. Shuffling papers absentmindedly, he had gotten two-thirds of the way through his talk when he abruptly read the conclusion. When he realized his mistake, he went back to the errant fork in the text and started in again. Not exactly the stuff of oratorical legends.

Nevertheless, during the two days he was at Columbia, I heard Kim Dae Jung whenever I could and asked him questions during some of the breaks. Like Koreans I had met in Seoul, he seemed to come alive in personal conversation and spoke about his prison experience and his political ideas with an intensity that was missing from the speeches.

He begins his argument by saying that it is the United States that "breathes life into the Chun Doo Hwan dictatorship." But he makes the distinction between American policy and action: "I am not asking the United States to restore democracy in our stead; we only ask that the United States not support military dictatorship but lend moral support to our democratic cause."

One by one he answers the justifications for the military government:

• That it provides security. He argues that even during the bleakest days of the struggle with the North, the South enjoyed all the freedoms he associates with American democracy: freedom of the press, direct election of the president, local autonomy, and an independent judiciary. "Today, in peace time," he says, "our people have lost all of the freedoms."

• That a military government means greater economic growth. "How is it," he asks again, "that we had all those freedoms during the Korean conflict when the per capita income was a meager sum of $60 but none today when Koreans earn an average of $2,000 a year?"

• That, by comparison, the government of the South is at least better than that of the North. But for Kim Dae Jung, simply to have leadership marginally better than one of the more backward regimes on Earth is not good enough. Nor should it justify American support. He believes that when a government has pretensions toward democracy and fails to deliver the appropriate representation, it builds resentment among the people. He sees this potential disenchantment as being as dangerous to the South as to the North Korean military. And he argues that "dictatorial governments which justify their existence by their stand against Communism have traditionally been corrupt. Wealth under such milder dictatorships tends to be concentrated in the hands of a few. Under such conditions, we cannot expect to see a real free-market system, but only a government-controlled economy. Thus milder dictatorships are vulnerable prey to the harsher Communist dictatorship."

Kim Dae Jung is not a powerful man. He stands on flat feet and walks slowly, with a slight limp and a cane for support. In the United States he often delivers his message in churches, because in South Korea churches remain one of the few outlets for the opposition. But he remains a political man, and with words and ideas he is fighting an entrenched system that on occasion has silenced the opposition with arrest and prison. In the U.S., Kim Dae Jung finds the contradiction of a rich democratic tradition—along the lines of the literature he read in prison—with a policy that is content to support in Korea men who are not worthy heirs to that same heritage.

He closed one speech with these words: "The restoration of democracy is desirable because it holds a key to many other problems facing South Korea today. For example, only a genuine democracy can promote stability and security by the realization of social and economic justice. Only a democratic Korea can, with confidence and popular support and legitimacy, approach and negotiate with North Korea toward peaceful coexistence, peaceful exchange, and, finally, peaceful unification. In a fundamental sense a democratic Korea is desirable for the United States as well, because it is the surest way to reduce tension in the Korean peninsula and consequently the military burden of the United States in the Far East."

Listening to him for the last time, I no longer concentrated on his delivery, but wondered when and if he might return home and what would be his fate.*

---

* In 1997, Kim Dae Jung was elected president of South Korea; in 2000, he was awarded the Nobel Prize for Peace.

Hello Again to All That

(1999)

Patriotism, in the trenches, was too remote a sentiment,
and at once rejected as fit only for civilians, or prisoners.

—Robert Graves, *Good-bye to All That*

John Keegan, the British military historian, finished his history of World War I (*The First World War*) before NATO's attack on Serbia was even a gleam in the president's photo opportunities. But the author of *The Face of Battle* and other histories of warfare asks of the earlier conflict in the Balkans: "Why did a prosperous continent, at the height of its success as a source and agent of global wealth and power and at one of the peaks of its intellectual and cultural achievement, choose to risk all it had won for itself and all it offered to the world in the lottery of a vicious and local internecine conflict?" We might ask the same question today of Messrs. Clinton and Blair.

In 1914, the tottering Hapsburg monarchy—the same kind of tangle of overlapping nationalism that NATO is today—decided to teach the Serbs a lesson for Belgrade's alleged involvement in the assassination of the Archduke Franz Ferdinand, who, ironically, was the one voice of restraint in an otherwise belligerent Vienna. The Hapsburg foreign office presented the Serbs with an ultimatum that included the acceptance of Austrian police within Serbia— similar to the NATO demand for its occupation forces within the Yugoslav republic. As Keegan writes of then and now: "Anyone of the characteristically world-weary officials of Hapsburg imperialism, if reincarnated today, might well ask what had changed."

In August 1914 the mobilization schedules of continental armies provided the great powers the momentum toward war, lest any of the European armies were literally to find themselves left at the station. Germany's support for Austria's Balkan adventure pushed the wooden wheels of the Russian army toward the Hapsburg frontier. "Russia, a great Slav brother, had tender feelings towards the Serbs but feelings are different from vital interests and certainly no motive for war," Keegan writes, in explaining that Europe descended into barbarism through miscalculation and the entanglements of its alliances, not from strong feelings for or against the nationalist passions of the Bosnian Serbs.

During the world war that followed, which included African skirmishes and Colonel T. E. Lawrence's revolt in the desert, 67 million soldiers were enlisted in the cause. One in six were killed, and of these, 4 million died along the trenches of the western front. France lost 2 million men, and ended the war with 650,000 war widows. Of the 1 million British soldiers killed, 500,000 were never found. Germany also lost 2 million soldiers, of whom 23 percent were officers. Austria mobilized 3.5 million men under arms, and one-third of them never came home. By 1917, 4 million Russian soldiers were prisoners of war and 1.3 million were dead. But, as Keegan writes, "In 1914, by contrast, war came, out of a cloudless sky, to populations which knew almost nothing of it and had been raised to doubt that it could ever again trouble their continent." In a similar vein today, who could have predicted that the administration of President Bill Clinton would take up the Hapsburgs' burden?

I first met John Keegan in the early 1980s. When I was a magazine editor, I commissioned him to write an essay on—of all things—the future of NATO (he didn't think it had one). I left the magazine before the essay was published, but when he traveled to America a few months later, I went with my father to pick him up at John F. Kennedy Airport in New York.

From a book jacket photograph, we recognized Keegan in the arrival-hall crowd and brought him home to begin a family friendship that, with only a handful of meetings, has lasted nearly twenty years. Tall, with dark swept-back hair and a voice that mixes warmth with authority, Keegan, an Oxford graduate, brings to the writing of history an undergraduate's enthusiasm for his subjects. Neither a retired officer nor a university don, his conversations are laced more with questions than with long answers. While he admires those who practice the profession of arms, at least in the cause of peace, he is not a battle enthusiast, believing that "if we hope to see war driven towards its end, we must not shrink from seeing its causes addressed."

Born in 1934, Keegan was too young for World War II, except to see it through a child's eye. In the introduction to *Six Armies of Normandy*, a history of each army that fought along the invasion beaches, he describes the summer of 1944. At the side of his father, a school superintendent who had survived the horror of the trenches, Keegan saw the night summer sky fill with American Dakotas, heading toward their Normandy encounters—an image he associates with both military accomplishment and his personal affection for America.

In 1960, Keegan became a lecturer at the Royal Military

Academy, Sandhurst, the West Point of the British Army, in which young officers study not just tactics but Tacitus. In 1986, Keegan left Sandhurst to serve as defense correspondent for the London *Daily Telegraph* and to continue writing books, many of which draw on his extensive readings from the two world wars, especially their memoirs.

If there is a theme that runs through John Keegan's histories, it is that wars are best understood listening to those who were there, a point he emphasized in his first and most influential book, *The Face of Battle*, in which the encounters at Agincourt, Waterloo, and the Somme are recounted from the perspective of the front lines or, to use one of his eloquent phrases, "the personal angle of vision."

The Mask of Command is a study of generalship, including a long chapter on Hitler's failings as a commander, which he describes as a "charade of false heroics." *The Price of Admiralty* is a sea companion to *The Face of Battle*, using Trafalgar, Jutland, and Midway to understand what drove sailors in these cruel seas. *Fields of Battle* visits the North American battlefields, from Bunker Hill to Little Big Horn, and includes, to my pleasant surprise, a succinct profile of my father, who commanded a Marine Corps rifle company during the Pacific island campaigns.

My own conversations with Keegan usually touch on the reading and writing of military history. Over the years I have noticed how much of my own reading has followed his syllabus. Last December, remembering his praise for Milovan Djilas's *Wartime*, I carried a copy to Belgrade, where I appreciated its recollection of earlier Yugoslav civil wars, if not the author's ruthless partisan convictions. But I consider Keegan's *The Battle for History*, a World War II annotated bibliography, as part of my life reading list.

Like Keegan, I also find myself drawn to World War I battlefields. On family vacations or during business trips,

without it being an obsession, I have toured the forts at
Verdun, climbed Vimy Ridge, bicycled through the Polish
lakes at Tannenberg, and seen Gallipoli at sunrise from the
rail of a steamship. Among the many strengths of *The First
World War* is how Keegan splices into the historical text his
own travel descriptions: "The smallness of the Gallipoli bat-
tlegrounds is the most striking impression left on the visitor."
Of Passchendaele (in Flanders) he writes: "There is one of the
dreariest landscapes in western Europe, a sodden plain of
wide, unfenced fields, pasture and plough intermixed, overly-
ing a water table that floods on excavation more than a few
spadefuls deep," an observation that explains his later conclusion: "On the Somme he [General Sir Douglas Haig] had
sent the flower of British youth to death or mutilation; at
Passchendaele he had tipped the survivors into the slough of
despond."

Keegan did not write his history of the First World War as
a cautionary tale, although it reads as such—given that much
of the war was fought over the landscape where NATO's
cheerleaders now wish to "introduce ground forces." In World
War I, for example rather than surrender to ultimatum when
attacked on all sides, Serbia retreated over the mountains to (of
all alleged non-Serb places) Kosovo and then the Adriatic, a
maneuver that cost 60,000 casualties—food for thought for
those who think taking out Belgrade's power stations will
break the nation. One-fifth of the Serbian population died in
the war. Nor, when "introduced," did Allied ground troops
have an easy time in the Balkans. In 1917, attacking north from
Salonika, British, French, and Serbian forces bogged down in
the mud of Macedonia, which one German commander called
"the greatest internment camp in the world."

Much today as we cling to a faith in air power (cf. the military doctrines of General Wesley Clark), the World War I
commanders saw artillery as the key to any breakthrough—

although, in the attack on the Somme River in 1916, one million British shells failed to cut the barb wire, let alone destroy German positions. On the morning of July 1, seventeen British and Canadian divisions attacked across farmland that today evokes the broad tranquillity of the Nebraska plains. Only five divisions made it across no-man's-land to find the uncut wire.

In the words of a German defender: "If only they had run, they would have overwhelmed us," but they walked, defiantly, a few kicking footballs. Of the 100,000 men in the first waves, 20,000 were killed and 40,000 wounded, and today all that breaks the sweep of farmland are the hollow squares of the war cemeteries, their headstones as symmetrical as the distant wheat and corn. "The Somme," Keegan writes, as many have before, "marked the end of an age of vital optimism in British life that has never been recovered."

Keegan writes critically of the lack of communication between the general staffs and the line officers who led the assaults. He contrasts Wellington, riding the front lines at Waterloo, to World War I generals, at the rear in well-fortified bunkers: "The iron curtain of war had descended between all commanders, low and high alike, and their men, cutting them off from each other as if they had been on different continents." In Vietnam, many officers rode in helicopters. In the war for Kosovo, it is easy to get the impression that NATO generals run their campaigns from AWACs or at press conferences in Brussels.

Not all of the lessons of the First World War apply today in Kosovo. The system of alliances that called each power to war is no longer present. Even the Russians are considering abandoning the Serbs for Western financial succor, and the NATO coalition includes many former enemies that, at least for now, agree on the further partition of the former Yugoslavia. But the inability of politicians and generals to control events in war is a theme that runs from the trenches of World War I to NATO's attack on the Chinese embassy in Belgrade. Keegan writes in *The Face of Battle* that "most wars are begun for reasons which have nothing to do with justice, have results quite different from those proclaimed as their objects, if indeed they have any clear-cut result at all, and visit during their course a great deal of casual suffering on the innocent."

One World War I legacy lingering today, especially within the administration, is the idea that only American military intervention can save Europe from its periodic ritual suicides. In the offensives of 1918, American divisions joined British and French troops, defeating a war-weary German army. (Perhaps the transition from the old world to the new took place at Belleau Wood, when retreating French officers told U.S. Marines that they, too, might like to pull back: "Retreat?" answered Captain Lloyd Williams. "Hell, we just got here.") But the Wilsonian peace sowed the seeds of World War II, just as President Clinton, with a sketchy view of European history, struggles now to impose the doctrines of self-determination in regions where rival nationalist claims are often more legitimate than the U.S. title to Texas.

Clinton and Blair, in rallying the attack against the Serbs, like to cite Munich as the precedent that is under fire in the Balkans. But in reading Keegan, one cannot help but fear that today's war for Kosovo could turn out to be yesterday's landing at Gallipoli—a military adventure in remote harsh terrain, planned by politicians.

The British war cabinet, urged on by Winston Churchill, thought to attack Europe's underbelly from Turkey, thus relieving pressure on the western front. But the invasion never got off the beaches of the rocky coastline and eventually cost 265,000 Allied casualties. Keegan describes the Australian troops in the first waves: "The ANZACs, clinging lost and leaderless to the hillsides, began, as the hot afternoon gave way to grey drizzle, to experience their martyrdom." His conclusion about the Dardanelles also speaks volumes about the current strategy in Kosovo: "Nothing was more improvised than the plan."

The State
of America's Newspapers

(1983)

In the winter of 1981–82, as part of my job as one of the directors of a newspaper syndicate, I visited the offices of more than fifty newspapers. The group I was representing proposed to edit magazine articles, transmit them over high-speed wires, and sell them to newspaper editors. I was selected to go on the road to find the appropriate editors and sell them the service.

"The road" turned out to be a succession of airports and bus and railroad stations—in addition to newspaper waiting rooms. The size of the papers varied from the *Juneau Empire* (circulation 6,650) to the *Chicago Tribune* (circulation 758,255), although I mostly concentrated on the one hundred largest dailies, as listed in *Editor & Publisher Yearbook*. In five months of travel, I got as far north and west as the *Anchorage Times* and *Anchorage Daily News*; as far south as the *Corpus Christi Caller-Times*; and as far east as the *Providence Journal*. I met with editors of every rank and description, and most were extremely generous with their time, if not with their purchases. Although the *Philadelphia Bulletin* was well known to be in financial difficulties, nearly all the top editors were happy to meet with me. At the *Allentown Morning Call*, I made my pitch at eleven-thirty at night. Only in Kansas City was I shown the door before my presentation was over.

The experience amounted to an education in American newspapers. I had worked in magazines and knew newspapers, aside from those I read, only by reputation. I started on the road with few expectations, but came to the conclusion that not all was well with the country's dailies, whatever their reputations. Hemingway is no longer on the staff of the *Kansas City Star*; the *New York Herald Tribune* isn't that city's second newspaper—Rupert Murdoch's *Post* is; and Carl Bernstein now works in television. But memories die hard.

My education began in Dallas with visits to the *Morning News*, the self-proclaimed leading newspaper of the Southwest, and the *Times Herald*, a colonial holding in the Times Mirror empire. In both cases I met with various editors—managing, news, features—and explained what the syndicate was trying to do and what articles it could provide. But quickly I learned that the last thing on any editor's mind—in Dallas or elsewhere—is news. Modern newsrooms, it should be noted, purr with the clickity-clack efficiency of word processors. The leitmotif is no longer the manual typewriter. Further, the job of editor or assistant editor, only in ceremonial ways, is to edit. Editors attend budget meetings, go over personnel issues, meet with the unions, or discuss plans for a new building. Rarely do they dispatch young reporters to fires or write editorials denouncing corrupt officials as thieves or rogues. Today's editors, by design, are middle management, and they preside over the news almost by remote control. They spend their days returning phone calls, and going to lunch, and as though by magic, the paper appears the next morning on the newsstand. Nevertheless, for all this absentee management, there is a cost.

For one thing, American newspapers suffer from the same blandness that has overtaken hotel chains and fast-food restaurants. Nearly all the papers look alike. After a while, I wondered if there wasn't some secret covenant among owners to give papers uniformity, so that the untrained eye can't tell the *Dallas Morning News* and the *Detroit News* apart. Even more alarming, most papers actually read the same. What is supposed to be news in Denver is about what it's supposed to be in Seattle except for a few schoolboard election stories. Besides which, outside of a few big-city dailies, there is the added homogenization of wire copy. Moving from city to city on the same day, I was often able to track a wire story from one paper to another, fostering the illusion that dispatches are still tossed from fast-moving trains and then printed in the next edition.

Yet most newspapers are doing well financially. Before the recent publishers' convention in New York, James Hoge, publisher of the *Chicago Sun-Times*, said: "Newspapering is a big and diverse industry. One part of it, the afternoon metros in the older cities, can get in trouble, but it was never as bad as it was painted." Translated, this means that despite the wreckage of such flagships as the *Philadelphia Bulletin*, the convoy keeps sailing and making lots of money.

Newspapers now have 62.4 million daily readers, up a million from last year. In 1980 there were 182 more Sunday papers than there were a decade earlier. Even medium-sized dailies are bloated with advertisements and supplements for consumers every day of the week. Such large papers as the *Washington Post* are thicker in newsprint on weekdays than, say, the London papers are on Sunday.

The reason for this economic well-being, not surprisingly, is that while there are 1,710 dailies in the United States, only 24 cities have newspapers competing for advertisers and readership. The rest are, in the words of A. J. Liebling, "one-paper towns," and the natural tendency in such places is to put out a paper inoffensive to the greatest possible number of readers. When Liebling was writing "The

Wayward Pressman" for *The New Yorker* in the forties, fifties, and early sixties, he was despairing because there were only seven competing newspapers left in New York and because in 1927 there were 502 cities with competition. Hence, as he watched the number of competitive newspapers in cities drop to around 60 in 1963, he observed that "as the number of cities in the United States with single newspaper ownership increases, the news becomes increasingly nonessential to the newspapers." In Liebling's day, the victor was usually an eccentric millionaire, who with his monopoly powers could inflict on the readership whatever version of the truth the traffic might bear. Today the monopolists are anything but eccentric, and the papers' mission is to serve as quasi-public utilities that strive to balance service and monopoly profits. It might be called the triumph of the bland, and it has done for newspapers what Howard Johnson did for home cooking.

The image of a monopoly press was brought home to me by the omnipresence of the large newspaper chains. Chains crisscross the landscape; despite all the clichés describing the newspaper as the stronghold of independence, a paper owned by an individual is the exception.* In effect, American cities are divided up among the chains much the way major league baseball distributes franchises in the minor leagues. After a while, I started to think of the cities I was calling on only in terms of their hierarchical affiliations. Seattle is divided between Hearst (the *Post-Intelligencer*) and Knight-Ridder (which owns forty-nine percent of the *Times*). Denver is Times-Mirror versus Scripps Howard more than it is a battle between the *Denver Post* and the *Rocky Mountain*

---

* One reason family newspapers are often sold to the chains is the inheritance tax imposed on heirs. Often these estate taxes are based on the newspaper's market value, and as communication companies often sell at high price/earnings multiples, this value can be greater than that of the paper. Hence the heirs have no choice but to sell — usually to one of the chains.

News, which are warriors in the symbolic way of medieval horsemen. Cleveland, Newark, and New Orleans are the sole possession of Newhouse. Gannett is boss in Rochester, Wilmington, and Oakland, to name but a few. Knight-Ridder has papers in Aberdeen (South Dakota), Akron, Boca Raton, Boulder, Bradenton (Florida), Charlotte, Columbus (Georgia), Detroit, Duluth, Fort Wayne, Gary, Grand Forks (North Dakota), New York, Lexington, Long Beach (California), Macon, Miami, Pasadena, Philadelphia, San Jose, St. Paul, State College (Pennsylvania), Tallahassee, and Walla Walla. A map of newspaper holdings in the United States would resemble one showing the European holdings of the Hohenzollerns, Wittelsbachs, Wettins, and Hapsburgs.

In terms of ownership, newspapers resemble not only sixteenth-century Europe but also the railroads after World War II—just before their decline. I came on this analogy while visiting the *Bulletin* in Philadelphia shortly before it folded. The offices of the top editors looked down on the freight yards that once belonged to the Pennsylvania Railroad. Now they are part of Conrail, what remains of the Penn-Central and other failed railroad mergers. Talking to the editors about the *Bulletin's* chances and looking out the window at switchers shunting freight cars in the yards, I couldn't help but draw a parallel between the decline and fall of American railroads and the present condition of U.S. newspapers. Like the railroads, newspapers flourished during and after the industrial revolution; like the railroads, they drew customers in and about American cities; and, like the railroads after the war, they are going through a period of intense consolidation. In the fifties and sixties, even though the pre-eminence of the airplane was about to supplant trains, railroads made record profits. Similarly, newspapers today, despite the advent of a host of mediums with which to distribute news, are reporting record earnings. Who is to say that Gannett today with its eighty-eight papers might not be the Penn-Central of tomorrow?

Because of their levels of concentration, the newspapers might well be a regulated industry, even though, officially, there is no Interstate Commerce Commission to adjust rates and apportion routes. Nearly 98 percent of all American cities and towns are in the hands of a monopoly. In turn, few of these monopolists compete with one another. The top ten newspaper publishers control 253 papers, which account for nearly 24 million readers—almost half of those in the United States. But it is as rare to find Knight-Ridder competing with Newhouse as it was, after a while, to find a robber baron who objected to sitting down with the competition and a map to figure out how both could make some money.

The irony of the newspaper business is that while some of the large chains are making, for them, record profits—in 1981 Gannett's net profit was $172 million—before the law they qualify as neediest cases. Bad enough that two-paper towns are vanishing like trolley systems; worse is that where vestiges of competition remain, the law has sanctioned newspaper oligopolies to ensure that one paper doesn't spoil the profits of another.

The newspaper as endangered species was an idea that gained currency during the Nixon Administration. Informal market-sharing arrangements had actually been around since 1933, when the *Albuquerque Tribune* and *Journal* merged operations, but a 1969 Supreme Court ruling threatened to overturn these divisions of the spoils. The publishers responded with intensive lobbying efforts, and the result was the Newspaper Preservation Act, which allows competitors—subject to approval from the Attorney General—to merge business, circulation, and mechanical departments while keeping editorial matters separate. The justification to the public and to the antitrust authorities was that economies of scale in business and advertising would allow weaker papers to continue publishing and thus provide at least a measure of competition—if only in the news columns. Time and again in my travels I found allegedly competing newspapers in the same building, their staffs separated either by an office partition or a floor—hardly the stuff of which newspaper wars are made.

Twenty-three cities now have both their papers run by some form of a Joint Operating Agreement (JOA). A twenty-fourth, Seattle, was approved by the Justice Department but subsequently blocked by a federal judge. The largest city on the list is San Francisco, where the relationship, as stated by *Editor & Publisher Yearbook*, is the following:

> The San Francisco Examiner and San Francisco Chronicle are independent and competitive newspapers, published by separate corporations. The San Francisco Sunday Examiner & Chronicle is produced jointly by the Hearst Corporation and the Chronicle Publishing Co., and includes sections independently edited by the San Francisco Chronicle. San Francisco Newspaper agency . . . is agent for the Examiner, the Chronicle and the Sunday Examiner & Chronicle, and operates their advertising, circulation, accounting and mechanical departments.

For good reason does Liebling repeatedly describe *Editor & Publisher Yearbook* as the "frightened handmaiden of the newspaper industry"; the word "independent" appears three times in the note on the JOA.

Other cities with JOAs are El Paso, Tucson, Tulsa, Chattanooga, Birmingham, Knoxville, Columbus, Pittsburgh, Nashville, and Miami. The smallest city on the list is Franklin-Oil-City, Pa., population 24,000. Lest anyone think JOAs are solely to benefit the struggling independent publisher trying to compete with the chains, it should be noted that Newhouse is party to two such agreements, Hearst two, Gannett six, Knight-Ridder two, and Scripps seven.

I saw a JOA in the making in Seattle, where the *Times*, the all-day paper forty-nine percent owned by Knight-Ridder, and the *Post-Intelligencer*, the Hearst paper that comes out mornings, were proposing to join business forces. If the agreement is approved, the *Times* will drop some of its early-morning editions to give the *Post-Intelligencer* a break in the morning, while Hearst will drop its Sunday edition, except for one of those independently edited inserts. For all practical purposes the *Times* will become the dominant paper in the city, because the Hearst paper, which is losing money, is in no position to dictate terms. It may even have to give up its building, a fixture on the Seattle skyline with its globe of the world standing proudly on the roof.

In arguing for the agreement, Hearst, which last year is estimated to have made $120 million, said that without it they would have to close the *Post-Intelligencer* or, worse, sell it to someone like Rupert Murdoch. The *Times* made the familiar plea to save competition, even though approval will leave the city—save for the intrusions of some suburban dailies—with mornings, afternoons, and Sundays as neatly carved up as the freight markets that fell in between the railroads of Mr. Vanderbilt and Mr. Gould.

According to the *New York Times*, which recently quoted "industry analysts," "most cities will only support one newspaper." The latest evidence supports this conclusion. Time Inc. poured an estimated $60 million into the *Washington Star*, and even that couldn't save it. Both the *Bulletin* and the *Cleveland Press* picked up readers during their last days, but it wasn't enough. Without a majority of readers—at least in the particular market you are aiming for—and consequently of advertisers, most owners, more than ever before, are content to pack it in. But what the *Times* means when it says cities will support only one paper is that advertisers will only flock to the leading daily: New York readers used to support fourteen papers.

Still, the reason for these failures goes beyond garnering advertisers. Odd as it may seem, many owners don't know why they want to own a newspaper, beyond the obvious reason of making money. Consider: Time Inc. bought the *Washington Star* because it wanted a "presence" in the capital; the Cowles Media Company bought the *Buffalo Courier-Express* because the paper had the only cable television franchise in the city. Once they lost their ability to sell advertising, they became expendable. Like passengers watching their favorite trains being pulled from service, the readers would have to make do with something else.

In my rounds I visited several of the papers that subsequently foundered. I had especially admired the editors of the *Minneapolis Star* and the *Bulletin* and wondered what they and all their reporters would do. For the crew, newspapers are a succession of Titanics. For the officers, safely removed from the action in their big glass corporate headquarters, newspapers are part of a fleet and, unfortunately, one occasionally hits an iceberg of low profitability. Little flags are then removed from the chains' strategic maps.

I can't help thinking that many of these losses could have been avoided. It wasn't just the drop in advertising revenues that doomed them. Many papers, including a host of those still publishing, have lost touch with their readers. Monopoly journalism is at best impersonal, and readers are now thought of in such terms as "market clusters," to use the phrase of *USA Today*. Whether it was always thus is difficult for me to gauge, but at least in the period that Liebling describes, newspapers stood for something—if only the bizarre notions of the owner. But now that the eccentric individual proprietor is gone, except in a few rare instances, newspapers are run on the same principles that guide any other monopoly industry.

Few of the papers I visited were willing to spend money on improving the quality of their coverage. Managing editors, in particular, are terrified of money. None that I met liked to talk about it, especially if they had to part with some for a good story. *The Rocky Mountain News* pays $65 for outside contributions. Period. No exceptions, even if the story is several thousand words long. An editor in Columbus once told me that she wasn't interested "in any story that costs more than $125." "I'll get back to you on that" was how most financial discussions abruptly ended, as though the editor had to poll the shareholders before spending $125.

I soon learned that what *does* interest editors is changing jobs. There are probably few professions whose work force is as mobile as that of newspapers. People I knew at the beginning of my travels had vanished by the end. Some of this movement, of course, was inside a chain. The Hearst chain has the habit of moving its talented young editors from city to city. But a lot of job switching was "intermural" and editors would frequently ask me in confidence, since I was traveling around, if I "knew of any openings in San Jose."

This peripatetic tendency was summed up to me in Dallas by an editor at the *Times-Herald*, who in his brief career had worked in as many cities as Alvin Dark, the baseball manager, did in his: "You can't shoot a moving target." The point was that no one could pin a defeat on his résumé if he had moved on by the time the critics caught up with the paper's performance. But what struck me most was the extent to which newspapermen are short-term journeymen, skilled only in the craft of producing a paper—using the staff and the wires as indistinguishable parts in a great assembly line. They rarely understand the politics of a city as someone might who was on the job for longer than a year. Nor do they become politically prominent themselves, as, say, Greeley was in his day; they're too intent on improving their careers with frequent hops. And the swarms of newspaper conventions and seminars are best understood as job fairs.

What makes it easier for editors to jump from paper to

paper is that many newspapers are now merely digests of available wire services. Staff reporters fill in on local stories, but the wires write the leading domestic and international dispatches. Thus any editor who can find the Associated Press in his computer file can find stories to fill most of the holes in the paper. What isn't there can be culled from any of the other services: United Press International; Knight-Ridder; Field; *Los Angeles Times/Washington Post; New York Times*; Hearst; etc. These wires pour into a newspaper's mainframe computer daily—wire editors are best thought of as flood-control experts—so all you need to worry about is keeping the word processors in working order.

When there is more than one paper in town, the syndicates are usually divided up so that the same *New York Times* reprint doesn't appear in both papers. In cases where one paper subscribes to the *Times*, the other might get the *Los Angeles Times/Washington Post*, as if to balance its power. Indeed, the strength of the major dailies in their coverage of the rest of the country is in their wire services, which have jointly eclipsed UPI as the second wire service behind AP. In fact, so many editors have come to rely on both the *Times* and the *Los Angeles Times/Washington Post* service that the *New York Times* and the *Washington Post* have launched national editions. Times-Mirror, which owns the *Los Angeles Times*, has papers in Dallas, Denver, Hartford, Long Island, Stamford, and Greenwich.

With the technology available in the form of satellites that shift copy around the country with the ease of a long-distance phone call, it is now possible to collect in one newspaper the best journalism from all over the country and the world. A paper in Texas, if it chooses, can subscribe to the foreign dispatches of the London *Observer*. But as Mort Rosenblum of AP wrote in *Coups & Earthquakes*: "On the surface, America's newsgathering apparatus appears sophisticated and all-encompassing. The carrier pigeons have been transistorized, and the battered trench coats have given way to drip-dry safari suits. . . . But for all the changes, there has been little real improvement." The reason for this is largely that there is no incentive to improve coverage unless competition forces it, as it has in Dallas, Denver, and Detroit—to list three cities whose newspapers are responding to the competitive impulse. But left on their own, without competition, newspaper editors can publish whatever the traffic will bear.

The gulf that has developed between most newspapers and their cities is symbolized by the fate of the newspaper offices themselves. For the most part, at least in the industrial sections of the country, these still tend to be clustered in the old, downtown section. If I was traveling by train or bus, it was often only a short walk from the station to a Gothic-inspired building. In Detroit, in Chicago, or in Seattle, the newspapers are as central to downtown life as the Agora was in Athens, harking to an era when the mission of the paper was stated in grandiloquent language on the masthead.

In recent years, however, newspapers have joined the flight to the suburbs, and when I didn't have a car it became nearly impossible to get to the offices of one of these exiles. *The Anchorage Daily News* is eight miles from center city, in an industrial area that appears to be waiting for the rest of the city to find it. Likewise, the *Houston Post* is off one of the many freeways outside the city, in a building that from a distance resembles a large white radiator. The *Madison* [Wisconsin] *Capital-Times* is inaccessible except by car.

Perhaps the best illustration of what has happened to the newspaper office as a symbolic part of the community is in Austin, where the *American-Statesman*, a Cox newspaper, has become the only one in town. Previously, the paper had offices not far from the capitol, in a building somewhat resembling a bottling plant. Now that the *American-Statesman* has the monopoly, the offices are housed in an unbelievably opulent structure. Like a medieval fortress, it sits on the south bank of the Colorado River. The parking lot is divided by hierarchical lines like any modern corporation, and, like most newspapers, it has an elaborate security system at the door.

The editor I saw had an office befitting that of a senior vice-president of a large insurance company. The carpeting and the walls were color coordinated in gray. The desk was spacious and hinted of Scandinavian design. If there were books in the office, I don't remember them. The first question the editor asked me was: "How long do you expect to be in business?" His tone was that of a banker about to be petitioned for a loan.

As the monopoly paper in Austin, the *American-Statesman* can pretty much do as it pleases, and that includes plowing all its profits into an architectural white elephant. Many of the papers I visited, even if they were short-staffed, were putting up new buildings or installing hugely expensive and elaborate computer systems. The *Dallas Morning News* is adding on a new wing. The *Spokane Spokesman-Review* is putting up a new building. The *Houston Post* is moving its newsroom upstairs and putting in a $3 million computer. Some of this, obviously, is the cost of doing business, but in newspapers today, I sensed it is a major preoccupation, at the cost of improved coverage. For example, the number of foreign correspondents for American papers has dropped to 450 from a postwar high of 2,500, and that is not because nobody can afford to send someone abroad.

The consequence of what Liebling called a "monovocal, monopolistic, monocular" press goes beyond the obvious loss to the political debate. Despite the profits that can be generated in a one-paper town, the habits of monopoly journalism—arrogance, indifference to the readership, wasting money—threaten the economic foundation of the newspaper industry. The current financial success enjoyed by so many papers may well prove short-lived.

Certainly the early success, at least with circulation, of *USA Today* points to the weaknesses of numerous daily papers. Gannett launched the national newspaper on September 15, 1982, in five cities. By October, circulation was 221,000; by January 1983, it was 531,000; and by April 1983, it reached 1,109,000, placing it third behind the *Wall Street Journal* and the *New York Daily News* in paid circulation.

Initially the audience for *USA Today* was to be the three million Americans who each day are traveling on business or for pleasure. Many of these, reasoned Gannett, have little interest in the news of another city and would therefore welcome a national paper that covered both national and international events, and also included blurbs of news from their hometowns. Consequently a distinguishing feature is "Across the USA," which is the journalistic equivalent of Willard Scott on the "Today" show inviting the entire nation to a bake sale in Ely, Vermont. A typical item, listed under Montana, for May 2, 1983, was: "HELENA—Area residents who engage in the frisbee-throwing sport of 'folf' may have to do their folfing elsewhere. A popular course, mostly on the private land in Tucker Gulch south of the city, has been fenced and subdivided for home development." The rest of the paper is a crisp division of news, weather, and sports—presented for quick perusal by Americans on the run. The short text is spliced with graphs and charts that highlight farm trends or the recent winners of the Stanley Cup.

Even if *USA Today* is the Holiday Inn of newspapers— readers know what they'll get no matter where they are—its circulation success is the first direct challenge to many monopoly journalists across the country. It may not be much—pre-packaged news, if you please—but its widespread appeal indicates the extent to which many readers are tired of their local fare. On a more pessimistic note, *USA Today* may even be described as the airplane that will replace the railroad-like local paper. Increasingly, newspaper chains are now rushing to produce their own versions of national newspapers, and it is not farfetched to imagine the day when the newsstand will resemble that familiar strip of neon motel signs present outside every city in America.

While the railroad analogy may not be precise, it bears repeating because so many newspapers now have monopolies and are deferring maintenance to their readers—in the form of just getting by editorially—much the way the railroads sealed their demise by putting off maintenance on their rights-of-way. By the time the interstate highway system was finished and airplane travel became commonplace, it was too expensive and too late for the railroads to catch up. So it may be for the newspapers, as the likes of *USA Today* arrive daily in the form of new technology, making it easier for department stores to advertise elsewhere or for AT&T to broadcast the news. In 1942, Owens-Corning Fiberglas ran an advertisement in *Fortune*: "How Will People Travel Tomorrow?" The answer, printed below: "By train, says the New York Central, as it plans increased travel comfort to woo passengers in post-defense period." From there, it is an easy leap to: "In Philadelphia, Nearly Everyone Reads *The Bulletin*."

In their monopoly phase, newspapers are investing their profits in everything—cable television, video-text satellite transmission, real estate, radio—but newspapers. The only exceptions are the national editions springing up across the country. By the end of 1983, Gannett plans to spend $40 million on *USA Today*. The *New York Times* and the *Wall Street Journal* already have their national operations. And the *Washington Post* is hoping to get its version off some time this year. But an investment advisory on the *Post's* stock summarizes the importance of these national operations in the future: "The *Post* may try to capitalize on its prestige by putting out a weekly national edition. It would be a news-in-review tabloid focusing on politics and finance. But the company's big ambition is to get a head start in the coming market for mobile (cellular) phone service by setting up service in several cities. If it wins the desired FCC franchises, system development would be costly for a few years. But the glamour of this new technology market might draw much more support for this stock by 1985-87 than we project."

That is a long way from Greeley: "The best use of a journal is to print the largest practical amount of important truth—truth which tends to make mankind wiser, and thus happier."

The Capital
of Underdevelopment

(1981)

It is the oldest city in the Americas, founded by the Aztecs in 1325 and originally named Tenochtitlán. The elevation is 7,350 feet above sea level, and the city spreads out in the bowl of a large plateau, surrounded by mountain peaks and volcanoes that resemble a string of unpolished pearls. The Spanish, led by Cortés, arrived in 1519, and one chronicler with the mission of conquest described their first glimpse of the city built on a lake as "like the enchantments they tell us of in the story of Amadis." Some of the other soldiers asked if they were looking at a dream, so ethereal were the temples and towers that rose from the water.

One vestige of the Spanish presence, Chapultepec Castle, still rises over Mexico City today, the capstone of the largest park. The headquarters of vice regents and the home of Emperor Maximilian and his sad wife, Carlotta, it sits in the downtown section like some baroque wedding cake of mortar and iron that has refused to melt in the warm tropic sun. It could be the Hofburg in Vienna or a New World Versailles. The top floor is a marble courtyard, where footsteps echo with the pomposity of an emperor's strut. But beyond the railing, almost like that on a cruise ship, are the dirt huts and sky-scrapers of a society that cannot decide whether it wants to live in the sixteenth or the twentieth century.

Late one afternoon, when the sun had settled on the ridges of the mountains, I stood at the railing and looked down on the labyrinth. The barrios, the slums of the poor, flew flags of drying laundry. The glass-sided office buildings, badges of bureaucratic progress, reflected the pale shimmer of dusk and smog. Cars raced around the narrow streets and the imperial boulevards like so many rats searching the maze. And in the distance I saw rows of houses, like the surf appropriat-ing a dune, washing up the sides of the hills. At its better moments it was Athens seen from the Parthenon, the push of democracy; at its worst, it was Los Angeles in a dish, the tyranny of the car.

Nothing better symbolizes the city today than its problems with traffic. At all hours the flow of the cars has a Gulf Stream quality, accompanied by a distant volcanic rumbling. Snarled intersections are legendary and dreaded, almost like the monsters that so fascinated the Aztecs. And getting from one place to another became, for me anyway, a serious pre-occupation; I spent many hours hunched over a map, plotting my course.

Many of the city's traffic problems stem from the narrow canals that the Aztecs used to get around in their floating city. As the city grew and the canals began to be filled in, they log-ically became the paths the streets took. Today they are a hon-eycomb, jutting out at all angles, like the tunnels in an ant farm. Because there are 2.5 million cars in the city, and because the same people shown clinging to the sides of over-stuffed buses in photos of the 1950s are now behind the wheels of small foreign imports, pedestrians are an endan-gered species. Even from the heights of Chapultepec they can be seen scurrying to safety. By the end of the century, Mexico

City will be the biggest city on earth, surpassing even New York and Tokyo. Population estimates for the year 2000 fluctuate between a low of 23 million and a high of 32 million. The present count is somewhere around 17 million, a figure that includes the federal district and the surrounding valley. But, as in the United States, census figures are imperfect, and even an army of pollsters would be hard put to tally up all the thousands upon thousands of people filling up the city at unprecedented rates. For contrast, the population was put at just under 8.5 million in 1970. But I have little faith in any of these numbers. The city is simply big, and getting bigger all the time.

It is little wonder, then, that the visitors and scholars of the city have chosen to interpret these elements as the ingredients of doom. Before going to Mexico City I talked with many people about its problems, and all seemed to agree that someday the combustible demographics of 32 million people, unemployment, and neighborhoods of mud hovels would spontaneously ignite to fill the air with the sparks of revolution. I found no reason to disagree, even after I arrived. During the course of my stay, I was handed pamphlets published by the United Nations, books by sociologists, reprints of articles; all pointed to dissolution. To borrow from Freud, the city had only a death wish and little impulse to survive.

Now that I have left the city, however, I am not sure whether these conclusions are correct. They have powerful and persuasive advocates, not to mention the backing of the dictates of common sense. The city gives every indication of decline. Merely guessing at how 32 million people could be fed, let alone given the chance for a satisfying life, makes one scoff at the vanity of civil administration. Many people with whom I spoke expressed this pessimism, but none more eloquently than Fernando Benitez, a historian of Mexico's Indians and the editor of *Sábado*, the literary magazine. The city will die not from a paucity of life but from a surfeit, like some unwieldy cancer whose cells are the growth of population and the stream of cars.

But there is another view, one of hope, which was expressed to me by Octavio Paz, the poet and essayist. It seems almost foolhardy even to consider such a position. And even Paz despaired of the exponential rise in population and the ghostly pollution that hovers over the cars. Nevertheless, out of all the discontent he was somehow able to salvage aspects of progress. Using another Freudian metaphor, it was the will to live. For Paz it was not an exercise in sophistry. He was quick to admit the loneliness of his position and the dearth of supporting evidence. But his faith was in the reason of ideas, and in the belief that the alternative to slow progress—in this case revolution—would be worse.

The visit with Paz came at the end of my stay. My talk with Benitez was earlier. Arranging the meeting over the phone, he suggested I take a taxi to his house in the south of the city. But being in something of a hurry, I decided instead to use the metro to get within striking range of Coyoacán, where Benitez lived, before paying a fortune to yet another mad cabdriver to idle his engine in traffic.

On this occasion I rode the metro south to Tasqueña, a maelstrom where buses and cabs hover like bandits, but I was no closer to Benitez than I had been in town. The directions I gave the cabdriver meant nothing; north seemed to mean south; west was any direction but west; and three blocks always worked out at about a mile. Whatever the cause, we spent the better part of an hour roaming Coyoacán, confirming the driver's random-walk theory of orientation.

Benitez wore slippers and dressed like a professor—which he is, part-time, in journalism; somewhere among the layers of his shirts and sweaters I spotted a necktie, although it did not seem rooted to any particular collar. He was about to celebrate his seventieth birthday, but a vitality, born of an absence of small talk, made him seem younger. An acquaintance who has known him a long time said he has looked the same for forty years.

Almost as soon as the introductions were over, Benitez began to harangue me, in the most enjoyable way, on the subject of foreign ownership—as far as he was concerned, the root of the city's destruction.

It is estimated, although I doubt anyone knows for sure, that two thousand people migrate to the capital each day. According to Benitez, the reason so many leave the small towns and farms is that foreign ownership of concerns, especially in agriculture, has driven the small farmer out of business. One could write an entire history of Mexico that dwelled only on its bad crops. But now the small, destitute farmers, instead of enduring their poverty, are moving to the barrios, "the belts of misery," which encircle the city like a poorly knotted noose.

To buttress his argument that emigration to Mexico City—or, for that matter, the flight across the border into Texas—is a function of profits registered in New York, Benitez disappeared into another room and returned with a clipping that listed the degree to which Mexican industries are controlled by foreigners and thus, presumably, siphon money away from the local population:

	%
children's food	*100*
canned and prepared foods	*90*
insecticides	*95*
tractors	*93*
fertilizers	*90*
vegetable oil	*75*
chocolates	*60*
soft drinks	*70*

By concentrating on large cash crops for export and by importing cheaper crops grown abroad—Mexico even imports grain—the multinationals, he argued, are driving small- and medium-sized farms out of business. As well they should, at least according to classical trade theories; but these eighteenth-century notions of prosperity succeed only when the workers dislodged by cheaper imports are put to work at something else, preferably producing goods that can be traded in their turn. In Mexico, however, they are not. Benitez estimated the city's numbers of unemployed or menial workers at about three million, which the sidewalks confirm. Everywhere you walk, blankets display trinkets for sale. And in pockets of the city, especially on the outer rings, small children and pariah dogs use the heaps of rubble as a playground.

What would relieve the growing population's siege of the city is an agricultural renaissance—the answer forever proposed in arm-waving speeches at election time or during revolutions—but, as Benitez explained, a cruel paradox is at once the cause of the problem and the obstacle to its solution: lack of water.

Oil is frequently touted as the savior of Mexico. It may indeed be so. Even Benitez called it "our last chance." But it cannot do away with the water shortage. The city is landlocked, adjoining neither a major body of water nor a river. The location of the city is only suitable as a defense against invaders; little else seems to recommend it. The lakes on which it was founded are now bogs, and the water under the city is full of volcanic ash and therefore undrinkable. In the introduction to his stories about the city, Carlos Fuentes has written:

> Burnt water, *alt tlachinolli*: the paradox of the creation is also the paradox of the destruction. The Mexican character never separates life from death, and this too is the sign of the city's destiny in the birth and rebirth.

All the drinking water must come from springs and wells, some of it from over the mountains via an elaborate system of aqueducts, similar to the waterworks evolved by the Aztecs.

In the last few years the city has grown by 15 or 16 percent, and it now consumes about 56 cubic meters of water per second. The only place to get this water is from the surrounding states and villages. Wells are tapped; there is talk now of diverting major rivers. Thus, in an ironic chain of shortage, the large numbers of people fleeing the small towns and moving to the city are denying those same towns the water needed for an agricultural revolution.

Yet however dry the city's grave, it will also be watery: Mexico City is sinking. Built on a lake bed, it often wakes up to find its foundations oozing into the mud. Only a Rube Goldberg assortment of pumps, drainage canals, and pipelines keeps the black water, as Benitez called it, from filling up the city's collective basement and the rest of the valley from becoming a sky-high Venice.

The Aztecs, faced with the problem of flooding, constructed an extensive series of dikes, still visible today, to keep the waters of Lake Texcoco from inundating Tenochtitlán. And in the seventeenth century the Spanish engaged German engineers to dig drainage canals. Today there are new drainage canals, deep in the earth, which carry the water to passes in the mountains and then to the valleys beyond. But they too seem a temporary solution, not unlike the dikes of the Aztecs or the hydroelectricity schemes of the 1920s.

At 11:00 P.M. Benitez offered to drive me to a spot from where it would be easy to get a taxi or a bus to the city. Despite his age and the hour, he remained full of enthusiasm. He kept pulling books from the shelves and reading crucial paragraphs out loud. On the ride to the Insurgentes—the city streets, if only in name, are alive with revolution—such was his excitement about explaining the importance of Mexican oil that his Ford LTD, a big car by Mexican standards, drifted across the road at high speeds, as did his hand from the steering wheel while he punctuated his speech. We said good-bye. I watched the bulky car do an incredible U-turn to head him toward home and then waited in the crisp night air for a bus that never came.

The morning routine began with an exercise I later heard denounced as an aspect of "cultural imperialism." Nevertheless, I was devoted to a segment of the local version of the "Today" show that reviewed professional football. Much more than bullfighting, although not rivaling soccer, American football is a Mexican national sport. The Tuesday press gave prominent coverage in the news sections to Monday-night games, and I was frequently told that in the poorest neighborhoods a television antenna comes before more basic necessities, so great is enthusiasm for football. Even the obscure college bowl games were broadcast; were I the NFL commissioner, I would not hesitate to give the city a franchise. The morning program was a highlight show, intended to explain the game to the uninitiated. One morning, for example, the announcers compared the quarterbacking styles of Danny White (Dallas *Vaqueros*, a local favorite) and Ron Jaworski (Philadelphia *Aguilas*). Many replays, plus commentary.

Part of bullfighting's diminished status may be attributed to labor unrest. During my stay the matadors were on strike, although, like golf pros, they can make $20,000 for an afternoon's work. The dispute involved the matadors' assistants, who hold the capes and occasionally step forward to distract the bull during tense moments. The matadors took the position that no matter how much bravery was required for the job, no one went to the fights to see their assistants perform—who knows the name of Arnold Palmer's caddie?—so the strike was on.

Only outside the city, in an obviously nonunion ring, was bullfighting in season. Minor-league matadors fought in front of a crowd of relatives, tourists, and a few professional scouts.

And the amateur flavor remained strong throughout the afternoon. One of the bulls chased a matador right out of the ring. Another bull refused to die—the numerous lunges with the sword had missed the mark—and grunted painfully while a perplexed gang of matadors, all wielding knives, tried to figure out how to get close enough to make the final stab. During the last fight of the afternoon, as even the sympathetic fans filed away in dismay, the matador lost both his shoes, and shod only in his colorful stockings, dodged the bull like a pajama-clad child frolicking before bedtime.

The power of the bullfight, even in a diminished setting, is its sense of tragedy. Unlike American sport, with its winners and losers, and its eternal hope for another tomorrow, bullfighting is the ordered killing of an animal by a man. The outcome is never in doubt. The variables are such things as the courage of the matador or, for that matter, the courage of the bull. Despite the flair, the music, the pomp, and the association with men such as Ernest Hemingway (at least in the United States), the ritual is delicate, almost balletic: the twists of the matador not unlike the pirouettes of the dancer. But the last scene is always tragic, and especially fitting in a place like Mexico City.

Since the Civil War, tragedy on a large scale has seldom visited American cities. Atomic bombs have not destroyed Chicago; plagues have not wasted Boston. In commenting on the differences between the United States and the rest of the world, Fuentes has noted that "for the West the notion of progress has replaced the notion of tragedy." Yet even in the wealthier quarters of Mexico City I sensed that prosperity was a precarious condition. The rich live behind high walls, as though readying for revolution. Some of the nicest suburbs look like the warehouse districts in Baltimore or Philadelphia. Many seem to feel that tragedy lurks at the front door.

Witness my friend Helen Escobedo, one of the country's leading sculptors. Her pieces, displayed on the university campus or in front of office buildings, have something of the puckish whimsy of Claes Oldenburg. Even her house, itself a witty collage of lava flows and doors that resemble keyholes, is an expression of her confidence and sense of well-being. She is one of the few people I know who can talk effortlessly about her work.

Even so, when we met for the first time—walking from the large gate on the street to her house, while she told me about the plants we were passing—she gestured around her yard and said: "If things became bad, I could sell off the front and live here"—pointing to the house and her studio. It was a casual remark during a rambling conversation that ranged from the Mexican reaction to the shooting of John Lennon ("Where were his henchmen?") to one of those earnest conferences on the improvement of Mexican-American relations, with Norman Podhoretz and Lillian Hellman on the U.S. squad. But the remark came back to me later when she happened to mention that she had once owned property several hours' drive from Mexico City, "in case things really got bad." This was an allusion to the possibility of revolution—nothing to be sneered at in a city of such poverty and multitudes; but the tone of her speech was not the New Yorker's panic about the tyranny of real-estate prices. Nor was it the whine of David Stockman, President Reagan's budget director, for whom cities like this one are abstractions on a ledger. It was matter-of-fact. And it was a recognition that everyday tragedies—the hovels creeping up the hillsides; the parched fields outside the city; the children using garbage as a sandbox—can lead to larger ones.

On my last evening in the city I went to see Octavio Paz, the author of, among other books, *The Labyrinth of Solitude*. My first impression of Paz was as a political man, in the way Henry Adams was a political man. Unlike almost the entire intellectual class, which lives in the fortress neighborhoods south of the city, Paz's home was downtown, five minutes from the United States embassy. It was a small point, perhaps, and I am sure there are others who have forsaken the comfortable suburbs for large apartment buildings, but just as Paz has deserted the enclaves of the affluent left, so has he deserted their thinking.

There is little overlap between the thought of Paz and that of a man like Benitez. They stand at odds, although, in the 1930s, living in Paris and sympathetic to the Left in the Spanish Civil War, Paz was attracted to Marxism. As late as 1972 he tried to form a political party to promote a Mexican brand of socialism. But today, whatever his reservations about capitalism and the West, he has broken with the Left, with the social democrats, as he calls them. He condemns the Russian invasion of Afghanistan as strongly as he does the interference of the United States in the affairs of others. In short, he is a friend of democracy when few remain.

For Paz there are two cities, two Mexicos. One is that of the upper classes, economically and politically. It produces oil, owns houses, and goes on vacation. "Were this all there was to Mexico," he said, "it would be a country like Spain or Yugoslavia." The city might be Miami. Indeed, he noted a greater affinity between the rich in Mexico City and, say, the rich in New York than between rich and poor in either city. All the frontiers are now economic. The other Mexico is that of the ruined little country towns, the barrios of the city, the quarter of the population that goes from year to year without eating meat. Its counterparts are in India and the poorer African countries. Thus, one of the great questions for Paz, and for the country, is whether the trickle-down theories of international capitalism are valid. In a country where, as Benitez said, some 70 percent of the population receives 30 percent of the income, will the gap between rich and poor ever narrow? Paz is not such a booster of Western capitalism that he could hang around comfortably with the Reagan cabinet, but he finds the alternative, social democracy, worse. He said: "What choice do we have? Some can go forward together and others can stay behind; or all can go forward together, very slowly, and accompanied by political repression." He observed that progress, unlike fiery rhetoric, advances at an often imperceptible rate.

Paz is one of the few Mexican intellectuals I met who did not regret, politically speaking, that the United States is Mexico's northern neighbor. Yes, Mexico may have more than its share of American influence—television, the automobile culture, Monday-night football—and this has by no means all been good. But he noted that since World War II, its proximity to the United States has spared Mexico international obligations. It is not Poland, Hungary, or Pakistan, always caught between feuding parties. "And," he said, "unlike Cuba or Czechoslovakia, Mexico has political freedom."

According to Paz, the threat to freedom, in Mexico and elsewhere, is the patrimonial state, the Visigoths of the bureaucracy. He has written a book called *The Philanthropic Ogre*, and while we talked he described Mexico City, like Washington or Moscow, as a bureaucratic city. It is not only the seat of government but also the center of the reigning political party, and there being only one in Mexico—at least one that matters—the patronage system of the party has become the patrimonial concern of the state. The party has even, to a large extent, eclipsed the church. As in Chicago ward politics, to get ahead, to do just about anything, it is helpful to be a party member. Had Stendhal's Julien Sorel been Mexican, he would have joined the local machine and fallen in love with the mayor's wife, so dominant is the party's position in all political and economic dealings.

Nevertheless, Paz remained optimistic. He noted that except for such places as Mexico and the United States, most nations and people today are cut adrift from their aspirations and are without a sense of hope or progress. "Maybe," he said, "in parts of Africa or China, people think that tomorrow will be better than today, but that is so in only a few places in the world." He gave as evidence of a brighter future the advances in the arts, literature, and the sciences (both in Mexico and the United States), in contrast to the inertia of so many intellectual and political classes around the world. Marxism, for him, has become the armor of despair rather than of progress.

When I said good-bye and left, it was dark. I rode the elevator down to the lobby and walked along the Reforma, the city's main boulevard. The cars, as always, bounced around like chrome enlargements of an atom. As a metaphor for the end of civilization, the city is amazingly vibrant.

What had impressed me most about Paz was his courage. He had spoken clearly about the threats to the individual, whether from poverty, corrupt bureaucracies, or Russian tanks. Before our meeting, I had read accounts that compare him philosophically and politically to Solzhenitsyn, but found none of them accurate. Paz struck me as more optimistic, more understanding of human failings and weaknesses—in a word, compassionate; Jefferson, not Tolstoy. He was not a long-bearded giant, deluded into thinking that he alone could roll up the Iron Curtain, but a man with ideas and the freedom to express them, who somehow symbolized the best of the city's chaos and emotion.

America Unplugged

(1997)

Growing up on Long Island, I watched my share of murders and sitcoms, as well as space shots and political assassinations. I always thought Maxwell Smart had a better grip on the Cold War than did Henry Kissinger. Everything I needed to know about Hollywood I learned from Jed Clampitt.

When I was at college in the 1970s, the appeal of television began to fade as if it were a shoe box of old baseball cards. In the eighties, I found myself estranged from the fusion of television and politics. I imagined the White House partitioned into stage sets, as government-by-story-board became hard to distinguish from the plots on daytime television. The sound-bite campaigns held no more interest than Home Shopping. In the early nineties, before C-SPAN had a following or the Sunday press shows had redefined themselves as Irish bars, I moved from New York to the Swiss countryside just outside Geneva. At the same time, my wife and I gave up TV, and thus, like pioneers in the nineteenth century, we connect to America only through mail and the columns of the daily newspaper. My up-link to the U.S. is hotel television.

Few things, however, are more discouraging than to fly to

a remote part of the globe, check into a hotel with ceiling fans, and then find the company of cable Americans beamed up on several channels. Even in Russia or on certain Pacific islands, I have been awake at odd hours watching real stories of the highway patrol or reruns of "Baywatch."

At these jet-lagged moments, lying on a great mattress, my head propped on extra pillows, I feel like Huck Finn adrift on a raft in the eddies of American culture. But in Bryant Gumbel or Peter Jennings, all I see are Mark Twain's king and duke playing the Royal Nonesuch along the banks of the Mississippi.

On these dark nights of the soul, I often wonder if, after an evening of television, Alexis de Tocqueville would again want to observe the American experiment. Would he stir from his native Normandy to make notes about a country that is spellbound by "Hard Copy" or "Live with Regis and Kathie Lee"? Or would he take comfort that he had already written: "I see an innumerable multitude of men, alike and equal, constantly circling around in pursuit of the petty and banal pleasures with which they glut their souls. Each one of them, withdrawn into himself, is almost unaware of the fate of the rest."

When my friend Bill Rodgers got rid of television in 1968, he tossed his into a lilac bush—giving the episode some biblical fire and brimstone. When we moved to Switzerland, we brought with us a VCR and a small black-and-white TV, the kind doormen watch in the lobbies of rundown apartment buildings. We talked about converting to Swiss television, perhaps even color. But it was summer, there were Alps to explore and local wines to taste, and Swiss TV on Saturday evenings features men in lederhosen playing the accordion to women in dirndls.

More to the point, our daughters, then four and two, were reaching an age that required explanations for prime-time rubouts or the civil war in Yugoslavia. So we followed the advice of the Oompa-Loompas in *Charlie and the Chocolate Factory*:

> The most important thing we've learned,
> So far as children are concerned,
> Is never, never, never let
> Them near your television set—
> Or better still, just don't install,
> The idiotic thing at all.
> In almost every house we've been,
> We've watched them gaping at the screen,
> They loll and slop and lounge about,
> And stare until their eyes pop out. . . .
>
> So please, oh please we beg, we pray,
> Go throw your TV set away,
> And in its place you can install
> A lovely bookshelf on the wall.

In place of TV, the children (now there are four) created a series of imaginary worlds that can be conjured as quickly as the changing of a channel. Old boxes are rafts that cross oceans. Sofa cushions are dogsleds speeding serum from Anchorage to Nome. As Robert Louis Stevenson wrote:

> We built a ship upon the stairs
> All made of the back-bedroom chairs,
> And filled it full of sofa pillows
> To go a-sailing on the billows

In the evenings we read them stories, and, after we surrender, they listen to books on tape. Over the years I have assembled, for the cost of a cable subscription, an extensive collection of full-length recordings, including *The Wizard of*

Oz, Peter Pan, Fantastic Mr. Fox, Charlotte's Web, Robin Hood.
The tapes link the children to the oral traditions of storytelling
that started with Homer and continued in children's lives until
TV muscled fireside radio out of the living room.

Since giving up television, I find myself drawn to others who
do without it, as if part of a smug club that has blackballed
Conan O'Brien. I also spend a lot of time reading about the
harmful effect that TV has on children. These books recite
the litany of gloomy statistics. By age eighteen, most
American children will have seen seventeen thousand televised murders and watched television for twenty thousand
hours, during which time they will have only spent eleven
thousand hours in a classroom. Last year, according to one
survey, prime-time television had sixty-five thousand sexual
references. The average American preschooler watches
twenty-seven hours of television a week. In most households,
the TV is on more than five hours a day.

Worse than its nightly refrain of violence, television de-
nies small children a life of the mind. With bedtime stories
and make believe, kids dwell in their imaginary worlds. They
visit hospitals, fly airplanes, or confront dragons under the
bed. Only through these fantasies can they try out future
character or come to terms with their fears—what Bruno
Bettelheim eloquently called "the uses of enchantment."

By developing these imaginative worlds children can start
to become happy in their own company—to rely on themselves, not Disney, to fill long afternoons. But TV makes it
difficult for children to dream. Neither "Sesame Street" nor
cartoons require imagination. "Watching television not only
requires no skills but develops no skills," as one educator put it.

From a life of TV, children expect only to be entertained.
I have heard schoolteachers complain that students sit at their
desks with the same expectations they have when watching
"Saturday Night Live." But the absence of "something to do"

is important in a child's development. As Jerry Mander writes in *Four Arguments for the Elimination of Television*: "Looking back, I view that time of boredom, of 'nothing to do,' as the pit out of which creative action springs. . . . Nowadays, however, at the onset of that uncomfortable feeling, kids usually reach for the TV switch."

Not only does television foster dependence on the entertainment world, it also ends the distinctions between children and adults, both of whom simultaneously digest the same disconcerting images of O. J. Simpson, the war in Somalia, or the ritual infidelities of afternoon talk shows. As Neil Postman observes in *The Disappearance of Childhood*, "The world of the known and the not-yet-known is bridged by wonderment." But wonderment happens largely in a situation where the child's world is separate from the adult world, where children must enter, through their questions, into the adult world. As media merge the two worlds, he adds, "the calculus of wonderment changes. Curiosity is replaced by cynicism or, even worse, by arrogance. We are left with children who rely not on authoritative adults but news from nowhere. . . . We are left, in short, without children."

Some of these adult-children in the big cities imitate their TV heroes by using a gun to settle an argument. I remember one interview with a child who killed a robbery victim in New York. He confessed that he had no idea guns actually killed people. He had seen many deaths on TV, but none of them had seemed real. After pulling the trigger, he had expected his victim to get up and be on his way, delayed only by a quick game of cops and robbers.

Another reason I do not want my children watching television is that I do not like how it projects the image of war. War may be a tragic element of the human condition, but unless adults interpret for children a land mine in Angola or a bomb in Jerusalem, such incidents become either another action drama in television's wonderland, no more real than

Superman, or as dreadfully immediate as the shadows on the bedroom wall.

"War makes no national or racial or ideological distinctions as it degrades human beings" is a lesson the writer John Hersey learned on Guadalcanal during World War II—where our children's grandfather had a similar education. But during the Gulf War in 1991, the television coverage of the fighting was delivered in tones of breathless excitement normally reserved for a Super Bowl. The allied air attack against Baghdad, with Peter Arnett down on the sidelines, lacked only a half-time show, and the slaughter of an army of frightened recruits touched off a national celebration as if Iraq had lost to Ohio State in the Rose Bowl.

Whether democracy can survive an electorate that watches five hours of television a day is an open question. Who can understand the complexities of Bosnia or the wealth of nations based on twenty-two minutes with Connie Chung? Would the minds of Thomas Jefferson, Daniel Webster, or F. Scott Fitzgerald have emerged from endless evenings with the Huxtables?

On the surface, nothing could be more democratic than a medium that projects the image of political leaders to 98 percent of the population. With interactive television, America could become a nation of parliamentarians, with citizens answering every roll call. But those judging either Messrs. Clinton or Gingrich are an audience, there to be entertained, not an electorate that is part of the debate. The Burbank studio is no more heir to the Greek *polis* than Tom Brokaw is Demosthenes.

For this reason, I expect TV to become a well-developed medium for show trials, since so many preconditions are present: an audience that needs ever more lurid tales to be entertained, the absence of history, and the popularity of judges second only to that of private detectives. Perhaps Time Warner can launch the Show Trial Station and each week have Wolf Blitzer introduce the victim and the crime for which he has already been condemned.

Television's threat to democracy lies also in its monarchist pretensions. Celebrities are the kings, while ideas live like monks in cold abbeys. Viewers are serfs, raking small patches of earth allotted them by Cablevision or Home Box Office. Audiences grovel before such court jesters as Jay Leno or Johnny Carson, who would be better understood if required by the Federal Communications Commission to wear Shakespearean tunics. Televised presidential addresses, however well-intentioned, are variations on the balcony scene in Evita.

Not only is the nostalgia of most television a rebellion against the future, its sense of history thinks nothing of rewriting the past. Only someone with the narrative sense of Franz Kafka could imagine the context in which most programs are set or the suspension of disbelief they require: FBI agents tracking aliens, happy people on bar stools, newspaper editors like Lou Grant. Thirty years later, I am still amazed that television could have broadcast a comedy about amusing Nazi prison guards. As Kafka wrote of another sitcom: "It turns lying into a universal principle."

Television was set up to sell things, not to inform. Its affiliations are to the advertising industry, not to the public library, and thus it measures its success by the amount of soap sold, not the number of spirits cleansed. Nor do I believe that with the expanding cable and satellite revolution the abundance of channels will produce a higher level of programming. For every C-SPAN or A&E, there are ten other channels preaching the spiritual value of time-sharing or showing reruns of "The A-Team." As Bruce Springsteen observed, "55 channels and nothing on."

Alas, I no more expect America to give up TV than I expect some day to visit Lake Wobegon and have lunch at the Chatterbox Café—attractive as both ideas might be. I do think, however, that young families, when it comes time to childproof the house, should remove television's live wire. Why protect children from Drano but not "The X Files"? From the experience of friends, even those who deplore TV, I know that for many people giving up the tube requires too great an act of penitence—as if it meant a move to an ashram or a cabin like that of the Unabomber.

Nevertheless, pulling the plug on television is a simple act of independence that requires neither a resolution of Congress nor an environmental impact statement. The cord comes easily away from the wall, and, in exchange, the average family will pick up lazy afternoons and quiet evenings for the pursuit of happiness.

Peleliu

(1998)

Over the captured ridge about the hurt battalion waited,
And hardly had sense left to prove if ghost or living passed
From hole to hole with sunken eyes and slow ironic orders,
While fiery mountains burst and clanged—
  and there your lot was cast.

—Edmund Blunden, "An Infantryman"

Peleliu may have the distinction of being the most remote American battlefield. For more than a few years, I made plans to get there, and often, after the children went to bed, I would study the *Official Airline Guide* for the best connections from Guam, Taipei, or Manila. On the map, Peleliu, a southern island in the archipelago of the Republic of Palau, is five hundred miles southeast of Manila, in what colonial mapmakers call the Carolines, part of Micronesia, although for many years in my travel dreams it was as remote as the dusty fields before Troy.

In September 1944, United States Marines, among them my father, launched an amphibious assault against Japanese forces on Peleliu. The strategic purpose of the landing was to protect the flank of General Douglas MacArthur's forces on their return to the Philippines. But instead of overrunning an obscure Japanese garrison and seizing the airstrip, the Marines attacked a network of interlocking caves and coral ridges. The ten thousand Japanese defenders, members of the Fourteenth Infantry Division, were eventually annihilated. But the three combat regiments of the First Marine Division, about the same number of men, suffered dreadful casualties, as if through a twist of fate they had attacked the Union center at Gettysburg.

In the landing my father served as executive officer of the First Battalion, 1st Marine Regiment. Prior to the invasion, as he wrote in recollection of the battle, "I moved up from captain to major, and became second in command of the nine-hundred-man combat unit. My friend Captain Everett Pope took over C Company which I had commanded for two-and-a-half years and shared with its men the unforgettable experience of war."

In recent years during family gatherings, when others are doing dishes or watching small children, our conversations have drifted to Peleliu. We talk about this general or that battalion, and read aloud from after-action reports, much as we once played with model trains. Like any child—even one now in his forties—I am interested to hear my father's stories of war. But I like to compare his memories with the written histories, not just because of Walt Whitman's remark about the real war not getting into the books. For me my father's recollections are a plumb line against which, at least on Peleliu, I try to measure the angles of history.

The standard accounts lined the shelves in the house where I grew up, although as a child I only looked at their pictures. One came inscribed to my father: "To a great CO," but it was not until the early 1980s, after I read E. B. Sledge's *With the Old Breed: At Okinawa and Peleliu*, that I sensed what the Marines had endured. At the same time I noticed that my father had, in a casual way, collected an extensive library about Peleliu. He had discovered the Sledge book, now recognized as a classic, in the flyer of an obscure military publisher and said offhandedly: "Here's one I think we ought to have." For Christmas and birthdays in the years that followed came other histories and memoirs. He gave me Bill D. Ross's *Peleliu: Tragic Triumph* at Christmas 1991 with the inscription: "To Matthew, whose devotion to my W.W. II battles widens our bonds of love."

Most of the larger histories of World War II, if they mention Peleliu at all, do so only in passing, calling it either "needless" or "forgotten." In his history of the Second World War, John Keegan bypasses the island. But in his recent *Fields of Battle*, about North America, I was surprised to come across a brief sketch of my father that captures his biography with elegant simplicity:

> I know the life story of a modest American hero, the graduate of a great Ivy League university, who decided on the day he got his degree that America would enter the Second World War, went down the street to the recruiting office, joined the Marines, and spent the next four years leading a company of infantry up island beaches in the Pacific until death and wounds brought him command of his battalion; the war over he married a childhood sweetheart, raised a large family, made a modest fortune, devoted his retirement years to traveling the United States, encouraging other sufferers from a progressive [eye] illness to which he had fallen victim to look on the bright side, see the best in life.

In our conversations my father casts himself neither as the hero of a wartime romance nor as an anonymous legionnaire, but as someone whose fate included a tour of duty in the underworld that is modern warfare. He tells these stories not to boast about his courage or even to prove that war is hell, but to recall friends long forgotten or sacrifices not foretold by the gods but dictated by the stress of battle. His tone is not that of Homer, describing the interventions of Zeus, but the grim humor and the sense of detached self-preservation that Alexandr Solzhenitsyn uses to remember another set of forgotten islands—*The Gulag Archipelago.*

My window of opportunity opened after several days of business in Manila. Early on a Saturday morning, I headed to the airport through the city's glittering high rises and street-level slums. Peleliu was a bloody footnote in the battle of the Philippines, and in September 1944, those islands were an American colony. Gazing from the taxi at the shanties, stray dogs, hanging wash, and occasional glass palace that are the mixed metaphors of most Asian cities, I found myself remembering Rudyard Kipling's epitaph for the Philippines, written about earlier colonial wars:

> Take up the White Man's Burden—
> The savage wars of peace—
> Fill full the mouth of Famine
> And bid the sickness cease;
> And when your goal is nearest
> The end for others sought,
> Watch Sloth and heathen Folly
> Bring all your hope to naught.

Air Micronesia, a subsidiary of Continental Airlines, makes the two-hour ocean hop from Manila to Koror, the capital of Palau. My fellow travelers were heading into the sunshine for rest and relaxation, if not snorkeling in the islands' pristine waters. Even though we flew south along the Philippine east coast, above volcanic peaks and mud flats, the flight felt like the shuttle to Houston until the Boeing 727 dropped below the clouds to make its approach across coral reefs and turquoise waters, which evoke idyllic dreams more than desperate attacks into no-man's-land.

By coincidence, my friend Doug Adler represented Palau in some of its dealings with the American government, which had a mandate for the islands until they gained limited independence in 1994. He arranged for the nephew of the president to meet my plane, and after I cleared customs, Steve Nakamura and his wife introduced themselves and carried my bag to a waiting taxi.

From my years of planning, I knew Peleliu was either fifteen minutes by air taxi from Koror or a more leisurely afternoon on an inter-island steamer, which one guidebook said cost five dollars. But Steve, a Palauan in his late twenties who wore an open shirt and a warm smile, discouraged me from either option. The planes, he hinted, were unreliable, and he said the steamer had departed. Instead for my account he had chartered a fishing boat for $350, making me think I might be the only catch of the week.

The bridge between the airport and Koror had recently collapsed, so the taxi took us to a makeshift ferry landing, and we waited under a thatched awning, like characters in *Lord Jim*, before crossing to the far shore. Because of the U.S. trusteeship, Koror feels like a small American town that has washed up on a tropical shore. The shops sell Budweiser, the post office has a ZIP Code, and many of the houses look like those on the fringes of American military bases. At the time of independence, the U.S. government agreed to large subsidies for the islands in exchange for Palau's consent to ports-of-call by ships armed with nuclear weapons—the kind of Faustian compromise that Joseph Conrad would understand better than Thomas Jefferson.

I expected my fishing boat to look like those that congressmen charter off Bimini. But this was an ordinary speed boat that had a few fishing poles thrown under the wheelhouse, and the captain, not exactly in dress whites, was asleep on the life jackets when we arrived at the pier. By water Peleliu is a little more than an hour south from Koror, and our boat made sweeping arcs among the reefs and sandbars that connect the chain.

After World War I, a League of Nations mandate gave control of Palau to the Japanese, who later began to fortify the islands, including the construction of an airfield on Peleliu. In response, the American military formulated contingency plans for a possible war with Japan, and, in particular, the U.S. Marine Corps developed the strategy of island hopping, which would allow it to leapfrog across the central and western Pacific toward the Japanese mainland—attacking some Japanese fortifications but leaving others to wither on the vine. The Marine Corps Lieutenant Colonel Earl H. (Pete) Ellis, who helped develop these plans, died mysteriously in 1923 in Koror, where he was posing as an American businessman—probably with shoes, a suitcase, and travel plans much like my own.

We made landfall in Peleliu alongside a concrete pier by climbing over a rusting steamer that I suspect was my five-dollar inter-island ferry. Near the dock was the kind of shed I associate with abandoned rail spurs and, with the tourist trade in mind, a sign proclaiming "Peleliu—Land of Enchantment," although at that moment the only spell cast seemed to be on the dogs sleeping in the shade of the afternoon sun.

From the guidebooks, not just the hand-painted sign, I had the impression that Peleliu was a tourist destination, and I imagined beach hotels where once there had been entrenched battalions. But we had to hitchhike to our guest house. We got a ride in the back of a pickup truck, and when Steve had it stop so that I could meet the governor, his excellency was outside mowing his lawn. Our rooms for the night were in the island's only lodging, run by a Japanese couple, who, as if in hiding since the end of the war, had the walls decorated with posters of zeros, Japanese cruisers and carriers launching their squadrons.

My weekend plan was to retrace my father's steps, starting at Beach White, where he landed with the First Battalion, and moving inland to The Blockhouse and finally Bloody Nose Ridge, where the invasion forces took dreadful casualties attacking a system of coral ridges that were as well defended as the cloisters at Monte Cassino. But when Steve and I, in a borrowed car, made a short excursion before dinner, we got lost immediately. At Anzio and Salerno you cannot see the landing beaches for the markers. But on the jungle roads that cross the small island, the battle for Peleliu is as faceless as an encounter at sea. When I expressed frustration to Steve, who grew up on Peleliu, about the fog of war that obscured the battlefield, he confessed: "In school, we studied American history, not Peleliu history."

That evening, as I pored over the maps in my regimental histories, a guardian angel arrived at the guest house in the form of Tangie Hesus. I knew before arriving that he was Peleliu's "state historian," but I despaired that I would find him on an island with so few telephones. But Steve rounded him up just after nightfall, and before me stood not an Oxford don but the happy presence of a Peleliu native in his mid-thirties wearing Marine Corps fatigues. When I said that I was a friend of Everett Pope, who had returned to the island in 1994, fifty years after the battle, such was his glee that I might well have invoked the image of a tribal god.

For Tangie, men like Pope or Ray Davis, who commanded the First Battalion, or my father, whom he knew by name, were legends whose spirits inhabited the desolate crags and jungle trails of the battlefield, where each day he guided returning veterans or accidental tourists who found their way to Peleliu. I discovered in Tangie not just a kindred spirit for the battle, but a one-man historical society and the curator of a museum, which, without funding from the National

Endowment for the Humanities, manages to keep Peleliu alive with displays devoted to personal narratives of the fighting—faithful, in its remote way, to John Keegan's thesis that the face of battle is best understood from those who were there.

The next morning I ate a breakfast of baked fish on the terrace overlooking the shallow waters encased by coral. The tide was low, revealing not a blue lagoon but a great reach of mud and rocks, as if it were a Maine potato field in springtime. It was through such murky waters that the three regiments of the First Marine Division launched their attack, from an armada of naval warships that had assembled beyond the reef. Over breakfast I was reading *The Devil's Anvil: The Assault on Peleliu* written by a Connecticut newspaperman, James H. Hallas, who quotes a D-Day tank crewman on this stretch of water: "When the tide went out that night, you could have walked 300 yards across the beach on the bodies of dead Marines."

Although there were discussions at the highest levels, including with President Roosevelt in Hawaii in July 1944, about canceling the landing at Peleliu, the decision was taken to proceed, in part because few of the commanding generals expected much resistance. General William Rupertus, who commanded the First Marine Division, said it would be a "quickie" and predicted the battle would be decided in three days. After shelling the island prior to the landings, one of the offshore admirals confessed that his warships had run out of targets. The legendary commander of the 1st Marine Regiment, Colonel Lewis ("Chesty") Puller, told his men, including my father, that after the naval bombardment they might only be asked to "police up the area with the bayonet."

Waiting to transfer to landing craft, my father remembers his first sense that the tides on Peleliu might run against the Americans:

As the boats loaded, circled and fanned out in the long line of the first assault wave, I felt the odds were with us. The first hint that they weren't and that all was not well came as Japanese mortar and artillery shells fell among the advancing boats, with two direct hits close by.

The three Marine regiments, about nine thousand combat troops, landed abreast along two horseshoe beaches, code-named White and Orange. On the left, as they landed from the west, the 1st Marines came ashore on Beach White, with the objective of pushing straight inland. The mission of the 5th Marines, in the center, was to capture the airfield, while the 7th Marines, on the right flank, were to wheel right and secure Peleliu's southern tip. Many of these best-laid plans, however, never got off the beach.

Most of the veterans I interviewed described their shock when they first realized that the burning wreckage along the shore had Marines, not Japanese, inside, reminiscent of the disaster at Tarawa. Many expressed the feelings that Sledge recorded:

> Up and down the beach and out on the reef, a number of amtracs and DUKWs were burning. Japanese machine-gun bursts made long splashes on the water as though flaying it with some giant whip. . . . I caught a fleeting glimpse of a group of Marines leaving a smoking amtrac on the reef. . . . I had tasted the bitterest essence of war, the sight of helpless comrades being slaughtered, and it filled me with disgust.

By driving down an unmarked jungle path, Tangie and I found Beach White, which almost until the water's edge sits under a gloomy mangrove canopy, as if in a backwater on the Georgia coast. Perhaps twenty yards across, the beach where the 1st Marines landed is covered with chunks of coral, some so gnarled as to resemble animal skulls. Not only was it impossi-

ble for the Marines to dig for cover in the rocky sand, but registered on the beach were Japanese mortars, artillery, and
machine guns that had withstood the naval barrage and now
raked the sands in search of casualties. An illustrator for *Life*
magazine who came ashore in the first waves, Tom Lea, recalls:
"Those marines flattened in the sand on that beach were dark
and huddled like wet rats in death." One of my father's close
friends, Fendall Yerxa, who served on Puller's regimental staff,
remembers the sand "popping" and how, weighed down with a
soaked pack, his mind moved off the beach faster than his
encumbered legs. He also remembers the withering fire that
came down the beach from what came to be known as The
Point, a redoubt on the left flank that in the legends of Peleliu
looms as large as an Arthurian castle.

K Company of the Third Battalion, commanded by
Captain George P. Hunt, had the mission after landing to
capture The Point and thus subdue the Japanese crossfire. Of
the 235 men who sought this objective, more than two-thirds
were killed or wounded, and the survivors, including Captain
Hunt, had to defend their gains on The Point against suicidal
counterattacks, which he describes in *Coral Comes High*, the
best book written about the landing.

I had expected The Point to loom like Pointe du Hoc,
which a Ranger battalion scaled and defended, in similar desperate circumstances, during the Normandy invasion. But
instead, Tangie and I climbed among scattered boulders and
what seemed like the neolithic roots of a petrified forest.
It was easier to imagine cavemen than twentieth-century
Americans carrying fire to such a primeval battleground.

"Imagine if an officer less brave than George Hunt had
the job of securing The Point?" is my father's rhetorical question about the savage battle for the flank and the consequences of failure. But my father never saw The Point, as the
First Battalion had pushed directly off the beach into a series
of bunkers and pillboxes, which inflicted heavy casualties, and

a fortified blockhouse that the navy had missed despite its "exhaustion of available targets."

Tangie and I walked to The Blockhouse along a small dirt road that, despite the walls of jungle vegetation that have grown since the battle, still evoked those quiet lanes that traverse the Antietam farmland. Several infantry assaults failed to break its resistance, which only gave way after sixteen-inch shells were called over the horizon from the battleship *Pennsylvania*.

As executive officer, my father set up the rear command post in The Blockhouse, which became, in addition to a supply base, the battalion aid station. Among other jobs, he organized the stretcher bearers and thus, like Charon on the River Styx, had to watch many friends—especially the men from C Company whom he led through Guadalcanal and Cape Gloucester—being ferried from the world of the living to that of the dead. Casualties among the 950 men in the First Battalion on Peleliu were 71 percent, but its three rifle companies were nearly wiped out. After six days of fighting, B Company had thirty-six enlisted men and two officers, C Company had fifteen men and two officers, and A Company had sixty-five men and two officers. To put this in perspective, Roman legions used the word *decimated* to describe casualties of one in ten. "Looking back," my father reflects,

> I have often felt that becoming battalion exec instead of remaining a company commander could have been the event that saved my life. No longer being required to lead a company directly into battle could have made the crucial difference between living and dying.

Casualties in the early assault regiments in Normandy, like those of combat Marines on Peleliu, were more than one in two. But once the Americans had pierced the outer walls of

Fortress Europa, they could move inland with tanks and artillery. Once Marines came off the beach at Peleliu and survived nightmares like The Point or The Blockhouse, they encountered coral hills, undetected in the pre-invasion intelligence, higher than the dunes above Omaha Beach.

Toward the end of the second day of fighting, the 1st Marines, with the First Battalion in the center, attacked what they called Bloody Nose Ridge. All the books about Peleliu describe the sharp ends of the Umurbrogol, its local name, but none is more compelling than a short memoir by Russell Davis, an infantryman with the Second Battalion, whose only book compares favorably to another he admires, *The Red Badge of Courage*:

> Old Marines talk of Bloody Nose Ridge as though it were one, but I remember it as a series of crags, ripped bare of all standing vegetation, peeled down to the rotted coral, rolling in smoke, crackling with heat and stinking of wounds and death. In my memory it was always dark up there, even though it must have blazed under the afternoon sun, because the temperature went up over 115 [degrees], and men cracked wide open from the heat. It must have been the color of the ridge that made me remember it as always dark—the coral was stained and black, like bad teeth.

Tangie and I drove his borrowed car up the narrow, dirt path that leads to a small plateau among the ridges. Halfway up we passed the only battlefield sign on the island—indicating the direction to Bloody Nose Ridge, where a small obelisk remembers the deeds of the First Marine Division and those from its ranks who won the Congressional Medal of Honor, including Everett Pope.

The monument has a commanding view of the surrounding valleys, like a box seat at the opera. But nowhere on the nearby ridges or down in the dark canyons was there a sign of civilization. I could hear the lonely caw of jungle birds or watch low clouds swirl on the distant hilltops, as if in a legend of Transylvania or the Black Forest. Nothing about this twisted ground connected to the American imagination except Edgar Allan Poe's description of the house of Usher: "An air of stern, deep, and irredeemable gloom hung over and pervaded all."

The sheer cliffs, almost parapets, the sense of a moat in the valleys recalled errant quests, and neither Americans nor Japanese would have been surprised had the defenders poured boiling oil on the assault forces—as, for most of those who tried to scale these ramparts, the experience of the heat and fire echoed medieval battles. As Russell Davis described the jousting:

> From the base of the cliff, we would pick out each man and follow him until he got hit, went to ground, or climbed to the top. Not many made the top. As they toiled, caves and gullies and holes opened up and Japanese dashed out to roll grenades down on them, and sometimes to lock, body to body, in desperate wrestling matches. Knives and bayonets flashed on the hillside. I saw one man bend, straighten, and club and kick at something that attacked his legs like a mad dog. He reached and heaved, and a Japanese soldier came end-over-end down the hill. The machine-gunners yelled encouragement.

Until the Marines attacked Bloody Nose Ridge, the invasion, while costly, had gone according to American military doctrine. Mobile, lightly armed assault troops had established a beachhead and seized the airfield. Offshore among the reserves was heavy armor and army regiments that could press the land campaign. But the Marine commanding general,

Rupertus, never called for the army and instead sent his badly depleted battalions, including the First, into the ridges, much the way World War I generals hoped that one more frontal assault would break the enemy trenches.

Among my father's books are some from World War II that he read during lulls in the fighting, and many are memoirs of the Great War, with titles like *Education Before Verdun*. Little did he realize that accounts of his own battalion would later read like those before Passchendaele or the Somme, such as this from Harry A. Gailey's *Peleliu*:

> The Marines of the 7th were exhausted and [Col.] Puller sent what was left of A Company of 1/1, a total of 56 men, through their lines to continue the attack. He did this because he assumed from his maps that there was a uniform slope to the hill mass. However, Company A encountered a nearly sheer 150-foot cliff. The Japanese hit the company with heavy small arms, machine-gun, and mortar fire. Only six men of the entire company regained the relative safety of the lines of 2/7 some 150 yards to the rear without being hit. The rest had been killed or wounded.

Nor did it help the Marines attacking Bloody Nose Ridge to call in either air cover, artillery, or naval gun ships. Dug in under the ridges, my father recalls:

> As the next hideous night fell, our men held what ground they had chewed out inside the limestone ridges. All the jungle foliage had long since been blasted away; the landscape seemed like the mountains of the moon. As the hours progressed, a forward observer, a young ensign from the battleship *Mississippi*, appeared and declared himself ready to direct fire from its big guns on the enemy positions if I could orient them to him.

They crept forward to a small ravine between the American and Japanese lines and

> . . . for the rest of the night we called in salvo after salvo, hour after hour, on the honeycombed ridges facing the fast dwindling strength of our companies. But as morning came, and our fire ceased, the Jap machine guns and mortars resumed their lethal chorus.

As Homer wrote:

> for all the world as if all Troy were torched and smoldering down from the looming brows of the citadels to her roots.

If the spirit of Achilles was alive on Peleliu, it was embodied in the personality of Lewis Burwell Puller, known throughout the war by his nickname "Chesty." In the 1950s, after the Korean War, he would retire from the Marine Corps as its most decorated officer. But by the time he landed on Beach White, he was already a legend. In the colonial wars of Haiti and Nicaragua, Puller won several Navy Crosses for leading assaults against rebel strongholds. On Guadalcanal and Cape Gloucester his battalions won important battles, although at the cost of heavy casualties. On Peleliu he commanded the three battalions of the 1st Regiment. As Craig Cameron writes in *American Samurai*: "Puller was not a man who would question Rupertus's wisdom in pressing costly frontal attacks or spare either himself or his men in carrying out his orders."

By my father's account, Puller was a short man, with steel gray eyes, a deep voice, and a swelling chest—almost like that of a bantam rooster—from which he took his nickname. He spoke with a southern, Tidewater drawl, and, had he been born in a different era, he might well have been one of Lee's lieutenants—the biographies of whom he often read in battle.

With the officers in his command, Puller was cool and direct. He resented the intrusions of military brass, especially parade ground generals and junior officers who perhaps did not share his zeal for combat. James Hallas writes that "to Chesty, low casualties among lieutenants indicated that the attack was not being pressed with sufficient vigor."

Puller was a mustang, meaning commissioned from the ranks, and with the enlisted men he had a natural affinity. "The men loved Chesty," is a phrase my father has often used, "and he loved them." During the thick of a battle, Puller would come forward, crouch low near a rifleman, and ask, "How's it going, old man?" Just as Jay Gatsby called everyone "old sport," Puller's name for everyone was "old man," with the usual prescription in battle to "just keep pushing." "Whenever he remembered a name," my father quips, "he usually mispronounced it."

Puller was physically brave but disinterested in tactics or strategy. Everett Pope remarks with both irony and apprecia- tion that he "was the greatest platoon leader in the history of the Marine Corps." But many of the officers and men I asked about Puller refused to answer, not wanting to be at odds with a legend.

Puller had a habit of humiliating junior officers, to the delight of the enlisted men. Jim Rogers, a battalion officer on Peleliu, remembers Puller, on Pavuvu, ordering him to stand at attention in a deep puddle. A man with Joycean sparkle, Rogers survived Peleliu to become a Catholic priest outside Boston. He wrote in one letter: "Your father and I were best friends, as you know, and I have the greatest respect and affec- tion for him. Puller thought highly of him and that's one of the few good things I can say about Chesty."

It was on Pavuvu, after telling the assembled Marines that all they might have to do on Peleliu would be to police up with the bayonet, that Puller added: "Still, I wouldn't mind having insurance on some of you boys," to which they responded with cheers. During the landing, the commander of the regimental weapons company, Bob Thomases, asked Puller: "During the attack, sir, where do you want me?"

"Just stick with me, old man," Puller replied with tactical insouciance. "That way I'll know you aren't yellow."

Puller's trademark was to have his command post far forward. But on Peleliu, Fendall Yerxa said that position led to permanent confusion in the regimental command, as much of the time staff officers were taking cover. Also, on Peleliu, Puller didn't have his legendary mobility, because a flare-up of a thigh wound from an earlier battle left him hobbling. "Puller had no idea what was going on," is Pope's assessment. "We never saw Chesty," is my father's.

As a consequence, gaps often developed in the lines of the 1st Marines. The official history describes one incident:

> As the exhausted Marines settled in, a more serious threat developed as the enemy discovered a gap between 2/1 and 1/1 and began to infiltrate the weak spot. To seal the hole, F Company, 7th Marines had to be committed. This outfit fought its way into position and managed to close the gap.

But it was my father who discovered this particular gap, and he tells the story whenever he is asked about Puller's habits of command:

> It was then that it became clear to me that there were no friendly troops on the battalion right flank. It was completely open, entirely vulnerable to a Japanese counterattack which, had it taken place, could have allowed them to surge all the way to the beach line and create near total havoc. I called Col. "Chesty" Puller, regimental commander, to warn him of the peril and the urgent need for reinforcements. When I reached him on the field tele-

phone he was true to form. First he confused me with Steve Sabol, commander of the Third Battalion. When this was cleared up, his gruff voice spoke its usual formula, "Just keep pushing, old man."

I stood transfixed, my runner beside me as we heard Japanese voices and the click of weapons on the far side of the vital road in question. Unbelieving I called again. This time I got Lt. Col. "Buddy" Ross, regimental exec, who instantly perceived the urgency. "Stay right there, Steve, don't move; I'm sending up a unit from the Seventh. Tie them into the line as soon as they get there." Within what seemed minutes, they appeared and immediately took up firing positions to plug the gap. No sooner was this done when there came wild shouts of "Banzai" as the Japanese poured across the road into the devastating but crucially effective fire of the newly arrived Marines. That day, or perhaps just a portion of it, was saved. More crises were to follow soon.

Craig Cameron sketches a portrait of Puller that makes him hard to distinguish from the fanatical enemy he was fighting. Of Peleliu he writes:

The course of the fighting began increasingly to take on the appearance of a test of wills between the implacable Japanese in their caves and Puller's regiment. On Guadalcanal it had been a test of wills between warrior representatives [i.e., each army]; on Peleliu, Puller made it more personal. It was, moreover, a test of endurance in which the Japanese did not play fully human roles but were instead faceless elements in the landscape, deadly, but to be conquered along with the heat and blasted coral ridges. He had strong and well-founded faith in his men, and they always responded to his repeated calls for attack.

But Puller, too, was a man in the chain of command. In another widely reported conversation, the divisional chief of staff, John Seldon, asked Puller, who like Honsowetz was requesting additional men to attack: "Anything wrong with your orders, Lewie?"

There is a famous photograph of Puller at his command post during the battle—shirtless, smoking a corncob pipe, and favoring his good leg—for which the caption could easily read:

> Towards thee I roll, thou all-destroying but unconquering whale; to the last I grapple with thee; from hell's heart I stab at thee; for hate's sake I spit my last breath at thee.

When the III Corps commander, General Roy Geiger, went forward to Puller's command post on the sixth day of the fighting, he decided, as Gailey writes, that Puller was "out of touch with reality." Shortly thereafter, the 1st Marines, with more than 50 percent casualties, were pulled from the line.

From the monument on Bloody Nose Ridge, Tangie and I came down the hillside into what is known as the Horseshoe, a vast amphitheater of death in which the 1st Marines played out the final acts of their tragedy. In Tangie's museum, there is a quote from Captain Hank Hough that describes this valley of decision:

> In broad daylight one could stand at the south of Horseshoe Valley and study at leisure the precipitous slopes and sheer cliffs that were its walls. It was eerie. You could almost physically feel the weightless presence of hundreds of hostile eyes watching you. Yet there was no sign of the enemy: no movement, no shots, only a lonely silence.

The only monument in the Horseshoe is Japanese, a small oriental shrine, but nothing to remember the hundreds of young Americans killed or wounded here. "War," my father likes to quote William Tecumseh Sherman, "is about dying in battle and then getting your name misspelled in the newspapers." On the right as you enter the Horseshoe is a hill covered with jungle brush that Tangie and I climbed like two boys playing in the woods after school. I wanted to reach the top because it was there that C Company made its last desperate stand and its captain, Everett Pope, won the Medal of Honor.

My father remembers Pope leading away the remnants of his old company:

> After another day of futile struggle against the fortified limestone catacombs, the battalion was withdrawn and regrouped. Ev Pope and what was left of "C" Company (90 men) were detached and sent in support of the Second Battalion. With a heavy heart I watched him go, knowing so well that in combat any attached unit is always given the dirtiest, the most dangerous assignment. Theirs was to be no exception.

Pope and his ninety men were ordered to take Hill 100, which on the Marine Corps maps appeared to be an isolated knob and might, if taken, give the Marines high ground to support the attacks, across the Horseshoe, against Bloody Nose Ridge. But Hill 100 turned out to be the head of a whale, and for one long night the Japanese attacked along the humpback against the few Marines who had struggled to the top.

One of the men who went up the hill was Joseph Seifts who remembers:

> We started up with about thirty men. By the time we got to the top there were only about twenty of us left. . . . We had no machine guns or mortars. The Japs hit us I believe

around ten or eleven at night. We had to hold the hill. Because at the bottom of the hill lay all of our wounded. We stopped attack after attack. . . . I was never so glad to see daylight. . . . I still have bad memories of Peleliu.

Another with a ringside seat to that night on the ridge was Russell Davis, who wrote:

The remnants of our Second Battalion spent a terrible night up there. But, for the few men up on the higher ridge—mostly from C Company, First Battalion—it was far worse. All through the night we could hear them screaming for illumination or for corpsmen, as the Japs came at them from caves which were all around them on the hillside. Men were hit up there and we could hear them crying and pleading for help, but nobody could help them. . . . The cries of Americans and Japanese were all mixed together.

Pope went to the Marine Corps from Bowdoin College in Maine, where he later served as chairman of the board of overseers. The previous Bowdoin graduate to win the Medal of Honor and who also was president of the college was Joshua Chamberlain, whose 20th Maine Regiment held the Union left flank at Gettysburg. While Little Round Top may be on the other side of the world from Hill 100, Chamberlain's account of the fighting could be Pope's account of Peleliu:

Squads of the enemy broke through our line in several places, and the fight was literally hand to hand. The edge of the fight rolled backward and forward like a wave. The dead and wounded were now in our front and then in our rear. . . . Rude shelters were thrown up of the loose rocks that covered the ground.

When dawn broke on Hill 100, Pope's perimeter was the size of a tennis court, he had no ammunition and about eight men, and he led the survivors off the hill. "I saw no good reason for us all to die there—as was about to happen." But he felt anything but a hero:

> My most vivid memory, after being driven off the hill, is that of expecting that Puller would have me court-martialed for having failed to hold—i.e., for not having died up there. As your father will recall, late on the afternoon, Puller ordered C-1-1 to take the hill again. Since there were only about 12–15 of us left, it was clearly to have been a suicide mission (ours, not Puller's).

As Pope prepared to lead his men back into battle and to their deaths, he received orders canceling the attack: "I have always believed that your father and Ray Davis succeeded in convincing Puller to call off the mission. Why Puller wanted us all dead on the top of that hill has never been clear to me."

My father wrote the citation proposing Everett Pope for the Medal of Honor. The language used is that of military decoration:

> . . . in order to hold ground won . . . remain on the exposed hill . . . attacked continuously with grenades, machine guns . . . suicidal charges . . . resorting to hand-to-hand combat. . . . eight remaining riflemen when daylight brought . . . he was ordered to withdraw.

On Pavuvu, Puller grilled my father about the nomination, and my father expected Pope to be "knocked back" to a Navy Cross. What he didn't know was that Puller tried to block the award. As Pope relates:

You must read my remarks about Puller with the knowledge that Puller attempted to prevent the award to me of the Medal of Honor. I have seen the files. He always maintained that none in his command would receive it until he did, and as far as I can determine, John Basilone and I are the only two serving under him whose awards were not posthumous.

But the Medal of Honor was awarded—instead of the court-martial Pope feared as he came off the ridge without orders. "I wear it proudly," he told me when we spoke at his summer house in Maine, "not because of anything I did to deserve it. But out of respect for my men who died up there and to prolong, at least for a moment of time, their place in our nation's history. As you know, it was 12 days before my dead on that hill were recovered."

During the night that C Company was fighting and dying for Hill 100, the rest of the First Battalion was across the Horseshoe, preparing for a final attack against the face of the ridge. My father remembers:

We received orders from Regiment that at six o'clock the next morning there would be an artillery barrage on Bloody Nose Ridge, followed at six thirty by a frontal attack by the remnants of the First and Second Battalions.

Without C Company, the First Battalion (normally about 950 men and officers) was reduced to a little more than 100 infantrymen and four officers. He continues:

A plea to Regiment to send forward any officers and men who could be spared brought old friend Fendall Yerxa back to us along with a dozen or two cooks, bakers and truck drivers, converted overnight into riflemen, and a 37 mm gun. Clearly it was to be the battalion's last throw of the dice. If Bloody Nose Ridge could be taken, our fire from its heights into enemy-held crevices below would eventually dislodge them and Peleliu would be won at last.

As first light broke, all hands took position and waited for the artillery barrage. Six ten, six twenty. Silence and growing horror that there would be none. There wasn't. But at six thirty sharp, Major Ray Davis gave the command and the men moved out in short rushes, starting up the slope toward the heights that now seemed miles away.

Russell Davis was part of the attack as a rifleman with the Second Battalion, which was mixed together on the First Battalion's right flank:

The whole motley lot—a fighting outfit only in the minds of a few officers in the First Regiment and in the First Division—started up the hill. I have never understood why.

As the men moved up the slopes, my father recalls:

Enemy fire quickened. Minutes later a runner came rushing up to me at the rear command post with a message, "Major Davis has been wounded and orders you to take command of the battalion." As I ran forward I found men still moving, trying to take what cover they could find, urged on by a young second lieutenant, Junior Thompson. On our right flank, the Second Battalion had not moved.

Until that moment, my father's role with the battalion, as its executive officer or number two, was supporting. He had kept the food, ammunition, water, and stretchers moving toward the front lines, but, unlike either Davis or Honsowetz in the Second Battalion, he had not had to carry out Puller's direct orders to assault the ridges. By contrast, Honsowetz had seen some of his men near mutiny when he gave the orders to continue the attack, and Jim Rogers was present when one Marine told the Lieutenant Colonel, pointing toward Bloody Nose Ridge: "I'll go—if you go with me."[1] As my father ran forward he realized that "to move farther would be suicide; no one would reach the crest alive." His crisis of command was not unlike Everett Pope's on Hill 100. He ordered the men to halt their attack, but now feared the wrath of Colonel Puller for disobeying orders. "I dispatched my runner, Cpl. Hauge, going at top speed to inform Regiment that we were pinned down by heavy enemy fire."

> At that critical moment the Japanese ceased their firing. An eerie, never-to-be-forgotten quiet fell, broken only by the faraway rattle of machine guns and the clump of distant mortars. We lay and crouched there, waiting. Waiting for we knew not what. The sun rose higher, turning helmets into ovens. At long last came a runner from Regiment, informing us that we were to be relieved by a fresh battalion, from the 7th Marines. Slowly we rose, formed two files on each side of the cart track leading back. The relief took place in full view of the Japanese atop Bloody Nose Ridge. If they had opened up, it would have been the final and apocalyptic carnage. Inexplicably, they did not. We marched slowly away.

Sledge describes the relief of the 1st Marines, passing the 5th Marines on their way down from the ridges.

> We in the 5th Marines had many a dead or wounded friend to report about from our ranks, but the men in the 1st

---

[1] The most quoted conversation on Peleliu took place between Puller and the commander of the Second Battalion, Russell Honsewetz, who had been given repeated orders to attack up Bloody Nose Ridge. In desperation, Honsewetz called Puller on the field telephone to complain that he had neither the ammunition nor the men to attack, to which Puller is said to have responded, in my father's version: "You're still there, ain't ya Hunnsecker."

Marines had so many it was appalling. . . . What once had been companies in the 1st Marines looked like platoons; platoons looked liked squads. I saw few officers.

For the men of First Marines, Peleliu was over. But the battle dragged on for more than a month, with the men of the 5th and 7th Marine Regiments, plus army units, fighting and dying among the coral valleys of the Umurbrogol. Only behind walls of sandbags and flame were American soldiers able to seal the last caverns of death.

Tangie waited for me in the car while I hiked to the top of Bloody Nose Ridge, where the Army Corps of Engineers has built a staircase and the kind of wooden deck found on houses in the Hamptons. From this perch, I could survey an American battlefield that will never be threatened with a K-Mart. The airport on Peleliu consists of a bench placed alongside the pock-marked runway, and no summer houses line the rocky, inhospitable shore as they do in Normandy. Where the fighting took place on Peleliu is as forlorn as a remote national park, although in this case one unencumbered with tourists, park rangers, or historical markers.

If Peleliu has any monuments, they are in its literature, as rich as any from a World War II battle. On the island, it may not be possible to study a diorama of the Horseshoe or buy postcards in a visitors' center. But as I walked beneath the cliffs of Bloody Nose Ridge or along the beaches, I could recall memoirs, histories, battalion reports, biographies, letters, and taped conversations—including those with my father—in which the fighting has the force of verses of *The Iliad*.

Although the Sledge memoirs were the first book I read about Peleliu, they remain the standard against which other histories and accounts are measured. During the fighting he kept notes secretly—some scribbled on the pages of a Bible—and wrote the first draft of the manuscript immediately after the war. In his history of wartime memoirs, *Soldiers' Tale*, Samuel Hynes describes Sledge's account as "one of the best of its kind." He continues:

> Everything is battlefield, and every action is battle. In his account of his thirty days there, nothing happens except fighting, killing, and dying: it is a personal war of an intensity beyond any other narrative I know.

After I read Sledge in the early 1980s, I mailed a copy to John Keegan, a family friend, in part to introduce him to what my father had gone through at Peleliu. In turn, he passed it on to Paul Fussell, who rescued the book from obscurity by convincing Oxford University Press to reissue a paperback with his own laudatory introduction. I also mailed a copy of the book to Sledge, whom I did not know, asking him to inscribe it for my father, and the intensity of his inscription captures the bond among those that survived Peleliu's underworld:

> Best wishes to the former company commander of C-1-1 and with greatest respect and admiration for a fine officer I knew by reputation—all I heard was the best about you and your leadership qualities and bravery. Also, with warm feelings for a fellow member of the Old Breed and a fugitive from the law of averages who knows what it feels like to put his life on the line day after day and night after night.

Sledge survived Peleliu, and subsequently Okinawa, in the infantry of the 5th Marines. The best memoirs of the 1st Marines, thus closer to my father's experiences, are *Marine at War* by Russell Davis, a book long out of print, which I tracked down through an Internet search service. In 1960 he wrote his battle memoirs to tell his sons about the war, noting that "it is very hard for a father not to make himself seem braver and wiser to his sons than he really was. . . . There is the way I dreamed I fought, and the way I wish I had fought. There is also the way I think I fought, and that is the story I have told here." Every passage from Davis I read aloud to my father is received with nodding approval.

Of the standard histories, most Marines admire *Peleliu: Tragic Triumph*, perhaps because Ross lays much of the blame in the foxholes of Rupertus and Puller. Hallas and Gailey get similar high praise. The two Marine Corps monographs, one after the war by Frank Hough and another more recent work by Gordon Gayle, are necessary sources to understand unit movements. But I was told that publication of Gayle's history was delayed for a year while military hierarchs debated what he could say about Chesty Puller.

That the memories of great wars can also be political is best illustrated in *The Story of Ray Davis*, the autobiography of the First Battalion commander who later won the Medal of Honor in Korea and retired a four-star general. The book's cover shows Davis in photographs with presidents Reagan, Kennedy, Truman, Bush, and Nixon, as if the most exposed flanks can be those in Washington. My father remembers Davis as "steady under fire." Everett Pope describes him on Peleliu as "an outstanding battalion commander."

In his memoirs Davis attaches himself firmly to the Puller legend: "Later, when I was asked how I knew what to do in the crunch situations I met in my first infantry command on Peleliu, I not only gave credit to Chesty's teachings, but I also noted . . . "

Although the incident appears nowhere else in the Puller encomia, Davis describes him during the battle getting carried forward on a stretcher:

While he was there Puller saw the bandage on my knee, he pulled it off, and told me that it was not bad enough to be evacuated. He was aware that they had wanted to haul me off to the hospital ship, but that I wouldn't go. He almost smiled at that.

But Davis is silent on the last suicidal attack, when he was wounded again, although in a letter he said that "Puller was under great pressure from Rupertus" when he ordered the men over the top. And inexplicably for a memoir, his account of Everett Pope's ordeal on Hill 100 is taken word-for-word from *The Devil's Anvil*.

Although it is not directly about Peleliu, *Fortunate Son*, the memoirs of Lewis Puller, Jr., is the most tragic book about some of its legacy. I had missed the book when it won the Pulitzer Prize in 1992 but knew from the newspapers that after it was published, Lewis, Chesty Puller's only son, who was dreadfully wounded in Vietnam, had died a suicide. At the time his friend Senator Bob Kerry, who also lost a leg in Vietnam, said: "He was an inspiration to everybody except himself."

In his autobiography, Lewis Puller, Jr., writes that only in war does he feel he can escape the shadows cast by his famous father. But as Craig Cameron writes in his excellent history of the First Marine Division: "Lewis Puller, Jr. literally and metaphorically carried the Pacific War imagery of his legendary father into the Vietnam War of the succeeding generation." His tragedy is that of Vietnam.

Fortunate Son came to my attention in winter 1995, when my father reviewed the book for a Long Island lecture series. In his review my father retold the lives of the Lewis Pullers as though they were the characters in a Greek tragedy. His empathy and grief for Lewis Puller, Jr., was like that for other young officers and friends—James Shanley, Bob Hoover, Andy Haldane, to name just a few—who died in the shadows of Bloody Nose Ridge. But it also reached out for the father who like Priam on the ramparts of Troy had to watch his son fall in battle. As Homer mourned: "Pitifully his loving father groaned."

I left Peleliu, on my same fishing boat, in the late afternoon as showers mixed with tropical sunshine. Steve, his wife, and I were joined on the return trip by the boat's owner, a businesswoman who gave the impression that she was less interested in deep-sea fishing than with the accounts receivable. The charter ended at the dock of the Pacific Palau Resort, where, dragging ashore my suitcase, I looked more like I was changing planes at O'Hare than getting ready for that evening's luau. I hitched a ride to the airport, but then discovered my flight to Taipei was delayed until 2:00 A.M. Because the bridge to Koror was out and none of the local restaurants held any appeal, I ate a box supper provided by the airline and wrote postcards in the coffee shop.

I felt weary satisfaction, despite the cost of the charter, to have seen Peleliu and to have forged a link to those who left so much behind on the island. In *The Great War and Modern Memory*, Paul Fussell quotes Siegfried Sassoon who said that "the man who really endured the War at its worst was everlastingly differentiated from everyone except his fellow soldiers." But I had found, not just in the conversations with my father but in all the letters and interviews with the men of C Company, a sense of intimacy and relief to retell their stories, lest Peleliu fulfill Abraham Lincoln's prophesy—that of a battle the world "will little note nor long remember."

Dozing on a bench with the comfort of a church pew, I thought about the uncomfortable nights my father spent among these islands, as Sledge wrote, "putting his life on the line," and about the alien landscape of the Horseshoe, even more remote to most Americans than the boulders in the Pennsylvania woods that mark Little Round Top. I tried also to equate the deaths of more than one thousand Americans on these forgotten shores with Lincoln's new birth of free-dom, and to believe that they died to defend a "government of the people" and not just trying to carry out confused orders.

In many hours of conversation, set in the lonely canyons about Bloody Nose Ridge, and in the books we shared on its dark history, my father and I had tried to fathom the reasons why. Only after my visit to Peleliu, after seeing its dark and harsh terrain, did I remember the ending to *Fathers and Sons*, when Turgenev writes about innocent eyes looking from the grave. He evokes "that immense peace of 'indiffer-ent' nature" but also, like the survivors of Peleliu, of the ties between generations that speak to us of "eternal reconcilia-tion and life without end."

American Notes

(1999)

*It was kind of solemn, drifting down the big, still river,
laying on our backs looking up at the stars, and we did-
n't ever feel like talking loud, and it warn't often that
we laughed—only a little kind of low chuckle.*

—Mark Twain, *The Adventures of Huckleberry Finn*

In spring 1976, during that eternal week between exams and
graduation, I said my good-bye to Lewisburg from a raft
floating gently down the Susquehanna. The captain was
Gerry Eager, a professor of art history, and even though we
weren't lighting out for the territories so much as for a boat
ramp in Sunbury, we did, for a few hours anyway, feel like
Huck and Jim playing hooky from our lives.

During my years in Lewisburg, sometimes when I should
have been studying, I had seen the river in various moods—
encased in winter fog, reflecting a spring moon, raging past
flood stage during a wet September. On this late spring day, it
might have been flowing through Claude Monet's gardens or
a similar slide in Gerry Eager's vast collection, despite the
scent of French fries that wafted from the Montandon shores.

After graduation, I drifted east toward New York rather

than South to the Chesapeake. Every few years, I returned to Lewisburg, once serving on a dean's committee that met as relentlessly as an eight o'clock class. But after moving to Europe in 1991, I had never been back, even though on summer evenings in Geneva, when nearby trains rattled through the darkness, I thought more of nights in Larison Hall than I did of the Paris express rushing to Evian.

In autumn 1998, like some distant Atlantic salmon, I decided it was time for another trip up the river. In an immediate sense, I wanted to see Charles Longley, my friend and a professor of political science, who was caught in the clutches of cancer. I also had an invitation from John Peeler, chair of the department, to meet with students and faculty. So too did I want to drive along the Susquehanna from Washington to Lewisburg, to see if my foreign eyes would recognize any of my undergraduate impressions.

"On my arrival in the United States, I was struck by the degree of ability among the governed and the lack of it among the governing"—words of Alexis de Tocqueville that described my landing in Washington during a week when Congress was debating original intent with references to a blue dress.

It was my second trip to the capital while it was under the siege of impeachment. On the first occasion, in October 1973, Charles Longley had loaded the Bison bus with his class on legislative behavior—as if on a sixth-grade field trip—and turned us loose in the corridors of power. I still remember our elation, riding home to Lewisburg, that we had discovered a government of men and women, not just the disembodied obfuscation of the evening news. Exactly twenty-five years later, I knew—more than I wanted to—that it was a government of men and women. So this time, up early with jet lag, I needed to be reminded that it was also one of ideals.

Walking alone among the Lincoln, Roosevelt, and

Jefferson memorials, it was easy to imagine Lincoln pardoning his successor, Bill Clinton, with one of those succinct presidential letters, sending him back to Arkansas with a revolver and a plow. Roosevelt, I sensed, would have relished the accounts of White House temptation, quoting passages from the afternoon tabloids to visiting labor leaders. For reasons obvious, Jefferson might have been more circumspect, perhaps writing a long letter to John Adams on how the press in America reminded him of the chambermaids at Versailles.

Before completing my loop around the Tidal Basin, I paused before the Korean and Vietnam war memorials—both of which struggle to explain the deaths of so many Americans on distant shores. The Vietnam memorial does not even try, preferring to list the names on somber marble, as though all hands had been lost at sea. The Korean memorial shows a platoon of riflemen advancing through a rice paddy, brave men following orders. But from where I stood—looking through the men to the Capitol dome—their angle of attack made me think of Edward Gibbon's account of Rome's decline and fall. I wondered when and if in our nation's history, with impeachment again in the air, the orders might get more confusing and similar soldiers might march on Washington.

By nightfall, I planned to be in Harrisburg. In a rented car, I escaped the Washington Beltway at signs for Frederick and, after a journey through some suburban sprawl, I found myself driving through a landscape of red barns and white silos, the kind of pastoral impression—Gerry Eager would have noted—that weaned the American imagination from Giverny.

At Bucknell, when I owned a Volkswagen worth less than the parking tickets on its windshield, I went several times to Gettysburg. Even though now I was pressed for time, I could not resist the temptation to revisit the battlefield. I drove the loops near the McPherson Farm and the Peach Orchard, still trying to equate the new birth of freedom with the large camper vans that were navigating Cemetery Ridge.

On this somber November afternoon, perhaps similar to the day on which Lincoln gave his address, I was struck again by the village qualities of the battlefield monuments, recalling the losses of this Maine regiment or that Alabama company. In Europe, the stones speak of national sacrifice. *Morts pour la patrie* is how the inscriptions read at Verdun or along the Marne. But the America that collided at Gettysburg was a nation of small towns, whose residents still today, in their loaded station wagons, need to make sense of the losses that were as local and inexplicable as the powder keg in Oklahoma City. What Lincoln did with his words, many towns tried to do with their monuments.

That evening in Harrisburg also had Lincolnesque qualities. Seeing Tom Leonard (my friend from the Class of 1974) in his federal-style parlor, surrounded by his many books, I found it easy to imagine Lincoln spending a similar evening in Springfield. By day, working as a labor relations judge, Tom traveled Pennsylvania, arbitrating disputes, much as Lincoln rode the circuit in Illinois. At night, he circulated petitions to preserve both the public library and historic buildings, clinging to the ideal that books, like row houses or even the union, are worth preserving.

After many years in England, Henry James wrote a series of essays, later published as *The American Scene*, about his return as a native. At Harvard, he wrote: "I went into the new Law Library, immense and supreme. . . . I saw in the distance a distinguished friend, all alone, belatedly working there, but to go to him I should have had to cross the bridge that spans the gulf of time and, with a suspicion of weak places, I was nervous about its bearing me."

I felt similar awe inside the renovated Ellen Bertrand Library, with its space-age stacks and rows of computer terminals. But in the department of political science, I picked up with friends and professors as if I had been away for spring break and not abroad for nine years.

John Peeler stationed me in the lounge, where I was on offer as a fountain of job experience. I credit an overheated economy, rather than the color of my parachute, to the paucity of students that drifted by, and then only to polish their résumés or chat about stock options.

Shortly before lunch, the head that poked into the lounge was that of Professor Robert Beard, of Russian studies and now Internet linguistics fame. In 1976, after graduation and his course on Yugoslav history, we had made a date to meet in Trieste, the Adriatic port, at noon on July 30th. Now was my chance to ask why he had never turned up.

"We got there a day late," was his professorial answer, as if maybe I had given him an extension. But from that moment, we were back in the Balkans, remembering Tito's origins or Russian warm-water ports. Together with John Peeler, we continued the conversation through lunch and coffee. Their curiosity and humor recalled a familiar dichotomy, at least during my undergraduate years: Students were interested in jobs, and professors in ideas.

After lunch, I dropped into Professor Peeler's class on geopolitics, in which, like Alfred Mahan or maybe a Pentagon briefing officer, he used wall maps and a long pointer to explain the choke points of South American politics. Far from the madding memos in my office, I could have spent five hours in that classroom, remembering the Chaco War or speculating whether now more drugs than oil passed through the Panama Canal. (Maybe college would be best between the ages of forty and forty-four? It would certainly make dating easier.) But I noticed that the students didn't share my enthusiasm. The slouch of some in their chairs made me think a few were in Barçaloungers, grasping for the remote control, eager to switch from John Peeler's worn notes to the more exciting *X-Files*.

I stayed the night in the home of Tom Travis, also a professor of political science, who was my freshman adviser and now is my mid-life friend. On a long walk across the campus, our feet shuffling through the leaves, we talked with the same intensity as we had in 1972. He had arranged for me to lecture that evening in Coleman Hall. Putting together a few notes on the Russian economy, I felt like Huck's duke or king, getting ready to play "the Royal Nonesuch" on the banks of the Mississippi—"Ladies and Children Not Admitted." In my case, there were no ladies or children or, for that matter, students—Russia's economy, to a job supplicant, being worth less than one of Tom Sawyer's cats. So we adjourned to a Route 15 restaurant, much as senior seminars ended with pitchers of Market Street beer.

Our Chinese dinner could easily have been a 1970s political science department meeting. Professors Peeler, Travis, and Gene Chenoweth were at the table, as if I were still a sophomore, except that the syllabus under discussion was Chenoweth's seminar on the 1960s (something that in 1973 was as inconceivable as Sonny Bono becoming a congressman). Did he teach in a tie-dyed shirt, we asked? Did his students think pigs were policemen or commodity futures?

The absent friend that evening at dinner, as during the day on campus, was Charles Longley, who died about the time that I was walking around Washington, remembering our field trip. The obituary, which I found on Tom Travis's kitchen table, outlined his life in the solemn language of the occasion, as if maybe he had fallen at Little Round Top. It spoke of his time in the Peace Corps, his doctorate from North Carolina, and his more recent collection of Americana. But like all obituaries, it missed the life and humor of his mind, not to mention his sentimental prediction in 1972 that George McGovern would beat Richard Nixon. ("Don't worry, Chuck," I liked to tease him, "at least you got it right in Massachusetts.") Among other interests, we shared a taste for bad political memoirs—what might be called the Dick Morris school of literature. When I stood outside what had been his Coleman office, I felt the loss of someone who would have enjoyed, with that flicker of mischievous delight, recalling other presidents who had flouted the dress code.

To make a meeting in New York, I left Lewisburg early the next morning, about the time I used to go to bed as a freshman. The gaslights in the historic district shimmered on the rain-slicked streets, and the Susquehanna that I crossed in the darkness might well have been an abyss, on this occasion more Géricault than Seurat.

Even as an undergraduate, leaving Lewisburg was bittersweet. While it pleased me to escape the confines of central Pennsylvania (I knew I was out when the VW radio came alive), before long I started to miss the intimacy of familiar surroundings and the presence of close friends—feelings I have today when, after a trip to America, I fly home to Europe. On this flight to Geneva, I read Peter Balakian's memoir, *Black Dog of Fate*, thinking only that I had picked up a history of the Armenian holocaust. The book jacket omitted any reference to Bucknell, and I did not place the author's name as someone who had been a senior when I was a freshman. As do my own memories of growing up, his connect the dots of the New York suburbs, high school football, Baker Field at Columbia, the sense of an immigrant past and—to my pleasant surprise—undergraduate years in Lewisburg (he graduated in 1973). I had never read a memoir set in my own place and time. "There was things which he stretched," Huck might have said, "but mainly he told the truth." But as the plane descended among the snow caps of the French Alps, it pleased me to find passages in which professors John Wheatcroft and Leo Ribuffo are given a hero's welcome, and to discover that I could drift a while longer in the currents pulling me ceaselessly into the past.

Matthew Stevenson was born in New York City in 1954 and grew up on Long Island. After graduation from Bucknell and Columbia universities, he worked as an associate editor of *Harper's* magazine and later in international banking, with emphasis on the Asia-Pacific region and the emerging markets of Europe. In 1991 he moved to Geneva, Switzerland, where he manages a Swiss bank. His writing has appeared in a number of national magazines, including the *American Scholar* and the *American Spectator.* He is married to Constance Fogler, and they have four children ranging in ages from thirteen to five. They live in Laconnex, Switzerland, which is near Geneva.

His e-mail address is: matthewstevenson@freesurf.ch